Justification
in Perspective

Before the Throne of God Above
Charitie Lees Bancroft, 1863

Before the throne of God above,
I have a strong, a perfect plea,
A great High Priest whose name is "Love,"
Who ever lives and pleads for me.
My name is graven on His hands,
My name is written on His heart;
I know that while in heav'n He stands
No tongue can bid me thence depart,
No tongue can bid me thence depart.

When Satan tempts me to despair,
And tells me of the guilt within,
Upward I look and see Him there
Who made an end to all my sin.
Because the sinless Savior died,
My sinful soul is counted free;
For God, the Just, is satisfied
To look on Him and pardon me,
To look on Him and pardon me.

Behold Him there! The risen Lamb,
My perfect, spotless Righteousness,
The great unchangeable I AM,
The King of glory and of grace!
One with Himself I cannot die,
My soul is purchased by His blood;
My life is hid with Christ on High,
With Christ, my Savior and my God,
With Christ, my Savior and my God.

Justification in *P*erspective

Historical Developments and Contemporary Challenges

Bruce L. McCormack,

EDITOR

BakerAcademic
Grand Rapids, Michigan

Rutherford
House

© 2006 by Rutherford House and Bruce L. McCormack

Published by Baker Academic
a division of Baker Publishing Group
P.O. Box 6287, Grand Rapids, MI 49516-6287
www.bakeracademic.com

and Rutherford House
17 Claremont Park
Edinburgh EH6 7PJ
Scotland, United Kingdom
www.rutherfordhouse.org.uk

Printed in the United States of America

Library of Congress Cataloging-in-Publication Data
Justification in perspective : historical developments and contemporary challenges / Bruce L. McCormack, editor.
    p.   cm.
    Includes bibliographical references and index.
    ISBN 10: 0-8010-3131-1 (pbk.)
    ISBN 978-0-8010-3131-1 (pbk.)
    1. Justification—History of doctrines. I. McCormack, Bruce L.
BT180.J8J87 2006
234'.7—dc22   2006016384

Contents

Preface

Bruce L. McCormack

The essays contained in this volume originated as lectures delivered at the tenth Edinburgh Dogmatics Conference, held in the Scottish city of that name from August 27–30, 2003, under the sponsorship of Rutherford House. Founded in 1983 by the Scottish Evangelical Research Trust as a center for theological study and research, Rutherford House is located in Leith (on the north side of Edinburgh). Through the years, its activities have expanded to include the arranging of conferences; the publication of books, training materials, and resources for church development and renewal and of two significant journals (the *Scottish Bulletin of Evangelical Theology* and the *Rutherford Journal of Church and Ministry*); and the sponsorship of study groups devoted to topics as diverse as Islam and the theology of John Calvin. The growing importance of Rutherford House on the Scottish scene is attested by the willingness of the Very Reverend Iain R. Torrance, then moderator of the Church of Scotland (now president of Princeton Theological Seminary), to interrupt a very busy schedule to bring words of greeting and encouragement to those attending the 2003 Dogmatics Conference.

One of the distinctive features of the biannual Dogmatics Conference has been the ability of its planners to bring together noted evangelical scholars who rarely get a chance to talk together because of differing ecclesial and guild commitments. Paul Helm, Kevin Vanhoozer, Henri Blocher, Donald Macleod, Stephen Williams, and D. A. Carson have regularly appeared alongside the likes of Colin Gunton, David Fergusson, Francis Watson, John Webster, and myself. The only conference like it in the States is the annual Wheaton College Conference, which takes place in the spring of each year.

The theme of the 2003 conference was justification. Not since the sixteenth century has the doctrine of justification stood so clearly at the center of theological debate as it does today. That this should be so is due not only to advances on the ecumenical front (the best-known example of which is the "Joint Declaration on the Doctrine of Justification," signed by representatives of the Lutheran and Roman Catholic churches in Augsburg, Germany, on Reformation Day, 1999) and challenges emanating from studies of Pauline literature in the last twenty-five years or so (the many variants of the so-called New Perspective); it is also due to growing anxieties among evangelicals regarding their own theological identity in a period of rapid change.

The theological heritage of the Reformation has been preserved by churches with a deep confessional consciousness. But today the old mainline churches of the Reformation are in decline throughout the West. Conservative splinter churches remain, of course, but while they are experiencing some growth their numbers remain relatively small. The future of Protestantism (if there is to be one) may well lie with non-denominational congregations—but this brings its own set of problems. One has to wonder what incentive there might be for nondenominational churches to promote a confessional theology that has its root in the writings of, say, a Luther or a Calvin in the absence of a denominational structure that requires such a thing. But even if, by some miracle, congregations will continue to be found that prize the Reformation, the lack of a strong confessional consciousness is bound to have an impact on the care with which old doctrines are studied and understood. Repetition alone is no guarantee of understanding; the use of any doctrinal formulation as a weapon to ensure conformity will serve only to further erosion of real understanding in the long run.

What we must *not* do, it seems to me, is simply lash out at those who, in our view, are departing from the Protestant understanding of justification. We must enter into thoughtful and gracious dialogue with all who offer challenges to the traditional conception—but especially with those who offer challenges from within the house of evangelicalism. The last point merits special emphasis. Not all those who are critical of this or that aspect of the traditional doctrine are "liberal" Christians or ecumenists with Catholic and/or Orthodox leanings. Many are evangelicals who, out of a desire to be faithful to the teaching of the New Testament (an evangelical virtue, to be sure!) have found it necessary to raise hard questions. In relation to them especially, it is my view that we need to proceed with great caution. It could be the case that the traditional doctrine will have to undergo some revision if it is to continue to be regarded as sound scriptural teaching by the many; it could also turn out to be the case that, after a period of rigorous testing, the traditional doctrine will emerge stronger (and certainly better understood) than it has been in the periods in which its adequacy was simply taken for granted. But we will only know which way we must go if we carry through rigorous and sustained examination of the issues involved, making use of the insights of biblical scholars, historians, and theologians—and not resting content with the provisional results of any one guild.

Taken together, the essays in this volume constitute a progress report on the state of the Protestant doctrine of justification today in the midst of challenge and change. They are a station on the way toward greater resolution, an aid that will assist theologians and church leaders in coming to a greater understanding of the issues (some of which are resident in the traditional formulation of the doctrine itself). No effort was made to ensure uniformity of perspective. Topics were assigned to individuals known to have expertise in the area in which they would be writing. The results, in each case, were left to the individual to decide. As a consequence, there is a fair bit of diversity not only on how the traditional doctrine should be interpreted in the details but also on the level of theological evaluation. But all of the participants are evangelicals; all are, in fact, Reformed in outlook and care deeply about the theological heritage of the Reformation. The debates that took place among us in Edinburgh were, in my view, the kind of in-house debates among evangelicals that one must expect in times of ecclesial upheaval and doctrinal uncertainty.

Thanks are due to David Searle, the former warden of Rutherford House, and my former colleague Professor David Wright of the University of Edinburgh, who put this conference together. Thanks, too, to Bob Fyall (successor to David Searle), who has been a friendly support to me as a first-time editor of essays for Rutherford House. I also wish to thank Mr. Robert Hosack of Baker Academic for his commitment to the project and the invaluable knowledge he brought to a publication of this sort. And, finally, I am very grateful to Michael Langford, Ph.D. candidate at Princeton Seminary, who served as my editorial assistant. Without his facility with a variety of computer programs, the task of bringing uniformity into the differing formatting decisions of American, Canadian, and British participants would have taken much longer than it did.

Abbreviations

General

art.   article
can(s).   canon(s)
ch(s).   chapter(s)
esp.   especially
fol(s).   folio(s)
LXX   Septuagint
q(q).   question(s)

Sources

ANF   *The Ante-Nicene Fathers.* Edited by Alexander Roberts and James Donaldson. 1885–1887. 10 vols. Repr. Peabody, MA: Hendrickson, 1994

Battles   John Calvin. *Institution of the Christian Religion.* Translated by F. L. Battles. Atlanta: John Knox, 1975

BJRL   *Bulletin of the John Rylands University Library of Manchester*

Bray   Gerald Bray, ed. *Romans.* Ancient Christian Commentary on Scripture: New Testament 6. Downers Grove, IL: InterVarsity, 1998

CD   Karl Barth. *Church Dogmatics.* Translated by G. W. Bromiley. 5 vols. in 13. Edinburgh: T&T Clark, 1956–1969

CT   *Concilium Tridentium. Diariorum, Actorum, Epistularum, Tractatuum Nova Collectio,* Edited by Societas Goerresiana. 13 vols. Freiburg: Herder, 1901–1976

DS   Heinrich Denzinger and Adolf Schönmetzer. *Enchiridion Symbolorum.* 34th ed. Barcelona: Herder, 1967

Edwards   Mark Edwards, ed. *Galatians, Ephesians, Colossians.* Ancient Christian Commentary on Scripture: New Testament 8. Downers Grove, IL: InterVarsity, 1999

Institutes	John Calvin. *Institutes of the Christian Religion*
KD	Karl Barth. *Die kirchliche Dogmatik*. 5 vols. in 14. Zollikon, Switz.: Verlag der Evangelischen Buchhandlun, 1932–1970
LW	Martin Luther. *Works*. Edited by Jaroslav Pelikan and Helmut T. Lehmann. 56 vols. St. Louis: Concordia; Philadelphia: Fortress, 1955–1986
NPNF[1]	*The Nicene and Post-Nicene Fathers*, Series 1. Edited by Philip Schaff. 1886–1889. 14 vols. Repr. Peabody, MA: Hendrickson, 1994
NPNF[2]	*The Nicene and Post-Nicene Fathers*, Series 2. Edited by Philip Schaff and Henry Wace. 1890–1900. 14 vols. Repr. Peabody, MA: Hendrickson, 1994
Owen	John Calvin. *Commentaries on the Epistle of Paul the Apostle to the Romans*. Edited and translated by John Owen. Grand Rapids: Baker, 1989
PG	Patrologia graeca [= Patrologiae cursus completus: Series graeca]. Edited by J.-P. Migne. 162 vols. Paris, 1857–1886
PL	Patrologia latina [= Patrologiae cursus completus: Series latina]. Edited by J.-P. Migne. 217 vols. Paris, 1844–1864
Scheck	Origen, *Commentary on the Epistle to the Romans, Books 1–5*. Translated by Thomas Scheck. Washington, DC: Catholic University of America Press, 2001
Hill	John Chrysostom, *Commentary on the Psalms*. Translated by Robert Charles Hill. 2 vols. Brookline, MA: Holy Cross Orthodox Press, 1998
StA	Philipp Melanchthon. *Werke in Auswahl*. Edited by Robert Stupperich. 7 vols. in 9. Studienauswahl. Gütersloh: Bertelsmann; G. Mohn, 1951–1975
WA	Martin Luther. *Werke*. Kritische Gesamtausgabe (Weimar Ausgabe). Weimar: Hermann Böhlau, 1883– (main series)
WA.Br	Martin Luther. *Werke*. Kritische Gesamtausgabe: Briefwechsel. 18 vols. Weimar: Hermann Böhlau, 1930–1985 (letters)
WA.Tr	Martin Luther. *Werke*. Kritische Gesamtausgabe: Tischreden. 6 vols. Weimar: Hermann Böhlau, 1912–1921 (table talk)

The Protestant Doctrine of Justification

The Heart of Protestant Preaching

1

Edinburgh Dogmatics Conference Sermon

Mark Bonnington

*But now, apart from law, the righteousness of God has been dis-
closed, and is attested by the law and prophets, the righteousness of
God through faith in Jesus Christ for all who believe. For there is no
distinction, since all have sinned and fall short of the glory of God;
they are now justified by his grace as a gift, through the redemption that is in Christ Jesus, whom God put forward as a sacrifice of
atonement by his blood, effective through faith. He did this to show
his righteousness, because in his divine forbearance he had passed
over the sins previously committed; it was to prove at the present
time that he himself is righteous and that he justifies the one who
has faith in Jesus.*

Romans 3:21–26 NRSV

*Heavenly Father, as we come to the foot of the cross of Christ, bring
us to that place of humility and hearing, and so send us out to pro-
claim this glorious gospel in the power of the Holy Spirit. We ask in
Jesus' name, Amen.*

Well, where are we to go for justification? I suppose it's a choice between
Galatians and Romans, and being more familiar with Galatians, I chose
the Epistle to the Romans 3:21–26—described by one commentator

as the Magna Carta of our whole faith, the hinge of the Epistle to the Romans. Like a mountain peak, everything that comes before our text leads up to it and everything that comes afterward flows from it. For those who love the words of commentators (and just to show I've read the commentaries!), C. E. B. Cranfield describes our text as "the centre and the heart of the whole Romans." Sin before, salvation afterward. Condemnation before, justification after. Sin leads us here, righteousness and salvation flow from it.

It's the first time in the body of the epistle that Jesus Christ is mentioned, and what is true of this letter is true of all human history, and what is true of all human history is true of your life and of mine. It's true of everyone who trusts in Jesus: when Jesus is brought in, everything changes. All is different. "But now" . . . "but now" . . . something is new, something has changed. God has acted.

In relation to us as humans, the opening chapters of Romans are as depressing as they are true to our human experience. Paul has cataloged in uncompromising terms the breadth and the depth of human sin and depravity. Sin is universal, sin is inescapable, and sin is inexcusable. The immoral and idolatrous Gentile has been lined up with the morally self-confident Jew, and both have been challenged to recognize that before God no flesh can be justified. All have sinned. But what Paul says about the human condition he says for theological reasons. It is because of two great facts about God that are central to his message that Paul treats sin in such detail and in such depth. What the apostle says with such clarity, with such depth, and with such power about human depravity should not hide our eyes from the truth about God that he is proclaiming.

The first great truth about God that Paul expounds in the opening chapters of the epistle is that *God is the Creator*. Humanity is without excuse because God has revealed himself as Creator in and through his creation. We could have seen that he was there, we should have known what he was like from the world around us, and we should have responded with acknowledgment and thanks. Every time that we look at the world in all its glorious beauty, we should turn from it to God. Every mountain stream, every sunset sky, every starry night, every tiny flower, every breath we take should breathe the praise of the Creator to the God who made us too. To put it simply: there is no excuse for atheism. Whether we deny God's existence in our minds and on our lips and say explicitly, "There is no God," or whether, as those who worship him with our mouths every week, we still allow him to become distant from our everyday living, from our decisions, and from our life in practical atheism, there is no excuse. We must not be among those who confess him with their lips but whose hearts are far from him. We are without excuse because God has revealed himself as the Creator. This is the first great truth about God.

The second great truth about God in the early chapters of Romans is that *God is the Judge of all*. If we are without excuse because he has revealed himself in creation, we are without hope because the same good God who called his creatures into existence will also call his creatures to account. The God who said, "Let light shine out of darkness," and saw that all he made was good, will shine again the goodness of his burning justice on every human life and into every human heart. Then every mouth will be stopped and all will be held to account. God's good judgment is coming. The God who is the Creator is also the Judge. The God who spoke at the beginning of history as the Creator also sits at the end of human history as the Judge.

These two great truths ring through the early chapters of the Epistle to the Romans. "But now" . . . "but now" . . . but now a third great truth about this good God is expounded. And the third great truth is that God is the Savior. He became the Savior at a specific time and in a specific place, in a specific way, in a specific person, and in a specific action. It happened in a Jewish teacher from Nazareth, two thousand years ago on a cross, by a quarry, outside a city wall. God has always been the Creator and he has always been the Judge and he has always been the redeemer God, but now his redemption is revealed, and the how and why of his redeeming purpose is seen on the human landscape. Horace's advice to a playwright in Greek drama was never to bring a god onto the stage to solve a problem unless the problem really required a god to solve it. Well, here in human sin there is a problem big enough to need God to solve it, and Jesus Christ is revealed.

So what has God done "but now"? And what is revealed about God in these six short verses? Three points for any evangelical sermon, I suppose, three simple things and yet three things profound and powerful. First, God's righteousness is revealed; second, God's grace is given; and third, God's perfection is proved—and all three things take place at the foot of the cross. And in each case, we will discover, there is a before and an after. There is what took place before the cross, "but now" there is what takes place after the cross of Christ. In each case, the situation has changed as God's salvation is shown.

First, God's righteousness is revealed. Before Christ, God's righteousness was known only through the law. If you wanted to know his character, his will, his saving ways, that's where you had to look. You had to look in the Old Testament, in the Torah, in the Prophets, in the old covenant. But now a new way has been revealed. You don't need the Commandments to know God. Righteousness is not the Ten Commandments plus, it is not morality, it is not human achievement, it is not human works in the face of a righteous God. Some were under the law; some didn't have the law, but they still knew right from wrong. In neither case would the law justify them on the last great Day. Whether the law is good or the law is bad, Paul simply says: it's beside the point when it comes to this new revelation of God's righteousness. Paul says here quite clearly that the relationship between the law and this new righteousness, this newly revealed righteousness, is double edged. The law is both irrelevant and a witness to this righteousness. It doesn't do the trick itself but it does point to God's work of salvation. Like John the Baptist, it is not the light but it does bear witness to the light. Like the saving acts of God in the past, the law foreshadows the ultimate saving act of God, which is now revealed in the blood and the cross and the death of Jesus.

"But now". . . God's righteousness is seen to be on a new basis: "through the faith of Jesus Christ." Whether we take the phrase as subjective or objective, both thoughts are in our passage. It is both to those who believe and also because of the redeeming self-giving of Jesus. Both are here: the redeeming work of the cross, appropriated by human faith. Just as the plight is universal, so are the salvation and the solution to all who believe. Whoever you are, you are a sinner. Whoever you are, justification through faith is available to all who believe. Then in Wesley's words we are "clothed in righteousness divine." But notice too that it is a qualified universalism: to all who believe; it is not automatic, it involves a coupling between God's action and our faith. All sin. Justification is to all who believe in Jesus. God's righteousness is revealed.

Second, grace is given. Here too there is a before and after. All fall short. As part of our summer holiday this year, with my family of young children, we stayed at Blair Athol, Scotland, just near Pitlochry on the A9 motorway. Many of you will know it even if you have only driven past it at seventy miles per hour as you drive through the deep and narrow pass at Killiecrankie. If you have visited Killiecrankie battle site, you will recognize it is one of the places where the seventeenth-century Jacobites trapped the government troops marching north. On a steep hillside they successfully scattered King William's men by driving them into the deep ravine. In the ravine, with the river swirling far below, is a point called Soldier's Leap, where one of the government soldiers found a narrow point of escape across the ravine. He leapt six and a half meters (that's just about twenty-five feet) from one side to the other and escaped with his life to tell the story. I took my children there, and I pointed them to it, and I asked them whether they thought they could jump it. The eldest, who's twelve, said, "No, I wouldn't make it halfway." The youngest, who's seven, said, "I could get about halfway." My middle son, who's very athletic, ten, and makes up for what he lacks in sporting prowess in confidence, said simply, "I could nearly make it, but I'd still be dead." I could nearly make it, but I'd still be dead. All have sinned and fall short of the glory of God. Sometimes, as twenty-first-century Western Christians, we find it so hard to see ourselves as sinners—as sinners without distinction, without discussion, without qualification, and without debate. We see the world around us: good or bad; better or worse; immoral and evil on the one hand, moral and good on the other. Paul proclaims over every human life: we are sinners without distinction, we all live in the prison of human sinfulness. Whether we are fibbing to the papers or committing mass murder, all are prisoners of human sin. God makes no distinction of degree or kind. How can I put it most sharply, most clearly? Without Christ, Mother Teresa is no better off than Adolf Hitler. Outside Christ, John Stott is no better than the British serial killer Harold Shipman. That is the reality of human sinfulness. In the face of God's holiness, if one link in the chain is broken, the whole chain is destroyed. "I could nearly make it, but I'd still be dead." We who are made for God's glory, to express his glory, to share his glory, have fallen short.

"But now" . . . "but now" . . . but now grace is given, and Paul leads us to three places, three buildings if you like, that show us the breadth and depth of what God has done. He leads us to the law courts and tells us of justification. He leads us to the marketplace and tells us of redemption, and he leads us to the Temple and tells us of the *hilastērion*, the mercy seat. First, we are taken to the law courts, to the Judge of all, to the One who is righteous without qualification and without question. How can we express this, this justification before God? By stories perhaps. Perhaps the story of the good judge, the judge who treats the woman who has failed and broken the law by fining her justly then pulling out the checkbook and paying the fine himself. Perhaps the story of the policeman who stopped a doctor driving out of town doing forty-five in a forty-mile-per-hour speed limit. She was going to visit a sick child, and the policeman pulled her over and said, "We're having a campaign on this bit of road, and we're stopping everybody. We've been told no exceptions, no excuses, book everybody doing more than 10 percent over the speed limit." She said "Well, I'm going to a sick child." He replied, "I can't let you off, but I can ask you to come back and pay your fine and fill in the ticket later. I'll be here all day—we're having a campaign . . ." So she drove off, dealt with the sick child, and went back to the policeman. He had thought about it and said, "Honestly, if I could, I would pay this for you. It's ridiculous, but I can't afford to pay for everyone who has a good excuse." God could afford to pay; God did so in Jesus Christ by the giving of his very self. In this way can God be both righteous and merciful.

The late Lord Chancellor Lord Hailsham, Quentin Hogg, was interviewed as an old man on the BBC radio program *Desert Island Discs*. Sue Lawley, perhaps someone without a detailed grasp of Christian verities, asked this deeply Christian man, "Lord Hailsham, as the highest judge in the land, what will you do when you face your maker on that last great Day as I know you believe you will? What will you say to him is your greatest achievement?" He didn't say, "You foolish young lady." He simply said, "I would do nothing but throw myself on the mercy of the court. There is nothing that will justify me before the face of Almighty God."

If the judge said to you, "Will you take a not-guilty verdict now or wait for a trial?" would you take it? That's the offer of grace. That's the offer of justification. The worst that can happen to us is that we get what we deserve; the rest is the mercy of God. You may know the tale of the young man who was serving in a hairdresser's, and an old lady came in, and she sat in the chair, and she looked at him warily and said, "I hope, young man, you're going to do me justice." Under his breath he replied, "It's not justice you need, madam, it's mercy."

Next, Paul leads us to the marketplace, to the language of redemption. And like the eighteenth-century antislavery campaigners who took their money and bought the slaves and manumitted them on the spot to prove they have the moral conviction to put their money where their mouth is, God redeems us in Jesus Christ. The price is paid and we are free. Steven Speilberg was interviewed about his wonderful black-and-white Holocaust film *Schindler's List*. He was asked, as a Jew, what he was saying in making the film. He said that ultimately it is about redemption. At the end, Oskar Schindler breaks down. He has no money left, but in his jacket he has a gold Nazi lapel badge, and he breaks down crying because though he has spent all the money, he could have sold his gold pin and bought a few more lives with it. *Schindler's List* is a redemption story. It is the story of a man buying people's freedom, freedom from death and condemnation. Schindler was buying back the lives of those condemned to die. That is redemption.

Finally, Paul takes us to the Temple, to the place of atonement, to the mercy seat, as I believe we should translate *hilastērion*, this very special and difficult word. He takes us into the holy of holies, into the inner sanctum where the high priest goes once a year to sprinkle blood for the sins of the nation. What was done by the high priest once a year for the sins of Israel God has done once and for all for the sins of all humanity, and not in the inner sanctum but on a hillside, not in a private place but publicly, on the top of a hill for heaven and earth to see. By the sprinkling of the blood of Christ, God has provided the mercy seat for all human sin and for all time. In Galatians, Paul explains what we are doing every time we read the gospel: "O foolish Galatians," he says in

3:1, "before whose eyes Jesus Christ was publicly portrayed as crucified" (RSV). When we preach the gospel, we are replaying, for all to see, the story of the death and the resurrection of Jesus.

How can God do all this? How can God who is just allow human beings to have their sins atoned for? How can his perfection be proved? This is the third great change that Paul says has happened in the redemption set forth in Christ. Again there is a before and an after. Before, God passed over sins. There is forgiveness and atonement before the cross, but it is divine forbearance. Prior to the cross, God forgave because of what he was going to do; afterward God forgave because of what he had already done. The cross is retrospective as well as prospective. It is postdated as well as predated. He died for the sins of Paul in the first century and for Mark Bonnington in the twenty-first century. He also died for the sins of David and Abraham and all who sinned before the cross. Forgiveness before the cross was possible because of what God would do. Forgiveness after the cross is possible because of what he has now done.

There are two things a human judge should never do: condemn the innocent and acquit the guilty. And only on the cross of Christ do perfect justice and perfect mercy meet. Here God exacts the perfect satisfaction for sin by providing the sacrifice himself and by being the sacrifice himself. So, repeating Charitie Bancroft's words, which are printed in the front of this book:

> When Satan tempts me to despair,
> And tells me of the guilt within,
> Upward I look and see Him there
> Who made an end to all my sin.
> Because the sinless Savior died,
> My sinful soul is counted free;
> For God, the Just, is satisfied
> To look on Him and pardon me.

Prior to the cross of Christ, we are lost in sin. After the cross of Christ, through faith we are justified. Before the cross of Christ, God's righteousness is seen only partially. At the cross of Christ, it is fully, completely, and publicly revealed for heaven and earth to see.

All have God as their Creator. All should know that, recognize him, and acknowledge and honor him as the One who gives them life and breath. God is also the Judge of every human life. Everyone should know that there is a difference between right and wrong, and they will one day give account. But God is also the Savior, the holy God who acts on behalf of his people in covenant-keeping love, in Old Testament and New. He is the God of the beginning who creates. He is the God of the end who comes in final judgment, but this good, holy, and just God is also the

God of the glorious middle, the center of time: he is the Redeemer, he is the Propitiator, and he is the Justifier. This is the good news of God in Jesus Christ.

Thanks be to God for his inexpressible gift.

Amen.

Part 2

The Protestant Doctrine of Justification

Its Antecedents and Historical Development

2

Justification
in the Early Church Fathers

Nick Needham

We trust in the blood of salvation.

Justin Martyr,
Dialogue with Trypho 24

Introduction

The patristic doctrine of justification, like its biblical counterpart, has always been a flashpoint of controversy between Protestants and Roman Catholics (and, to a lesser extent, between Protestants and Eastern Orthodox). Roman Catholics have boldly claimed the early church fathers as teaching the same doctrine as the Council of Trent; Protestants have equally boldly claimed at least some of the fathers, or some important strands of patristic teaching, as holding or foreshadowing the Reformation doctrine. The latter claim, in a particularly intrepid form, has recently been made by Thomas Oden in *The Justification Reader*.[1] The

---

1. Thomas Oden, *The Justification Reader* (Grand Rapids: Eerdmans, 2002).

same claim was made in the nineteenth century by Anglican scholar George Stanley Faber in his lengthy and learned volume *The Primitive Doctrine of Justification*, written in response to Alexander Knox, the Irish Anglican forerunner of the Oxford movement.[2] Indeed, if we go right back to the sixteenth century, we find the great Lutheran theologian Martin Chemnitz (the "second Martin without whom the work of the first Martin would have perished")[3] producing eight pages of patristic testimonies to the true doctrine of justification in his *Examination of the Council of Trent* (although Chemnitz, reflecting an older usage of the term "fathers," included within its scope Anselm of Canterbury, Bernard of Clairvaux, Bonaventure, and Jean de Gerson).[4]

This paper offers a brief survey of some important strands of patristic teaching on justification within a number of clearly defined parameters. First, I am using the term "father" in a broad sense to include any early Christian writer, even if the later church refused him the title "father" (e.g., Tertullian and Origen). Second, I am limiting myself to the fathers of the first four centuries. My terminus ad quem among Eastern fathers is John Chrysostom, who died in 407, and, among Western fathers, Jerome, who died in 419 or 420. Third, I am excluding Augustine of Hippo from my survey, partly because he both needs and deserves a separate treatment on account of his massive output and unique influence on Latin theology and partly because David Wright is giving us that separate treatment in this volume. For the same reason, I have excluded Pelagius from consideration, since his thought and its impact are so inextricably bound up with those of Augustine. Fourth, I have excluded from consideration all mere patristic quotations of biblical texts, since mere quotation tells us nothing about how those texts

2. George Stanley Faber, *The Primitive Doctrine of Justification*, 2nd ed. (London: Seeley and Burnside, 1839).

3. The quote is from a seventeenth-century epigram: "If the second Martin had not come, the first Martin would scarcely have endured" (Fred Kramer, "Martin Chemnitz, 1522–1586," in *Shapers of Religious Traditions in Germany, Switzerland, and Poland, 1560–1600*, ed. Jill Raitt [New Haven and London: Yale University Press, 1981], 51).

4. Martin Chemnitz, *Examination of the Council of Trent* (St. Louis: Concordia, 1971), vol. 1. Jaroslav Pelikan delivered a more cautious estimate when he was still a Lutheran: "The Council of Trent selected and elevated to official status the notion of justification by faith plus works, which was only one of the doctrines of justification in the medieval theologians and ancient fathers. When the reformers attacked this notion in the name of the doctrine of justification by faith alone—a doctrine also attested to by some medieval theologians and ancient fathers—Rome reacted by canonizing one trend in preference to all others. What had previously been permitted (justification by faith and works), now became required. What had previously been permitted (justification by faith alone), now became forbidden. In condemning the Protestant Reformation the Council of Trent condemned part of its own catholic tradition" (*The Riddle of Roman Catholicism* [London: Hodder & Stoughton, 1960], 50).

were understood. There is also a class of patristic comment where it is decidedly unclear how key terms are being used; such comments have not entered into the construction of this survey.

Let me also preface with two caveats. Caveat one: I make no claim to an exhaustive or definitive treatment of the subject. This is more in the way of a tentative exploration. If you have ever looked at the massed ranks of weighty tomes that compose J.-P. Migne's Patrologia, you will appreciate the vast volume of material to be mastered and how much of it is yet untranslated into English. So, although I have extensively consulted the original Latin and Greek of Migne,[5] this paper—for the purposes of accessibility—is primarily based on English translations of the patristic corpus. It is a tentative exploration.

Caveat two: It is easy to be misled by terms such as "patristic teaching" and "patristic corpus." We need to bear in mind that this survey takes in three hundred years of Christian thinking and writing. If we consider the last three hundred years, from 1700 to the present, we will immediately see how misleading it might be to speak about "Christian teaching" or "the Christian corpus" over that period (or we could replace the word "Christian" with "Roman Catholic" or "Protestant" to the same effect). The phraseology could imply a uniform body of thought when the reality is anything but. When therefore I speak about different strands of thought in the fathers of the first four centuries, I am not claiming that all these strands always existed together in a single coherent monolith that was universally embraced by the fathers (or even in the writings of the same father). I am simply highlighting various aspects of Christian thought and piety that can be found within the documentary residue of the first three hundred years of postapostolic church life. I am not convinced that these formed a monolith, and doubt whether the "consensus of the fathers" over that period extended much beyond the Apostles' Creed.

Justification Language

The language of justification occurs reasonably often in the fathers.[6] What does the language mean? Although it does not always have the

---

5. I have checked in Migne all the occurrences of "justify" and its cognates where these are found in the English translations, and all my examples use *dikaioō* and its cognates in the Greek text, and *justificare* and its cognates in the Latin. I have also found and translated some other examples.

6. It is not, however, the dominant language model for soteriology, as it became in significant forms of Protestantism. I am not entirely sure that there is a single dominant model in the fathers.

same precise connotation, it seems clear that there is a very prominent strand of usage in which it has a basically forensic meaning. That is, it means something like "to declare righteous," "to acquit," "to vindicate."[7] Commenting on Romans 3:4b ("that You may be justified in Your words" NKJV), Chrysostom offers a definition of justification: "What does the word 'justified' mean? That if there could be a trial and an examination of the things He had done for the Jews, and of what had been done on their part towards Him, the victory would be with God, and all the right would be on His side."[8] Chrysostom understands clearly that justification means a verdict in which right is pronounced to lie with one party in a dispute. It would seem a minor strand of patristic teaching that sees justification as meaning moral transformation, what Protestant theology calls "regeneration" or "sanctification."[9]

7. Occasionally, "to show to be righteous" (Clement of Rome, *First Epistle to the Corinthians* 30).

8. John Chrysostom, *Homilies on Romans* 6, on 3:4. (Unless otherwise stated, the quotations from the church fathers are taken from *ANF, NPNF¹*, and *NPNF²*. I have sometimes modernized the English to make it more readable.) Cf. Origen, who equates "justify" with "deem righteous": "To be justified before God is completely different from being justified before men. That is to say, in comparison with other men, one man can be deemed just if he has lived relatively free from faults; but in comparison with God, not only is a man not justified, but even as Job says, 'But the stars are not pure before Him.' They are certainly pure to us, that is, in comparison with men they are deemed pure and holy; but they are not able to be pure in comparison with God" (*Commentary on the Epistle to the Romans* 3.6.8 [Scheck]). Cf. 3.2.11, 13. Quotations from Origen's commentary on Romans must be taken with the qualification that they are filtered through Rufinus's Latin translation. For other references, like Chrysostom's, where God or Christ is said to be justified (hence "declared righteous," "shown to be righteous"), see Clement of Rome, *First Epistle to the Corinthians* 16; Justin Martyr, *First Apology* 51; *Dialogue with Trypho* 13; Origen, *Romans* (Scheck) 2.14.17; Hippolytus, *Refutation of All Heresies* 7.22.

9. Indeed, justification and sanctification are occasionally distinguished in the fathers: "We know that a man is not justified by the works of the law but through faith and the faith of Jesus Christ. . . . It is faith alone that gives justification and sanctification" (Marius Victorinus, *Commentary on Galatians* 2:15–16, in *Justification by Faith*, ed. H. George Anderson, T. Austin Murphy, and Joseph A. Burgess, Lutherans and Catholics in Dialogue 7 [Minneapolis: Augsburg, 1985], 114); "And by riches here he means the knowledge of godliness, the cleansing away of sins, justification, sanctification, the countless good things which He bestowed upon us and purposes to bestow" (John Chrysostom, *Homilies on 2 Corinthians* 17.1). Cf. Chrysostom's distinction between righteousness and sanctification in *Homilies on John* 28.1, and *Homilies on 2 Corinthians* 12.1. When Chrysostom wants to speak of sanctification within the *dik-* word group, he seems to use the verb *poieō* ("to do" or "to make") with *dikaios* ("righteous"), rather than *dikaioō* ("to justify"). See, e.g., *Homilies on Matthew* 3.6, where he says that humility makes sinners righteous, and *Homilies on Matthew* 16.3 and *Homilies on Romans* 7, on 3:31, where he says that the original purpose of the law was to make people righteous. In *Homilies on 2 Corinthians* 11.5, however, he also uses *poieō dikaios* to mean "declare righteous," "treat as righteous," in apposition to *poieō hamartia*, Christ's being "made sin," which can hardly be morally

Apart from Chrysostom's explicit definition, the evidence for justification language bearing a forensic meaning in this major strand in the fathers is parallel to the evidence for its having this meaning in the Bible. For example, the fathers frequently set "justify" and "condemn" antithetically against each other, as equal and opposite verdicts or judgments. Justification thus becomes the positive judgment, a declaration of approval. Sometimes the fathers speak in this way outside strictly theological discourse.[10] Cyprian, for instance, says about restoring the lapsed, "You have judged quite correctly about granting peace to our brethren, which they, by true penitence and by the glory of a confession of the Lord, have restored to themselves, being justified by their words, by which before they had condemned themselves."[11] Athanasius reports Antony as giving this advice: "Let him abide in that which is good, without being negligent, neither condemning his neighbors, nor justifying himself."[12] Ambrose says, "What is more unjust than to justify yourself in that wherein you condemn another, whilst you yourself are committing worse offenses?"[13] And so forth.

We frequently find the same justify/condemn antithesis in strictly theological patristic discourse: "He always justifies the poor, condemns in advance the rich";[14] "Set me free from the yoke of condemnation, and place me under the yoke of justification";[15] "Whom God has condemned, who shall justify?";[16] "For where sin abounded, grace did much more abound; and if a taste condemned us, how much more does the passion of Christ justify us?"[17]

---

transformative. Christ was regarded and treated as a sinner and sin but did not become actually sinful in heart or life. See the discussion below.

10. "Theological discourse"—i.e., where God is the subject or where human justification is salvific *coram Deo* ("before the face of God").

11. Cyprian, *Letters* 19.

12. Athanasius, *Life of Antony* 55.

13. Ambrose, *On Repentance* 1.8.38. Cf. John Chrysostom, *Homilies on the Acts of the Apostles* 52.1, contrasting justification with condemnation in Paul's trial before Festus. See also Clement of Alexandria, *The Parable of the Prodigal Son* 4; Basil of Caesarea, *Letters* 204.4; Jerome, *Dialogue against the Pelagians* 1.21.

14. Tertullian, *Of Patience* 7.

15. Methodius, *Oration on Simeon and Anna* 8.

16. Athanasius, *To the Bishops of Egypt* 19.

17. Gregory of Nazianzus, *Orations* 38.4. Cf. Origen: "For the Creator makes vessels of honour and vessels of dishonour, not from the beginning according to His foreknowledge, since He does not condemn or justify beforehand according to it" (*De principiis* 3.1.20). Ambrose: "But the flesh of Christ condemned sin, which He felt not at His birth, and crucified by His death, so that in our flesh there might be justification through grace, in which before there had been pollution by guilt" (*On Repentance* 1.3.13). John Chrysostom: "If faith in Him, he says, avails not for our justification, but it is necessary again to embrace the law, and if, having forsaken the law for Christ's sake, we are not justified but condemned for such abandonment, then we shall find Him, for whose sake we forsook

The law court framework is particularly clear in Hilary of Poitiers as he reflects on our position before the judgment seat, arguing, in this context, for the oneness of Christ the Savior-Judge against any splitting up of his natures:

> Is He Who rose again other than He Who died? Is He Who died other than He Who condemns us? Lastly, is not He Who condemns us also God Who justifies us? Distinguish, if you can, Christ our accuser from God our defender, Christ Who died from Christ Who condemns, Christ sitting at the right hand of God and praying for us from Christ Who died. Whether, therefore, dead or buried, descended into Hades or ascended into Heaven, all is one and the same Christ.[18]

"Justifies" here is the counterpart of "defends" and the opposite of "accuses" and "condemns," in the setting of divine judgment.

Sometimes justification language is set antithetically against some other corresponding negative from the forensic sphere, such as guilt. Ambrose exclaims, "In Adam I fell, in Adam I was cast out of Paradise, in Adam I died. How shall the Lord call me back, unless He finds me in Adam, so that as I was liable to guilt and owing death in him, so now in Christ I am justified?"[19]

The fathers also speak of justification in a way that makes it equivalent to forgiveness, remission, pardon, or acquittal. Origen, for instance, uses justification, forgiveness, and remission of crimes as synonyms: "If anyone acts unjustly after justification, it is scarcely to be doubted that he has rejected the grace of justification. For a person does not receive the forgiveness of sins in order that he should once again imagine that he has been given a license to sin; for the remission is not given for future crimes, but for past ones."[20] Ambrose pursues a similar equivalence between justification and pardon:

---

the law and went over to faith, the author of our condemnation" (*Homily on Galatians*, on 2:17). See also Bardesan, *Book of the Laws of Divers Countries* (*ANF* 8:724, 729, from a Syriac original whose language I have been unable to check); Tertullian, *Against Marcion* 4.36; Athanasius, *Letters* 52.3; Ambrosiaster, *Commentary on Paul's Epistles* (Bray); Chrysostom, *Homilies on 2 Corinthians* 4.7; *Homilies on Philippians* 5 (*NPNF¹* 13:206); *Homilies on Hebrews* 9.8; Rufinus, *Apology* 1.14.

18. Hilary of Poitiers, *On the Trinity* 10.65. The forensic meaning is also clear in Ambrose: "So he [the publican] was justified by the judgment of the Lord rather than the Pharisee, whom overweening pride made so hideous" (*On the Duties of the Clergy* 1.18.70). Cf. John Chrysostom: "There is no human being on earth who could come to judgment in the face of precepts from You and be justified; so the verdicts are overwhelmingly in Your favour" (*Commentary on the Psalms* [Hill, 2:298]).

19. Ambrose, *On the Decease of His Brother Satyrus* 2.6 (PL 16:1374). (The *NPNF²* translation is somewhat defective.)

20. Origen, *Romans* (Scheck) 3.9.4.

Why do you fear to confess your sins to our good Lord? "Set them forth," He says, "that you may be justified." The rewards of justification are set before him who is still guilty of sin, for he is justified who voluntarily confesses his own sin; and lastly, "the just man is his own accuser in the beginning of his speaking." The Lord knows all things, but He waits for your words, not that He may punish, but that He may pardon.[21]

Chrysostom illustrates justification in the following way. He is rebutting an imaginary Jewish legalist who objects to the apostle Paul's teaching on the grounds that he can justify himself by his own righteousness: "If anyone still contradicts what Paul says, they do the same as a person who, after committing great sins, is unable to defend himself in court, but is condemned and about to be punished, and then is forgiven by royal pardon—yet has the effrontery, after his forgiveness, to boast and say that he had committed no sin!"[22] Here "royal pardon" and "forgiveness" are synonymous with justification.[23]

21. Ambrose, *On Repentance* 2.7.53.

22. John Chrysostom, *Homilies on Romans* 7, on 3:27. Chrysostom's use of a law court analogy here prompts the observation that we find the same equivalence between the language of justification and the language of pardon/acquittal in the purely secular sphere. E.g., Chrysostom says of Paul's trial before Festus, "Mark how he accuses them, while he acquits him. O what an abundance of justifications! After all these repeated examinations, the governor finds no ground on which he may condemn him" (Chrysostom, *Homilies on the Acts of the Apostles* 52.1).

23. John Chrysostom again: "Consider that the publican was justified by one word, although that was not humiliation, but a true confession. Now if this has power so great, how much more power has humiliation. Remit offenses to those who have transgressed against you, for this too remits sins. And concerning the former He says, 'I saw that he went sorrowful, and I healed his ways' (Isa. 57:17–18, LXX); and in Ahab's case, this appeased the wrath of God (1 Kings 21:29). Concerning the latter He says, 'Remit, and it shall be remitted to you.' There is also again another way which brings us this medicine; condemning what we have done amiss; for, 'Declare first your own transgressions, that you may be justified' (Isa. 43:26, LXX)" (*Homilies on 2 Corinthians* 4.7). Here justification, the remission of sins, the remission of offenses, and appeasing God's wrath are all used to signify the same reality. Cf. the famous passage in *Epistle to Diognetus* 9: "He Himself took on Him the burden of our iniquities, He gave His own Son as a ransom for us, the holy One for transgressors, the blameless One for the wicked, the righteous One for the unrighteous, the incorruptible One for the corruptible, the immortal One for them that are mortal. For what other thing was capable of covering our sins than His righteousness? By what other one was it possible that we, the wicked and ungodly, could be justified, than by the only Son of God? O sweet exchange! O unsearchable operation! O benefits surpassing all expectation! that the wickedness of many should be hid in a single righteous One, and that the righteousness of One should justify many transgressors!" Here justification is equivalent to "covering" and "hiding" sins in Christ as the sinner's ransom. See also Ambrosiaster, *Commentary on Paul's Epistles* (Bray, 119, 147); Ambrose, *Concerning Repentance* 2.6.40; *De Jacob et vita beata* 1.6 (PL 14:637) and 2.2 (PL 14:648); Chrysostom, *Homilies on 1 Corinthians* 2.5; 8.8; 23.5; *Homilies on Philemon* 1 (*NPNF¹* 13:549, col. 2, par. 3); Jerome, *Expositio Quatuor Evangeliorum Mattheus* (PL 30:568).

The forensic framework of this justification language is further illustrated by another strand of patristic teaching that employs the concept of imputation—reckoning or crediting something to someone's account, a synthesis of legal and financial metaphors, where the books that are being kept are "judgment books." Justin Martyr teaches a bold doctrine of imputed righteousness: "For the goodness and the loving-kindness of God, and His boundless riches, hold righteous and sinless the person who, as Ezekiel tells, repents of sins; and reckons sinful, unrighteous, and impious the person who falls away from piety and righteousness to unrighteousness and ungodliness."[24] That is, God graciously regards the penitent person as though that person were righteous and sinless.[25]

Irenaeus interprets the nonimputation of sin as the remission and forgiveness of sin and debt. Commenting on Christ's physical healing and spiritual forgiveness of the bedridden paralytic, he says,

> Therefore, by remitting sins, He did indeed heal the man, while He also manifested Himself who He was. For if no one can forgive sins but God alone, while the Lord remitted them and healed men, it is plain that He was Himself the Word of God made the Son of man, receiving from the Father the power of remission of sins; since He was both man and God, so that having suffered for us as man, He might have compassion on us as God, and forgive us our debts, in which we were made debtors to God our Creator. And therefore David said beforehand, "Blessed are those whose iniquities are forgiven, and whose sins are covered. Blessed is the man to whom the Lord has not imputed sin." David points out in this way the remission of sins which follows upon Christ's advent, by which He has destroyed the handwriting of our debt, and fastened it to the cross, so that as by means of a tree we were made debtors to God, by means of a tree we may obtain the remission of our debt.[26]

24. Justin Martyr, *Dialogue with Trypho* 47.

25. Cf. Jerome: "The soul therefore that has not sinned shall live. Neither the virtues nor the vices of parents are imputed to their children. God takes account of us only from the time when we are born anew in Christ" (*Letters* 60.8).

26. Irenaeus, *Against Heresies* 5.17.3. Clement of Alexandria, who, as we shall see, was not fond of using justification language in a forensic sense, nonetheless occasionally employs imputation language: "For it is in the power of God alone to grant the forgiveness of sins, and not to impute transgressions" (*Who Is the Rich Man That Shall Be Saved?* 39). For further patristic use of imputation (or reckoning) language as equivalent to forgiveness of sins, see Clement of Rome, *First Epistle to the Corinthians* 50, and the longer version of *Epistle* 60; Justin Martyr, *Dialogue with Trypho* 141; Irenaeus, *Against Heresies* 4.27.2; Clement of Alexandria, *Stromata* 2.15; *Constitutions of the Holy Apostles* 2.53; Ambrose, *On Repentance* 2.35; John Chrysostom, *Homilies on John* 39.4.

Generally it is this negative nonimputation of sin that we find in the fathers, but sometimes we also discover a more positive imputation of righteousness, as, for example, in Ambrosiaster:

> This he says, that without the works of the law, to an impious person (that is, a Gentile) believing in Christ, his faith is imputed for righteousness, as it was to Abraham. How then can the Jews imagine that through the works of the law they are justified with Abraham's justification, when they see that Abraham was justified not from the works of the law, but by faith alone? Therefore there is no need of the law, since an impious person is justified with God through faith alone.[27]

Here the imputation of righteousness is synonymous with justification.

The concept of imputation also bears on how the atonement is understood. We certainly find many passages in the fathers where Christ is seen as carrying vicariously the weight of humanity's guilt on the cross. Quite often this is stated very clearly in terms of penal substitution. This view of the atonement is sometimes ascribed exclusively to the Reformers, but wrongly, for it is quite pervasive in the fathers too. Justin Martyr, for instance, says,

> For the whole human race will be found to be under a curse. For it is written in the law of Moses, "Cursed is everyone that continues not in all things that are written in the book of the law to do them." And no one has accurately done all, nor will you venture to deny this; but some more, and some less than others, have observed the ordinances enjoined. But if those who are under this law appear to be under a curse for not having observed all the requirements, how much more shall all the nations appear to be under a curse who practice idolatry, who seduce youths, and commit other crimes? If, then, the Father of all wished His Christ to take upon Himself the curses of all for the whole human family, knowing that, after He had been crucified and was dead, He would raise Him up, why do you argue about Him, Who submitted to suffer these things according to the Father's will as if He were accursed, and do not rather bewail yourselves? For although His Father caused Him to suffer these things on

27. Ambrosiaster, *Commentary on Paul's Epistles*, on 4:5 (PL 17:86). Cf. Tertullian: "In short, faith in one of two gods cannot possibly admit us to the dispensation of the other, so that it should impute righteousness to those who believe in him, and make the just live through him, and declare the Gentiles to be his children through faith. Such a dispensation as this belongs wholly to Him through whose appointment it was already made known by the call of this selfsame Abraham, as is conclusively shown by the natural meaning" (*Against Marcion* 5.3). See also Irenaeus, *Against Heresies* 4.16.2; Eusebius, *Church History* 1.4.

behalf of the human family, yet you [Jews] did not commit the deed as in obedience to the will of God.[28]

Perhaps the strongest statement comes from Chrysostom, who starkly affirms that Christ became a sinner and sin itself on the cross:

And what has He done? "Him that knew no sin He made to be sin, for you." For if He had achieved nothing else but done only this, think how great a thing it is to give His Son for those that had outraged Him. But now He has truly achieved mighty things, and besides, has allowed Him that did no wrong to be punished for those who had done wrong. Yet Paul did not

28. Justin Martyr, *Dialogue with Trypho* 95. Gregory of Nazianzus adopts a similar outlook, referring to Psalm 22 (which he calls Psalm 21 according to the LXX numbering) as christological in meaning:

> But look at it in this manner: that as for my sake He was called a curse, Who destroyed my curse; and was called sin, who takes away the sin of the world; and became a new Adam to take the place of the old; just so He makes my disobedience His own as Head of the whole body. As long then as I am disobedient and rebellious, both by denial of God and by my passions, so long Christ also is called disobedient on my account. . . . Of the same kind, it appears to me, is the expression, "My God, My God, why have You forsaken Me?" It was not He who was forsaken either by the Father, or by His own Godhead, as some have thought, as if It were afraid of the Passion, and therefore withdrew Itself from Him in His Sufferings (for who compelled Him either to be born on earth at all, or to be lifted up on the Cross?). But as I said, He was in His own Person representing us. For we were the forsaken and despised before, but now by the Sufferings of Him Who could not suffer, we were taken up and saved. Similarly, He makes His own our folly and our transgressions; and says what follows in the Psalm, for it is very evident that the Twenty-first Psalm refers to Christ. (*Theological Orations* 4.5)

Cf. John Chrysostom:

> And that you may learn what a thing it is, consider this which I say. If one that was himself a king, beholding a robber and malefactor under punishment, gave his well-beloved son, his only-begotten and true, to be slain, and transferred the death and the guilt as well, from the robber to his son, who was himself of no such character, that he might both save the condemned man and clear him from his evil reputation; and then if, having subsequently promoted him to great dignity, he had yet, after thus saving him and advancing him to that unspeakable glory, been violated by the person who had received such treatment: would not that saved man, if he had any sense, have chosen ten thousand deaths rather than appear guilty of so great ingratitude? This then let us also now consider with ourselves, and groan bitterly for the provocations we have offered our Benefactor. (*Homilies on 2 Corinthians* 11.6)

For other references to penal substitution in the fathers, see Irenaeus, *Against Heresies* 5.17.2; Origen, *Commentary on the Gospel of John* (PG 14:160); Cyprian, *On the Advantages of Patience* 6–7; Eusebius (PL 22:726–27); Athanasius, *On the Incarnation of the Word* 6–7, 25; *Orations against the Arians* 1.60; 2.7; 2.47; 2.55; 2.67; 2.69; 3.33; *On Luke 10:22* 2; *Letter to Epictetus* 8; *Letters* 60.6; Hilary of Poitiers, *On the Trinity* 10.47–48; Cyril of Jerusalem, *Catechetical Lectures* 13.2, 13.33; Gregory of Nazianzus, *Orations* 30.5; 30.20; 38.1; 40.45; *Letters* 101, to Cledonius; Epiphanius of Salamis, *Against Heresies* 42.8; 66.79; Ambrose, *Sermon against Auxentius* 25; Chrysostom, *Homilies on Galatians*, on 1:19, 3:13–14; *Homilies on Colossians* 6, on 2:14; *Homilies on 1 Timothy* 7, on 2:6; *Homilies on Hebrews* 17.4.

say this, but mentioned that which is far greater than this. What then is this? "Him that knew no sin," he says, Him that was righteousness itself, "He made sin," that is allowed Him to be condemned as a sinner, as one cursed to die. "For cursed is he that hangs on a tree" (Gal. 3:13). For to die like this was far greater than simply to die; and this he also elsewhere implies, saying, "Becoming obedient unto death, even the death of the cross" (Phil. 2:8). For this thing carried with it not only punishment, but also disgrace.

Reflect therefore what great things He bestowed on you. For it would indeed be a great thing for even a sinner to die for anyone whatever; but when He who undergoes this is righteous and yet dies for sinners; and not only dies, but even dies as one cursed; and not as cursed only, but thereby freely bestows upon us those great benefits which we never anticipated (for he says that "we might become the righteousness of God in Him")—what words, what thought shall be adequate to realize these things? "For the Righteous One He made a sinner," he says, "that He might make the sinners righteous." Indeed rather, he did not even say this, but what was greater by far; for the word he employed is not the habit [sinner], but the quality itself [sin]. For he did not say "made Him a sinner," but "made Him sin"; not only, "Him that had not sinned," but "that had not even known sin; so that we also might become," he did not say "righteous," but "righteousness," indeed "the righteousness of God." For this is the righteousness of God, when we are justified not by works, in which case it would be necessary that not even a spot should be found, but by grace, in which case all sin is done away. And this, at the same time that it does not allow us to be lifted up (for it is entirely the free gift of God), teaches us also the greatness of what is given. For what came before was a righteousness of the law and of works, but this is the righteousness of God.[29]

Here is what the Reformers were to call "the wonderful exchange": Christ being made sin with humanity's sin, so that we might become righteous with a divine righteousness.[30]

29. John Chrysostom, *Homilies on 2 Corinthians* 11.5. Cf. Jerome: "Christ who was without sin is said to have been made sin for us, because for our sins He died. Christ who knew no sin, the Father made sin for us: that, as a victim offered for sin was in the law called 'sin,' according as it is written in Leviticus, 'And he shall lay his hand upon the head of his sin'; so likewise Christ, being offered for our sins, received the name of sin. 'That we might be made the righteousness of God in Him': not our righteousness, nor in ourselves" in *Expositio In Primam Epistolam Ad Corinthiios* (PL 30:820).

30. Tertullian brings together justification by faith, imputation, and penal substitution in the following dense passage, arguing against Marcion's attribution of the Old Testament law to a god other than the Father of Jesus Christ:

For he remembered that the time was come of which the Psalm spoke, "Let us break their bands asunder, and cast off their yoke from us"; since the time when "the nations became tumultuous, and the people imagined vain counsels"; when "the kings of the earth stood up, and the rulers were gathered together against the Lord, and against His Christ," in order that thenceforward man might be justified by the liberty of faith, not by servitude

We have, then, in the fathers of the first four centuries, this major strand of justification teaching where the meaning is forensic: a not-guilty verdict, an acquittal, a declaration of righteousness, a nonimputation of sin, an imputation of righteousness. We see this in the way they use the language of justification in both human and theological discourse, its

---

to the law, "because the just shall live by his faith." Now, although the prophet Habakkuk first said this, yet you have the apostle here confirming the prophets, even as Christ did. The object, therefore, of the faith whereby the just man shall live, will be that same God to whom likewise belongs the law, by doing which no man is justified. Since, then, there equally are found the curse in the law and the blessing in faith, you have both conditions set forth by the Creator: "Behold," says He, "I have set before you a blessing and a curse." You cannot establish a diversity of authors because there happens to be a diversity of things; for the diversity is itself proposed by one and the same author.

Why, however, "Christ was made a curse for us," is declared by the apostle himself in a way which quite helps our side, as being the result of the Creator's appointment. But yet it by no means follows, because the Creator said of old, "Cursed is every one that hangs on a tree," that Christ belonged to another god, and on that account was accursed even then in the law. And how, indeed, could the Creator have cursed by anticipation one whom He knew not of? Why, however, may it not be more suitable for the Creator to have delivered His own Son to His own curse, than to have submitted Him to the malediction of that god of yours,—in behalf, too, of man, who is an alien to him? Now, if this appointment of the Creator respecting His Son appears to you to be a cruel one, it is equally so in the case of your own god. If, on the contrary, it is in accordance with reason in your god, it is equally so—nay, much more so—in mine. For it would be more credible that that God had provided blessing for man, through the curse of Christ, who formerly set both a blessing and a curse before man, than that he had done so, who, according to you, never at any time pronounced either. "We have received therefore the promise of the Spirit," as the apostle says, "through faith," even that faith by which the just man lives, in accordance with the Creator's purpose.

What I say, then, is this, that that God is the object of faith who prefigured the grace of faith. But when he also adds, "For you are all the children of faith," it becomes clear that what the heretic's industry erased was the mention of Abraham's name; for by faith the apostle declares us to be "children of Abraham," and after mentioning him he expressly called us "children of faith" also. But how are we children of faith? and of whose faith, if not Abraham's? For since "Abraham believed God, and it was accounted to him for righteousness"; since, also, he deserved for that reason to be called "the father of many nations," whilst we, who are even more like him in believing in God, are thereby justified as Abraham was, and thereby also obtain life—since the just lives by his faith,—it therefore happens that, as he in the previous passage called us "sons of Abraham," since he is in faith our (common) father, so here also he named us "children of faith," for it was owing to his faith that it was promised that Abraham should be the father of (many) nations. As to the fact itself of his calling off faith from circumcision, did he not seek thereby to constitute us the children of Abraham, who had believed previous to his circumcision in the flesh? In short, faith in one of two gods cannot possibly admit us to the dispensation of the other, so that it should impute righteousness to those who believe in him, and make the just live through him, and declare the Gentiles to be his children through faith. Such a dispensation as this belongs wholly to Him through whose appointment it was already made known by the call of this selfsame Abraham, as is conclusively shown by the natural meaning." (*Against Marcion* 5.3)

equivalent terms, and its implicit or explicit meshing with a frequently employed penal substitutionary model of atonement in which Christ bears our sins.

The only individual father of note who appears to stand out strongly and quite consistently as an exception to this pattern is Clement of Alexandria. Although Clement can use forensic concepts, his use of the terminology of justification usually places it in a nonforensic spectrum. When Clement says "justify," he mostly seems to mean "sanctify." For example, he says that "at one time philosophy justified the Greeks," although "not conducting them to that entire righteousness" that Christ gives.[31] "Justified" here seems to mean something like "trained in moral conduct." Or again, Clement depicts Christ saying to the rich young ruler, "haste to the ascent of the Spirit, being not only justified by abstinence from what is evil, but in addition also perfected, by Christ-like beneficence."[32] While "justified" here could mean "shown to be righteous," it is perhaps more likely that Clement is contrasting the positive perfection of "Christlike beneficence" with a negative "abstinence from what is evil." The latter justifies but does not perfect; it is a step on the path of moral renewal, but only a first step. Or again: "'Wherefore,' he says, 'you are justified in the name of the Lord.' You are made, so to speak, by Him to be righteous as He is, and are blended as far as possible with the Holy Spirit."[33] George Stanley Faber in his *Primitive Doctrine of Justification* argues that Clement is using "justified" forensically here,[34] but it seems more plausible that his meaning should be gauged from the parallel clause, "and are blended as far as possible with the Holy Spirit."[35]

31. Clement of Alexandria, *Stromata* 1.20.
32. Ibid., 4.6. "Christlike" is literally "Lordlike."
33. Ibid., 7.14. Cf. 1.4; 6.18; *Comments on 1 John 3:2*; *Fragments from the Book on Slander* (*ANF* 2:580). It is unclear what Clement means by "justified" in *Stromata* 1.7, 2.4, or 4.23, although clearly 1.7 denies salvific value to all works done by unbelievers. The 4.23 reference to Abraham ("justified by obedience") could mean "shown to be righteous by his obedience." In *The Parable of the Prodigal Son* 4, Clement employs "justification" as the antithesis of "condemnation" and "accusation": a rare occurrence of a clearly forensic usage.
34. Faber, *Primitive Doctrine of Justification*, 119.
35. Other patristic references where "justified" seems equivalent to "sanctified" are Shepherd of Hermas, book 3, *Fifth Similitude* 7, and probably book 1, *Third Vision* 9; *Epistle of Barnabas* 4. It is interesting that Martin Chemnitz highlights Hermas as a notable corrupter of the apostolic doctrine of justification. See Chemnitz, *Loci Theologici*, 2 vols. (St. Louis: Concordia, 1989), 2:468–69. Chemnitz also singles out the *Pseudo-Clementine Recognitions* and Clement of Alexandria. The fluidity of patristic terminology, however, is shown by Cyprian in *On the Lord's Prayer* 6, where he uses "sanctified" to mean "justified."

The Christian Life: Initial Justification

How does this justification first take effect in a person? There is a strong strand of patristic teaching that ascribes initial justification to faith—either to faith in an unqualified way, or to faith in contrast with works, or even specifically to "faith alone." When I speak of "initial justification," I mean justification as it applies to the new convert. We shall have to go on to consider separately how, in the patristic corpus, justification continues to apply to the Christian in the course of his earthly pilgrimage. In this section, we will examine patristic teaching where it is clear that initial justification is the focus or where this is not clear but justification in a general unspecified sense is in view.

The ascription of justification to faith, at least initially, is quite frequent in the fathers. Let us take it under the three headings mentioned in the previous paragraph. First, justification is attributed to "faith" in a simple and unqualified way: "The Lord, therefore, was not unknown to Abraham, whose day he desired to see; nor again was the Lord's Father unknown, for Abraham had learned from the Word of the Lord, and believed Him; therefore it was accounted to him by the Lord for righteousness. For faith towards God justifies a person";[36] "For when a human being is once a believer, he is immediately justified."[37] There are many expressions equivalent to these where the word "justification" is not used:

> Oh the great loving-kindness of God! For the righteous were many years in pleasing Him: but what they succeeded in gaining by many years of well-pleasing, this Jesus now bestows on you in a single hour. For if you shall believe that Jesus Christ is Lord, and that God raised Him from the dead, you shall be saved, and shall be transported into Paradise by Him who brought in the robber there. And doubt not whether it is possible; for He who on this sacred Golgotha saved the robber after one single hour of belief, the same shall save you also on your believing.[38]

36. Irenaeus, *Against Heresies* 4.5.5.

37. John Chrysostom, *Homilies on Romans* 7, on 3:30. Cf. Eusebius: "For he [Abraham], having renounced the superstition of his fathers, and the former error of his life, and having confessed the one God over all, and having worshipped him with deeds of virtue, and not with the service of the law which was afterward given by Moses, was justified by faith in Christ, the Word of God, who appeared to him" (*Church History* 1.4). Ambrosiaster: "Whoever has faith in God and Christ is righteous. . . . No one is justified before God except by faith" (*Commentary on Paul's Epistles* [Bray, 103]). See also Justin Martyr, *Dialogue with Trypho* 23; Irenaeus, *Against Heresies* 4.9.1; 4.25.1; 5.32.2; Tertullian, *Against Marcion* 4.18; 5.3; Origen, *Romans* (Scheck) 3.8.1; Pseudo-Athanasius, *Synopsis scripturae sacrae* (PG 28:413); Marius Victorinus, *Epistle to the Galatians* 2.3.25–26 (Edwards, 50); Hilary of Poitiers, *On the Trinity* 4.27; 5.15; 10.68–9; Ambrosiaster, *Commentary on Paul's Epistles* (Bray, 63, 107, 115); Chrysostom, *Homilies on Romans* 9, on 4:25; *Homilies on Galatians*, on 2:17.

38. Cyril of Jerusalem, *Catechetical Lectures* 5.10.

Yet He came not to judge or to inquire, but to pardon and remit transgressions, and to grant salvation through faith.[39]

Often faith is contrasted with works and law in justification or salvation:

Then, as they [the Jews] made great account of the patriarch, he brings his example forward, and shows that he too was justified by faith. And if he who was before grace,[40] was justified by faith, although plentiful in works, much more we. For what loss was it to him, not being under the law? None, for his faith sufficed unto righteousness. The law did not then exist, he says, neither does it now exist, any more than then. In disproving the need of the law, he introduces one who was justified before the law.[41]

39. John Chrysostom, *Homilies on John* 28.2. Cf. Tertullian: "And eternal righteousness was manifested, and a Holy One of holy ones was anointed—that is, Christ—and vision and prophecy were sealed, and sins were remitted, which, through faith in the name of Christ, are washed away for all who believe in Him" (*An Answer to the Jews* 8). Basil of Caesarea: "Those who have not yet put on Christ's yoke do not recognize the laws of the Lord. They are therefore to be received in the church, as having remission in the case of these sins too, as of all sins, from their faith in Christ" (*Letters* 199). See also *Epistle of Barnabas* 16; the anonymous *Treatise on Rebaptism* 5, 18; Clement of Alexandria, *Exhortation to the Heathen* 11; *The Instructor* 1.6; *Stromata* 6.6; Cyprian, *On the Lapsed* 17; Cyril of Jerusalem, *Procatechesis* 17; Basil of Caesarea, *On the Holy Spirit* 18.44; *Letters* 234.2; Gregory of Nazianzus, *Orations* 43.72; Gregory of Nyssa, *Against Eunomius* 10.2; Jerome, *Letters* 51.7; Chrysostom, *Homilies on Romans* 8, on 4:15; *Homilies on 1 Corinthians* 1.1; *Homilies on Hebrews* 22.1; *Homilies on Eutropius* 2.15.

40. I.e., Abraham lived before the age of New Testament grace.

41. John Chrysostom, *Homilies on Galatians*, on 3:6. Cf. Chrysostom: "Do not doubt, then: for it is not by works, but by faith. And do not shun this righteousness of God, for it is a blessing in two ways: first, because it is easy, and second, because it is open to all people. And do not be embarrassed and ashamed. For if God Himself openly declares Himself to do this, and He finds a sort of delight and pride in doing it, how is it that you are dejected and hide your face at what your Master glories in?" (*Homilies on Romans* 7, on 3:25). Tertullian: "He enjoins those who are justified by faith in Christ and not by the law to have peace with God. With what God? Him whose enemies we have never, in any dispensation, been? Or Him against whom we have rebelled, both in relation to His written law and His law of nature? Now, as peace is only possible towards Him with whom there once was war, we shall be both justified by Him, and to Him also will belong the Christ, in whom we are justified by faith, and through whom alone God's enemies can ever be reduced to peace" (*Against Marcion* 5.13). Origen: "Therefore the righteousness of God through faith in Jesus Christ reaches to all who believe, whether they are Jews or Gentiles. It justifies those who have been cleansed from their past crimes and makes them capable of receiving the glory of God; and it supplies this glory not for the sake of their merits nor for the sake of works, but freely to those who believe" (*Romans* [Scheck] 3.7.13). See also Tertullian, *Against Marcion* 5.3; Clement of Alexandria, *Stromata* 2.4; Origen, *Romans* (Scheck) 3.8.1; Lactantius, *Divine Institutes* 6.25 (the exhortation not to trust in one's own "integrity and innocence" but in God's mercy, albeit the advice is couched rather moralistically); Marius Victorinus, *Commentary on Galatians* 2.15–16, in Anderson, Murphy, and Burgess, *Justification by Faith*, 114; *Epistle to the Galatians*

   This quotation also illustrates a strand in patristic teaching that refused to restrict nonjustifying works to the ceremonial Mosaic law. Abraham was justified by faith, not by his moral works that were done prior to the ceremonial law, even though those moral works were abundant. Often the fathers do speak about nonjustifying works in a ceremonial sense,[42] but at other times they recognize that no works at all done prior to faith, by Jew or Gentile, according to Mosaic or natural law, can justify.[43]

   Finally, there is the strand of teaching that insists quite explicitly on justification by faith alone:

> They are justified freely because, neither working anything nor returning payment, they are justified by faith alone as a gift of God.[44]

> Further, they were possessed with another apprehension; it was written, "Cursed is every one who does not continue in all things that are written in the book of the law, to do them" (Deut. 27:26). And this he removes, with great skill and prudence, turning their argument against themselves, and showing that those who relinquish the law are not only not cursed, but blessed; and those who keep it, not only not blessed but cursed. They said that he who did not keep the law was cursed, but he proves that he who kept it was cursed, and he who did not keep it was blessed. Again, they said that he who adhered to faith alone was cursed, but he shows that he who adhered to faith alone is blessed.[45]

> When an ungodly man is converted, God justifies him through faith alone, not on account of good works which he did not have. Otherwise he ought

---

2.3.21 (Edwards, 48); Hilary of Poitiers, *On the Trinity* 9.16; Ambrosiaster, *Commentary on Paul's Epistles* (Bray, 31, 113, 121, 127); Ambrose, *Letters* 73.11, in Anderson, Murphy, and Burgess, *Justification by Faith*, 127; Chrysostom, *Homilies on Matthew* 26.5; *Homilies on Romans* 7, on 3:25–28; *Homilies on Romans* 8, on 4:1–3; *Homilies on Romans* 16, on 9:28; *Homilies on Galatians*, on 3:6–12; *Homilies on Colossians* 6, on 2:13–15; Jerome, *Dialogue against the Pelagians* (PL 23:568).

   42. E.g., Justin Martyr, *Dialogue with Trypho* 23, 92; Irenaeus, *Against Heresies* 4.16.2; Marius Victorinus, *Epistle to the Galatians* 3.10 (Edwards, 40); Ambrosiaster, *Commentary on Paul's Epistles* (Bray, 104); John Chrysostom, *Homilies on Galatians*, on 5:3.

   43. This point is brought out in many of the passages that speak of justification (or its equivalent) through faith alone (see below). For other references, where the law (understood as "natural law"), works, or the curse of the law are seen as involving Gentiles as well as Jews, see Clement of Alexandria, *Stromata* 1.7; Origen, *Romans* (Scheck) 2.7.5; Arnobius, *Against the Gentiles* 2.65–66; Epiphanius of Salamis, *Panarion* 42.12.3 (Edwards, 40); Ambrosiaster, *Commentary on Paul's Epistles* (Bray, 65, 95); John Chrysostom, *Homilies on John* 25.3; Jerome, *Letters* 133.8; *Epistle to the Galatians* 1.2.16 (Edwards, 30–31).

   44. Ambrosiaster, *Commentary on Paul's Epistles*, on 3:24 (PL 17:83). For some reason, in Bray, 101, the first occurrence of the phrase *justificati sunt* in this passage has been translated "justified" whereas the second has been translated "made holy." This obscures Ambrosiaster's meaning. Perhaps the translator was working from a variant text.

   45. John Chrysostom, *Homilies on Galatians*, on 3:8.

to have been punished on account of his ungodly deeds. . . . God purposed to forgive sins freely through faith alone.[46]

This strongly attested strand on initial justification by faith, even faith alone, must, however, be coordinated with the patristic teaching that forgiveness is mediated through baptism. In the words of Chrysostom: "For these two things most of all declare His unspeakable love, that He both suffered for His enemies, and that having died for His enemies, He freely gave to them by baptism entire remission of their sins."[47] There seems to have been no necessary friction between these two ideas (jus-

46. Jerome, *Expositio Quator Evangelorium Matthaeus* (PL 30:568). Cf. Origen: "Who has been justified by faith alone without works of the law? Thus, in my opinion, that thief who was crucified with Christ should suffice for a suitable example. He called out to Him from the cross, 'Lord Jesus, remember me when you come into Your kingdom!' In the Gospels nothing else is recorded about his good works, but for the sake of this faith alone Jesus said to him, 'Truly I say to you, today you will be with Me in paradise.' . . . For through faith this thief was justified without works of the law, since the Lord did not require in addition to this that he should first accomplish works, nor did he wait for him to perform some works when he had believed. But by his confession alone, the One who was about to begin His journey to paradise received him as a justified traveling companion with Himself" (*Romans* [Scheck] 3.9.3). Ambrosiaster: "He speaks of the blessed, concerned whom God ratifies this, that without work or any observance they are justified before God by faith alone" (*Commentary on Paul's Epistles*, on Rom. 4:6 [PL 17:87]). John Chrysostom: "For, on a sudden, to have brought men more senseless than stones to the dignity of angels, simply through bare words, and faith alone, without any laboriousness, is indeed glory and riches of mystery: just as if one were to take a dog, quite consumed with hunger and the mange, foul, and loathsome to see, and not so much as able to move, but lying cast out, and make him all at once into a man, and to display him upon the royal throne" (*Homilies on Colossians* 5, on 1:26–8). See also Origen, *Romans* (Scheck) 3.9.2; Ambrose, *Letters* 63.87; Ambrosiaster, *Commentary on Paul's Epistles*, on Rom. 4:5 (PL 17:86); *Epistle to the Galatians* 3.18.1–3 (Edwards, 45); Marius Victorinus, *Epistle to the Ephesians* 1.2.14–15 (Edwards, 138); Chrysostom, *Homilies on Acts* 32, on 15:1; *Homilies on Romans* 2, on 1:17 ("For you do not achieve it [salvation] by toilings and labors, but you receive it by a gift from above, contributing one thing only from your own store, believing"); 7, on 3:28; 9, on 5:2; *Homilies on Ephesians* 5, on 2:13–15 ("for by faith alone He saved us"); *Homilies on 1 Timothy* 4, on 1:15.

47. John Chrysostom, *Homilies on John* 27.1. Cf. Justin Martyr: "In order that we may not remain the children of necessity and of ignorance, but may become the children of choice and knowledge, and may obtain in the water the remission of sins formerly committed, there is pronounced over him who chooses to be born again, and has repented of his sins, the name of God the Father and Lord of the universe" (*First Apology* 61). Cyprian: "In baptism remission of sins is granted once for all" (*On Works and Alms* 2). Methodius: "Her very name also presignifies the Church, that by the grace of Christ and God is justified in baptism. For Anna is, by interpretation, grace" (*Oration on Simeon and Anna* 12). Chrysostom: "If you are to receive a gift, if baptism conveys remission, why delay?" (*Homilies on Acts* 7); "In the Law, he that has sin is punished; here, he that has sins comes and is baptized and is made righteous, and being made righteous, he lives, being delivered from the death of sin" (*Homilies on 1 Corinthians* 6.2).

tification by faith and by baptism) in the minds of at least some of the fathers. Basil of Caesarea says,

> Faith and baptism are two kindred and inseparable ways of salvation: faith is perfected through baptism, baptism is established through faith, and both are completed by the same names. For as we *believe* in the Father and the Son and the Holy Spirit, so are we also *baptized* in the name of the Father and of the Son and of the Holy Spirit; first comes the confession, introducing us to salvation, and baptism follows, setting the seal upon our assent.[48]

Basil's approach effectively makes initial justification itself a twofold process: faith introduces us to salvation, and baptism perfects the introduction. Basil's use of "seal" imagery may indicate that he regarded baptism as the public and official declaration of a justification that until then has been private and unofficial.[49]

The Christian Life: Justification after Conversion/Baptism

The question of the believer's continued justification after conversion and baptism is far more complex in the fathers than the previous issues. A definite strand of patristic teaching denies the sufficiency of faith after initial conversion. Chrysostom often speaks vigorously in this vein. For

48. Basil of Caesarea, *On The Holy Spirit* 12.28. Cf. Ambrose's conflation of grace, faith, and baptism: "Let no one glory in his own works, since no one is justified by his deeds, but one who is just has received a gift, being justified by baptism. It is faith, therefore, which sets us free by the blood of Christ, for he is blessed whose sin is forgiven and to whom pardon is granted" (*Letters* 73.11, in Anderson, Murphy, and Burgess, *Justification by Faith*, 127). John Chrysostom also conflates baptism and "being saved by faith" in *Homilies on Ephesians* 11, on 4:7.

49. Cyril of Jerusalem describes a similar twofold initial salvation in the case of Cornelius the centurion and his God-fearing friends in Acts 10: "Cornelius was a righteous man; God honored him with a vision of angels, and his prayers and gifts of charity were set up as a good memorial before God in heaven. Peter came; the Spirit was poured out on those who believed; they spoke in other tongues and prophesied; and after the grace of the Spirit was given, Scripture says that Peter 'commanded them to be baptized in the name of Jesus Christ' (Acts 10:48). Why? So that when their souls had already been born again by faith, their bodies also might share in the grace by the water of baptism" (*Catechetical Lectures* 3.4). Tertullian, however, denies any salvific value to faith prior to baptism (*On Baptism* 13). So, in effect, does John Chrysostom in *Homilies on John* 25.3. Other fathers, however, notably Origen, were equally clear on the reality of the believer's initial salvation prior to baptism. For Origen, see *Romans* 5.7.3 (Scheck, including n. 376). Others insisted that catechumens dying before baptism were nonetheless saved by their inward disposition. See esp. Ambrose, *De obitu Valentiniani* 51–53.

example, commenting on the fate of the wedding guest who lacked a wedding garment, he says, "Therefore, beloved, let not us either expect that faith is sufficient to us for salvation; for if we do not show forth a pure life, but come clothed with garments unworthy of this blessed calling, nothing hinders us from suffering the same as that wretched one."[50] It does not seem clear, however, whether this patristic strand is affirming a strict justification by works in the postconversion believer or whether its true intention may be to polemicize against "dead faith." If the latter, it can be matched by equally stringent statements from the most impeccably evangelical sources. "Faith is not sufficient for salvation" and parallel statements in the fathers could then mean, "A faith that is alone, devoid of fruit, will not save." This seems to be Jerome's import when commenting on Galatians 3:10:

> It is of course inquired from this place, if faith alone is sufficient for a Christian: and whether he is not cursed who despises the precepts of the gospel. But faith is effective for this, that it justifies those who approach God in their initial believing, if afterwards they remain in justification: however, without works of faith (not works of law) faith is dead. For he who does not believe the commands, and those who despise the precepts of the gospel, are alike cursed, as the Savior teaches.[51]

It perhaps reminds us of the forceful argument of François Turrettini, prince of seventeenth-century Reformed systematic theologians, that the "alone" in "faith alone justifies" applies not to the subject (faith) but to the predicate (justifies): justification is only by faith, yet this faith is never alone but is invariably and inseparably allied to holiness and good works, without which it is like an eye torn out of its socket, dead and useless.[52]

50. John Chrysostom, *Homilies on John* 10.3. Cf. his *Homilies on Matthew* 69.2: "Then in order that not even these should put confidence in their faith alone, He discourses to them also concerning the judgment to be passed upon wicked actions; to them that have not yet believed, of coming to Him by faith, and to them that have believed, of care with respect to their life. For the garment is life and practice. And yet the calling was of grace; why then does He take a strict account? Because although to be called and to be cleansed was of grace, yet, when called and clothed in clean garments, to continue keeping them so, this is of the diligence of those who are called. The being called was not of merit, but of grace." See also Chrysostom's comments in *Homilies on Matthew* 47.3; *Homilies on Romans* 5, on 2:7; *Homilies on Galatians*, on 5:6; *Homilies on Ephesians* 1, on 1:4; 4, on 2:8–10; *Commentary on the Psalms* (Hill, 2:50), all of which deny the postbaptismal sufficiency of faith, or faith alone, for salvation.

51. Jerome, *Epistle to the Galatians* (PL 30:848).

52. François Turrettini, *Institutes of Elenctic Theology* (Phillipsburg, NJ: P & R, 1994), 2:677. Cf. John Owen:

More germane to any discussion of justification in the fathers is the strand of patristic teaching that affirms the salvific efficacy of works of penance, especially almsgiving, in the life of the postconversion believer. Chrysostom again: "First the font cleanses, afterwards other ways also, many and of all kinds. For God, being merciful, has even after this given to us various ways of reconciliation, of all which the first is that by alms-doing. 'By alms-deeds,' it says, 'and deeds of faith sins are cleansed away' (Ecclus. 3:30)."[53] This strand can easily lend itself to a form of language that, at least on the surface, looks like a scheme of salvation by mercenary calculation, in which the aim is to make the merits of one's almsgiving outweigh the demerits of one's sins.[54]

On the other hand, the apparently merit-laden ethos of this view of almsgiving and other good works is offset by several other factors. First, the works themselves are often seen not as independent human contribu-

---

Suppose a person freely justified by the grace of God, through faith in the blood of Christ, without respect unto any works, obedience, or righteousness of his own, we do freely grant,—(1.) That God does indispensably require personal obedience of him; which may be called his evangelical righteousness. (2.) That God does approve of and accept, in Christ, this righteousness so performed. (3.) That hereby that faith whereby we are justified is evidenced, proved, manifested, in the sight of God and men. (4.) That this righteousness is pleadable unto an acquitment against any charge from Satan, the world, or our own consciences. (5.) That upon it we shall be declared righteous at the last day, and without it none shall so be. And if any shall think meet from hence to conclude unto an evangeli-cal justification, or call God's acceptance of our righteousness by that name, I shall by no means contend with them. And wherever this inquiry is made,—not how a sinner, guilty of death, and obnoxious unto the curse, shall be pardoned, acquitted, and justified, which is by the righteousness of Christ alone imputed unto him—but how a man that professes evangelical faith, or faith in Christ, shall be tried, judged, and whereon, as such, he shall be justified, we grant that it is and must be, by his own personal, sincere obedience. (*The Doctrine of Justification by Faith*, ch. 6, in *The Works of John Owen* [Edinburgh: Banner of Truth, 1965], 5:159–60)

Owen probably grants here all that Chrysostom could wish.

53. John Chrysostom, *Homilies on John* 73.3. Cf. Ambrose: "You did not dedicate yourself to the Lord on purpose to make your family rich, but that you might win eternal life by the fruit of good works, and atone for your sins by showing mercy" (*On the Duties of the Clergy* 1.30.150). See also the whole of Cyprian, *On Works and Alms*.

54. John Chrysostom: "Let us reflect then how many burdens of sins each of us has about him, and let us make our acts of mercy counterbalance them; nay rather, far exceed them, that not only the sins may be quenched, but that the acts of righteousness may be also accounted unto us for righteousness. For if the good deeds be not so many in number as to put aside the crimes laid against us, and out of the remainder to be counted unto us for righteousness, then shall no one rescue us from that punishment, from which God grant that we may be all delivered, through the grace and loving-kindness of our Lord Jesus Christ, with whom to the Father, etc." (*Homilies on Ephesians* 24). It has been argued that Chrysostom's final appeal in this passage to "the grace and loving-kindness of our Lord Jesus Christ" as the source of deliverance may relativize his previous talk of good deeds counterbalancing bad. Cf. n. 63, below.

tions but as instrumental means appointed by a gracious God whereby we may appropriate God's mercy. This thought is clear in the quotation above from Chrysostom, where he makes almsgiving and other charitable works parallel with baptism, given by God in his mercy as "various ways of reconciliation." This removes almsgiving from a strictly meritorious framework. Second, even almsgiving itself could be denounced as useless unless it was a genuine expression of faith. Ambrose says, "God requires not money but faith. And I do not deny that sins may be diminished by liberal gifts to the poor, but only if faith commends what is spent."[55] Seen in this perspective, almsgiving and other good works may become simply faith in action.[56] One wonders if the real intent of this strand of

55. Ambrose, *On Repentance* 2.9.82–83. Cf. Lactantius, *Divine Institutes* 6.13, where, however, he relates almsgiving ("bounty") to the demonstration of the sincerity of one's repentance, rather than to faith, warning his readers not to rely on their almsgiving if, in the rest of their lives, they prove morally unchanged. Bounty to the poor gives no license to sin.

56. The ultimate sovereignty of God's grace over all human almsgiving and other works is affirmed very clearly in a lengthy passage just outside our time frame, by John Cassian:

You see then what great means of obtaining mercy the compassion of our Savior has laid open to us, so that no one when longing for salvation need be crushed by despair, as he sees himself called to life by so many remedies. For if you plead that owing to weakness of the flesh you cannot get rid of your sins by fasting, and you cannot say: "My knees are weak from fasting, and my flesh is changed for oil; for I have eaten ashes for my bread, and mingled my drink with weeping," then atone for them by profuse almsgiving. If you have nothing that you can give to the needy (although the claims of want and poverty exclude none from this office, since the two mites of the widow are ranked higher than the splendid gifts of the rich, and the Lord promises that He will give a reward for a cup of cold water), at least you can purge them away by amendment of life. But if you cannot secure perfection in goodness by the eradication of all your faults, you can show a pious anxiety for the good and salvation of another. But if you complain that you are not equal to this service, you can cover your sins by the affection of love. And if in this also some sluggishness of mind makes you weak, at least you should submissively with a feeling of humility entreat for remedies for your wounds by the prayers and intercession of the saints.

Finally who is there who cannot humbly say: "I have acknowledged my sin: and my unrighteousness have I not hid"; so that by this confession he may be able also to add this: "And You forgave the iniquity of my heart"? But if shame holds you back, and you blush to reveal them before men, you should not cease to confess them with constant supplication to Him from Whom they cannot be hid, and to say to Him: "I acknowledge my iniquity, and my sin is ever before me. Against You only have I sinned, and have done evil before You"; as He is accustomed to heal them without any publication which brings shame, and to forgive sins without any reproaching. And further besides that ready and sure aid, the divine condescension has afforded us another also that is still easier, and has entrusted the possession of the remedy to our own will, so that we can infer from our own feelings the forgiveness of our offenses, when we say to Him: "Forgive us our debts as we also forgive our debtors."

Whoever then desires to obtain forgiveness of his sins, should study to fit himself for it by these means. Let not the stubbornness of an obdurate heart turn away any from the saving remedy and the fount of so much goodness, because even if we have done all these things,

patristic teaching was to affirm that faith must *continually* appropriate God's undeserved mercy and that such appropriation takes place in faith's actions—in living faith, not fruitless faith.[57]

In a more general sense, we find a broad strand of patristic teaching that daily repentance and a reliance on Christ's intercession are essential to the continued enjoyment of God's mercy. Chrysostom joyously extols the power of simple repentance:

> Tell me, if we fall into any difficult trouble, from whom do we not request help? And if we soon obtain our request, we breathe freely again. What an advantage it would be for you, to have a friend to whom you could go with your request, who will be ready to take it as a kindness, and be obliged to you for your asking! What an advantage, not to have to go about and seek someone to ask for his help, but to find one ready! And to have no need of others through whom to solicit his aid! What could be greater than this? Here then is One who does most for us, when we do not make our requests from any others than Himself: just as a sincere friend most complains of us for not trusting in his friendship, when we ask others to make our request to him. So let us act towards God, as our sincere Friend. "But what," you will ask, "if I should have offended Him?" Cease to give offense, and weep, and so draw near to Him, and you will quickly render Him propitious to your former sins. Say only, "I have offended." Say it from your soul and with a sincere mind, and all things are remitted to you. You do not so much desire your sins to be forgiven, as He desires to forgive you your sins. For proof that you do not so desire it, consider that you have no mind either to practise vigils, or to give your money freely; but He, that He might forgive our sins, spared not His Only-begotten and True Son, the partner of His throne. Do you see how much more He desires to forgive you your sins than you desire to be forgiven? Then let us not be lazy, let us put this off no longer. He is merciful and good: only let us give Him an opportunity.[58]

---

they will not be able to expiate our offenses, unless they are blotted out by the goodness and mercy of the Lord, who when He sees the service of pious efforts offered by us with a humble heart, supports our small and puny efforts with the utmost bounty, and says: "I, even I, am He that blots out your iniquities for My own sake, and I will remember your sins no more." (*Conference of Abbot Pinufius* 8)

57. Perhaps this is Cyril of Jerusalem's meaning in an otherwise puzzling passage: "There is much to tell of faith, and the whole day would not be time sufficient for us to describe it fully. At present let us be content with Abraham only, as one of the examples from the Old Testament, seeing that we have been made his sons through faith. He was justified not only by works, but also by faith: for though he did many things well, yet he was never called the friend of God, except when he believed. Moreover, his every work was performed in faith. Through faith he left his parents; left country, and place, and home through faith. In like manner, therefore, as he was justified, be justified yourself also" (*Catechetical Lectures* 5.5).

58. John Chrysostom, *Homilies on Acts* 36. Cf. Chrysostom, *De beato Philogonio* (PG 48:754): "I certify and bear witness to every individual one of us who has sinned, that if he gives up his previous sinning, and sincerely promises God to sin no more, God will demand

Commenting on 1 John 1:8–2:2, Jerome argues against perfectionism in the Christian life by appealing to the reality and necessity of Christ's ongoing ministry of intercession:

> I suppose that John [the apostle] was baptized and was writing to the baptized: I imagine too that all sin is of the devil. Now John confesses himself a sinner [in 1 John 1:8–2:2], and hopes for forgiveness of sins after baptism. . . . But that we may not utterly despair and think that if we sin after baptism we cannot be saved, he immediately checks the tendency: "And if anyone sins, we have an advocate with the Father, Jesus Christ the righteous, and He is the propitiation for our sins. And not for ours only, but also for the whole world." He addresses this to baptized believers, and he promises them the Lord as an advocate for their offences. He does not say: If *you* fall into sin, *you* have an advocate with the Father, Christ, and He is the propitiation for *your* sins: you might then say that he was addressing those whose baptism had been destitute of the true faith: but what he says is this, "*We* have an advocate with the Father, Jesus Christ, and He is the propitiation for *our* sins." And not only for the sins of John and his contemporaries, but for those of the whole world. Now in "the whole world" are included apostles and all the faithful, and a clear proof is established that sin after baptism is possible. It is useless for us to have Jesus Christ as an advocate, if sin is impossible.[59]

On occasion this is presented with a clear note of evangelical elation, as by Chrysostom: "If then the Spirit even makes intercession for us with groanings that cannot be uttered, and Christ died and intercedes for us, and the Father spared not His own Son for you, and elected you, and

---

from him nothing more for his greater discharge." See also Chrysostom, *Homilies against the Anomoeans* 5.7. Cf. Ambrose, speaking of the believer fallen into sin: "So the Lord Jesus, seeing the heavy burden of the sinner, weeps, for He does not allow the Church alone to weep. He has compassion together with His beloved, and says to him that is dead, 'Come forth,' that is, 'you who lie in darkness of conscience, and in the squalor of your sins, as in the prison-house of the guilty, come forth, declare your sins that you may be justified. For with the mouth confession is made unto salvation'" (*On Repentance* 2.7.57).

59. Jerome, *Against Jovinian* 2.2. Cf. Cyprian on the Lord's Prayer: "Let us therefore, brethren beloved, pray as God our Teacher has taught us. It is a loving and friendly prayer to beseech God with His own word, to come up to His ears in the prayer of Christ. Let the Father acknowledge the words of His Son when we make our prayer, and let Him also who dwells within in our breast Himself dwell in our voice. And since we have Him as an Advocate with the Father for our sins, let us, when as sinners we petition on behalf of our sins, put forward the words of our Advocate. For since He says, that 'whatsoever we shall ask of the Father in His name, He will give us,' how much more effectually do we obtain what we ask in Christ's name, if we ask for it in His own prayer!" (*On the Lord's Prayer* 3). For Christ's intercession, see also Cyprian, *Letters* 7.5; 51.18–19; Ambrose, *On Repentance* 1.3.14; Gregory of Nazianzus, *Fourth Theological Oration* 14. For the efficacy of simple repentance, see also Cyprian, *On the Lord's Prayer* 6; John Chrysostom, *Concerning Lowliness of Mind* 2; Jerome, *Dialogue against the Pelagians* 3.14.

justified you, why be afraid any more? Or why tremble when enjoying such great love, and having such great interest taken in you?"[60]

Sometimes, in a postconversion/postbaptismal context, we find the fathers specifying simply faith, or faith rather than works, or even explicitly "faith alone," as the indispensable requisite for justification. Clement of Rome, for example, says,

> All these, therefore, were highly honored, and made great, not for their own sake, or for their own works, or for the righteousness which they wrought, but through the operation of His will. And we, too, being called by His will in Christ Jesus, are not justified by ourselves, nor by our own wisdom, or understanding, or godliness, or works which we have wrought in holiness of heart; but by that faith through which, from the beginning, Almighty God has justified all men; to whom be glory for ever and ever. Amen.[61]

Ambrose says of Christians, "We are not justified by works but by faith, because the infirmity of our flesh is an impediment to works; but the brightness of faith overshadows the error of works and merits forgiveness of our faults."[62] (Ambrose's use of merit language here is a topic we will examine in a moment.) Chrysostom provides this antithesis: "For the law requires not only faith, but also works; but grace saves and justifies by faith."[63] Jerome, addressing the Christian reader of his commentary on Galatians, says, "Abraham believed in God, and it was imputed to him for righteousness. Thus likewise for you, faith alone is sufficient for righteousness."[64] At greater length, Basil of Caesarea, commenting on the apostle Paul's postconversion avowal of his reliance on Christ's righteousness alone in Philippians 3:8–9 and pointing to an ongoing lesson for the believer, says,

> This is the true elevation of man; this is his glory and greatness: truly to know that which is great, and to adhere to it, and to seek glory from the Lord of glory. The apostle says: Let him that glories glory in the Lord; declaring that Christ is made by God to be our wisdom and righteousness and sanctification and redemption, in order that, as it is written, Let him that glories glory in the Lord. For this is the true and perfect glorying in God, when a man is not lifted up on account of his own righteousness,

60. John Chrysostom, *Homilies on Romans* 15, on 8:34.
61. Clement of Rome, *First Epistle to the Corinthians* 32.
62. Ambrose, *De Jacob et vita beata* 2.2 (PL 14:648).
63. John Chrysostom, *Homilies on Galatians*, on 3:12. The fact that Chrysostom can speak in this vein, whereas elsewhere he denies the postbaptismal sufficiency of faith, requiring works also, lends some credence to the view that the latter denials were essentially a polemic against dead faith.
64. Jerome, *Epistle to the Galatians* (PL 30:848).

but has known himself to be wanting in true righteousness and to be justified by faith alone in Christ. And Paul glories, in that he despises his own righteousness, and seeks the righteousness which is through Christ, even the righteousness which is from God in faith, to know Him and the power of His resurrection and the fellowship of His sufferings, being conformed to His death, if by any means he might attain to the resurrection of the dead. Here all the elevation of pride falls to the ground. Nothing is left to you for boasting, O man: inasmuch as your whole boasting and hope consist in the mortification of your own will and in living henceforth the life which is in Christ. The first-fruits of this we have in the present time: for we live altogether in the grace and free gift of God.[65]

There are passages in the fathers where, although the language of justification by faith is not used, the sentiment of trust in God's grace and mercy in Christ is expressed as the sole ultimate hope of the Christian:

65. Basil of Caesarea, *Homilies on Humility* 22 (PG 31:529–32). Cf. Cyprian's vibrant Christ-centered assurance in the face of death: "But we who live in hope, and believe in God, and trust that Christ suffered for us and rose again, abiding in Christ, and through Him and in Him rising again, why either are we ourselves unwilling to depart hence from this life, or do we bewail and grieve for our friends when they depart as if they were lost, when Christ Himself, our Lord and God, encourages us and says, 'I am the resurrection and the life: he that believes in me, though he die, yet shall he live; and whosoever lives and believes in me shall not die eternally'? If we believe in Christ, let us have faith in His words and promises; and since we shall not die eternally, let us come with a glad security to Christ, with whom we are both to conquer and to reign for ever" (*On Mortality* 21). Gregory of Nyssa: "Now the tenet which has been held in common by all who have received the word of our religion is, that all hope of salvation should be placed in Christ, it being impossible for any to be found among the righteous, unless faith in Christ supply what is desired. And this conviction being firmly established in the souls of the faithful, and all honor and glory and worship being due to the Only-begotten God as the Author of life, Who doeth the works of the Father, as the Lord Himself says in the Gospel" (*Answer to Eunomius' Second Book* [*NPNF*[2] 5:255]). John Chrysostom:

"For I put you this question," Paul would say, "were you not liable for countless sins? Were you not in despair? Were you not under sentence? Were you not all out of heart about your salvation? What then saved you? It was your hoping in God alone, and trusting to Him about His promises and gifts; and you had nothing besides to contribute. If it was this, then, that saved you, hold it fast now also. For that which afforded you so great blessings, most certainly will not deceive you in regard to things to come. For it found you dead, and ruined, and a prisoner, and an enemy, and yet made you a friend, and a son, and a freeman, and righteous, and a joint-heir, and yielded such great things as no one ever even expected! How, after such bounty and generosity, will it betray you in what is to follow?" Do not say to me, "Hopes again! Expectations again! Faith again!" For it is in this way you were saved from the beginning, and this dowry was the only one that you brought to the Bridegroom. Hold it fast, then, and keep it. (*Homilies on Romans* 14, on 8:24)

For other similar references, see Cyprian, *Letters* 62.4; Athanasius, *To the Bishops of Egypt* 21; Marius Victorinus, *Epistle to the Galatians* 1.3.7 (Edwards, 39); Chrysostom, *Homilies on Romans* 2, on 1:17; 8, on 4:1–2; *Homilies on Galatians*, on 3:5; 5:5; *Homilies on Titus* 3, on 1:14; *Homilies on Hebrews* 7.6.

An eternal rest remains to those who, in the present life, have wrestled legitimately, which rest is not given according to the debt of works as just payment, but is bestowed according to the grace of an abundantly bountiful God to those who have hoped in Him.[66]

We are then righteous when we confess that we are sinners, and when our righteousness depends not upon our own merits, but on the mercy of God, as the Holy Scripture says, "The righteous man accuses himself when he begins to speak," and elsewhere, "Tell your sins that you may be justified." "God has shut up all under sin, that He may have mercy upon all." And the highest righteousness of man is this—whatever virtue he may be able to acquire, not to think it his own, but the gift of God.[67]

Ambrose could be particularly clear and forceful on this point:

Therefore the Lord our God tempers judgment with mercy. Who of us can survive without the divine pity? What can we do that is worthy of heavenly rewards? Who of us so rises in this body that he lifts his soul to a continual adherence to Christ? By what human merit, in short, is it procured that this corruptible flesh should put on incorruption, and this mortal put on immortality? By what labors, by what injuries inflicted on ourselves, can we take away our sins? The sufferings of this present age are unworthy toward the gaining of future glory. Not according to our merits, therefore, but according to the mercy of God, the form of heaven's decrees proceeds towards human beings.[68]

It has however been beneficial for me to begin to confess what I used to deny; I have begun to become acquainted with my crime, and not to cover up my unrighteousness. I have begun to pronounce against my unrighteousness before the Lord, and You have forgiven the impieties of my heart. But it is also beneficial to me because we are not justified by the works of the law. Therefore I do not have grounds on which I can glory in my works, I have no grounds on which to boast, and therefore I will glory in Christ. I will glory, not because I am righteous, but because I am redeemed. I will glory, not because I am free from sins, but because my sins are forgiven me. I will glory, not because I have done good, nor because someone has

---

66. Basil of Caesarea, *Homilies on the Psalms*, on 114:5 (PG 29:491). Cf. Basil's exhortation against despondency and to trust in God's mercy: "Anxiety is a good thing; but, on the other hand, despondency, dejection, and despair of our salvation, are injurious to the soul. Trust therefore in the goodness of God, and look for His succour, knowing that if we turn to Him rightly and sincerely, not only will He not cast us off forever, but will say to us, even while we are in the act of uttering the words of our prayer, 'Lo! I am with you'" (*Letters* 174).

67. Jerome, *Dialogue against the Pelagians* 1.13.

68. Ambrose, *Psalm 118* 42 (PL 15:1574).

done good to me, but because Christ is my advocate with the Father, and because Christ's blood has been shed for me.[69]

We find the same sentiment in the liturgy: "We trust not in our own righteousness, but in Your good mercy, by which You purchase our race."[70]

We can summarize this strand of patristic evangelical spirituality with a quotation from Theodoret of Cyrrhus, which expresses the matter so pithily that I may be forgiven for venturing just outside my self-imposed time frame: "I own myself wretched—aye, thrice wretched. I am guilty of many errors. Through faith alone I look for finding some mercy in the day of the Lord's appearing."[71] In the sixteenth century, the main architect of post-Luther Lutheranism, Martin Chemnitz, effectively rested the bulk of his patristic case on such passages, arguing that trust in God's mercy as one's sole ultimate hope was the inner meaning of the Reformation doctrine of justification, even if that doctrine is not semantically stated as such. Of these patristic passages, Chemnitz says,

They show the practice and the use of the article of justification most beautifully, because they place their conscience before the tribunal of God; and they contain such delightful statements that while reading them I feel myself touched by them in my inmost heart; and I do not read anything in the writings of the fathers with greater pleasure than their pious meditations. Also in the struggle of death the fathers both

69. Ambrose, *De Jacob et vita beata* 1.6 (PL 14:637).

70. *Liturgy of James* 25. The liturgy of James is thought to have its roots in the fourth century and so falls within our time frame.

71. Theodoret of Cyrrhus, *Letters* 83, to Dioscorus. For other passages with this note of ultimate appeal to, or reliance on, God and His grace and saving power, cf. *Letter of Barnabas* 12; Irenaeus, *Against Heresies* 5.2.3; Theophilus of Antioch, *Apology to Autolycus* 1.8; *Constitutions of the Holy Apostles* 8.11; Cyprian, *Letters* 53.5; Athanasius, *Festal Letters* 5.3; Ambrose, *On the Sacraments* 5.4.19 (Edwards, 133); Jerome, *Dialogue against the Pelagians* 3.14; *Letters* 69.4; 133.9; John Chrysostom, *Homilies on 1 Corinthians* 2.3; 24.7; *Homilies on 2 Corinthians* 1.3. Also to be noted is the way Chrysostom always concludes his sermons with an appeal to God's grace and love for final salvation, e.g., "From all worldly things, therefore, let us withdraw ourselves, and dedicate ourselves to Christ, that we may both be made equal to the apostles according to His declaration, and may enjoy eternal life; to which may we all attain, by the grace and love towards man of our Lord Jesus Christ to whom be glory and might forever and ever. Amen." (*Homilies on Matthew* 46.4); "Flee then wickedness, that you may have power over such [demons]; and pursue virtue with all your might. For if this is the case here, consider what it will be in the world to come. And as being evermore possessed with this love, lay hold on the life eternal; to which may we all attain, through the grace and love towards men of our Lord Jesus Christ, with Whom to the Father together with the Holy Spirit, be glory, might, honor, now and ever, and world without end. Amen." (*Homilies on 2 Corinthians* 26).

learned to know and expressed that same true marrow of the article of justification.[72]

Finally, let us address the use of merit language, which forms a solid strand in the Latin patristic corpus. Merit is sometimes ascribed to good works: "There is need of righteousness, that one may deserve well of God the Judge; we must obey His precepts and warnings, that our merits may receive their reward."[73] Sometimes merit is ascribed to faith: "He declares that Abraham by his faith merited the blessing which he received in begetting his son."[74] It is not easy to determine what exact content the Latin fathers were placing in such language or whether it had different meanings in different authors (or even at different times in the same author). The ascription of "merit" to works or faith may mean nothing more than identifying them as those qualities that "obtain" God's blessing. The Latin *meritum* derives from *mereo*, the Latin form of the Greek *meromai*, "to receive one's share." In itself it carries no necessary connotations of "just deserts" and can simply denote "that which obtains."[75] Sometimes, however, it does go beyond "that which obtains" to express the idea of inherent moral virtue. Even here, though, care is

72. Chemnitz, *Loci Theologici*, 1:510. A similar "underlying essence" or "metatheological principle," which is seen as being articulated and safeguarded by the doctrinal formulation "justification by faith," was proposed by the Lutheran/Roman Catholic dialogue in the United States: "Of everything from buttresses to boycotts, from catechesis to chant, from decretals to dogmas, one question had to be asked: 'Is it conducive to bringing people to put their trust and hope in the God of Jesus Christ *alone?*'" (Anderson, Murphy, and Burgess, *Justification by Faith*, 304). Recognizing this does not necessarily lead to a relativistic downgrading of justification by faith as merely one (fallible, human) attempt to formulate the metatheological principle, for one could always argue that (a) the formulation is found in Scripture and (b) nothing else will so effectively safeguard the principle.

73. Cyprian, *On the Unity of the Church* 15. Cf. Tertullian, *On Repentance* 6; *Pseudo-Clementine Recognitions* 2.21; 6.8; Lactantius, *Epitome of the Divine Institutes* 73; Ambrose, *On the Duties of the Clergy* 1.31.162; 1.48.246.

74. Jerome, *Against Jovinian* 1.5. Cf. Tertullian, *Against Marcion* 4.20; Cyprian, *Letters* 62.12; 75.12; Hilary of Poitiers, *On the Trinity* 10.68; Ambrosiaster, *Commentary on Paul's Epistles* (Bray, 123).

75. Cf. Alister E. McGrath, *Iustitia Dei: A History of the Doctrine of Justification*, 2 vols. (Cambridge: Cambridge University Press, 1989), 1:14–15. Faber (*Primitive Doctrine of Justification*, 385–87) reprints material from Archbishop Ussher arguing that the language of merit in the fathers means "to procure or to attain, without any relation at all to the dignity either of the person or the work" (385). Ussher cites from secular sources such as Tacitus, who says of Agricola "that by his virtues he merited the anger of Caius Caesar," and from Augustine, who says that the good works of Catholics had, "instead of thanks, merited the flames of hatred" from Donatists (385–86). In these instances "merit" clearly means "incur," "bring upon oneself." In my judgment, this does explain much of the Latin patristic language of merit, but I still think that some of it goes further than this to implications of righteous deserving, e.g., in the *Pseudo-Clementine Recognitions*.

needed; the use of the concept of virtue does not necessarily imply some quid pro quo human claim on God (especially when the same author, e.g., Ambrose or Jerome, elsewhere disavows human merit in favor of divine mercy). Hilary of Poitiers, while recognizing merits in the sense of virtues that obtain divine reward, also makes it clear that the reward is ultimately gracious in nature: "For these very works of righteousness would not suffice to merit perfect blessedness, unless in our righteous will the mercy of God overlooked the defects of human changes and impulses. From this comes the saying of the prophet, 'Your mercy is better than life' [i.e., better than our life deserves]. . . . Through the mercy of God, more will follow than is merited."[76]

And when a Latin father positively renounces or denounces merit, it seems it must then imply righteous human deserving, as when Rufinus represents Origen as saying of the saved, "It is by the grace of God and not by their own merit that they have been placed in that final state of happiness."[77] The shifting nuances of Latin patristic merit language probably make it impossible to discern a unitary body of thought on this issue in the first four centuries. Perhaps the most obvious function of Latin merit terminology was to underscore the point made in other terms by the Greek fathers, that faith without works is dead and that God takes our Christian obedience seriously, both now and when we stand before God's judgment seat.

76. Hilary of Poitiers, *Tractatus in LI Psalmum* (PL 9:322). Cf. John Chrysostom on the reward of the righteous in the parable of the sheep and the goats: "So for this cause, while the one are punished justly, the others are crowned by grace. For though they had done ten thousand things, the munificence were of grace, that in return for services so small and cheap, such a heaven, and a kingdom, and so great honor, should be given them" (*Homilies on Matthew* 79.2).

77. Origen, *De principiis* 2.3.3. Cf. 3.1.12; Marius Victorinus, *Epistle to the Ephesians* 1.2.7; 1.3.7–8 (Edwards, 132, 148); Jerome, *Dialogue against the Pelagians* 1.16 (of the Virgin Mary: "Where, observe, she says she is blessed not by her own merit and virtue, but by the mercy of God dwelling in her"); 2.7 (PL 23:568) ("He manifestly shows that righteousness is not in human merit but in God's grace, who accepts the faith of believers without the works of the law"); 2.25 (PL 23:590) (of Jerusalem in Ezek. 16:14, 60–61: "She is saved not by her merit but by His mercy"); 2.29 (PL 23:593) ("Whence we say that we human beings are just and holy, and—after our sins—pleasing to God, not so much by one's merit but by His clemency, to which every creature is subject and needs its mercy").

3

Justification in Augustine

DAVID F. WRIGHT

It is a frustrating business writing on a subject that Augustine did not write on—at least did not write on in the manner we would assume of a modern writer who had "written on justification." Augustine never addressed the topic of justification in a precise and focused way in any of his works and certainly never devoted a treatise or a sermon or a letter, and barely even a whole chapter or section of one of these, to it. So a good case could be made for holding that Augustine did not have a doctrine of justification. Within that theological complex often called Augustinianism, encompassing particularly "the doctrines of grace" in a later sense, he did clarify at great length his teachings on issues ancillary to justification, such as grace and faith, merit and election, forgiveness and freedom. But he scarcely answered key questions raised by later debates, and he nowhere systematized his position, which explains why his interpreters have not always agreed about him.

Alister McGrath draws attention to "a virtual absence of studies dealing with his doctrine of *justification*," finding this to be the more astonishing given the importance of Augustine's doctrine of justification as the earliest discussion at the twilight of Western theology.[1] He proceeds to

1. Alister E. McGrath, *Iustitia Dei: A History of the Doctrine of Justification*, 2nd ed. (Cambridge: Cambridge University Press, 1998), 24. The section on Augustine (pp. 23–36)

set out Augustine's "new understanding of justification"—new, that is, in relation to Augustine's earlier belief—exposed in *Various Questions to Simplician*, written in the year 396, soon after he became bishop in Hippo. In responding to Simplician's request for clarification of Romans 9:1–29, as Augustine himself put it in his *Reconsiderations* thirty years later, "I tried hard to maintain the free choice of the human will, but the grace of God prevailed."[2] "Augustine's teaching on justification altered . . . radically at this point," remained constant hereafter, and "henceforth would be known as the 'classic Augustinian theology of grace.'"[3] It must, however, be insisted that "doctrine of justification" and "theology of grace" are not synonymous and, more precisely, that Augustine's understanding of the former did not change around 396. *Various Questions* does not discuss or define justification and may be more truly said to presuppose the meaning or meanings of "justify," and so on, that it deploys.

What, then, does Augustine mean by the Latin verb *justifico*, which he found in the Old Latin Bible texts (and could have found later in the Vulgate)? There is general agreement that he took it to mean "to make righteous" and held to this throughout his writing career. The position is not as straightforward as this, quite apart from his ability, according to McGrath, to embrace within this one understanding of the term both "the *event* of justification" and "the *process* of justification" without always distinguishing between the two.[4] There is evidence that Augustine was aware of a declarative sense of *justifico* ("I justify"), but I know of no place in his corpus where he directly addresses the meaning of *justifico* as a question to be resolved. Latin is unable to express the English language's distinction between "justice" and "righteousness," between "just" and "righteous," and so, in encountering translations of Augustine's works, one may meet variations between the two in English that go back to a single Latin original.

How Augustine interpreted *justifico* is best revealed en passant, as it were. In one of his first anti-Pelagian writings—in the view of many, perhaps his finest, *The Spirit and the Letter* (AD 412)—he asks, "Must then the unrighteous [*injustus*], in order that he may be justified [*justificetur*]—that is, become righteous [*fiat justus*]—use the law lawfully . . . ?"[5]

---

is unchanged from the first edition of 1986 (1:23–36). I am grateful for suggestions made by A. N. S. Lane after this paper was delivered, which have helped to improve its final form.

2. Augustine, *Reconsiderations* 2.1.1 (PL 32:629). The Latin *Retractationes* does not mean "retractions" in the sense of "recantations," but more "reviews, revisions." All quotations from Augustine in this chapter are the author's translation.

3. McGrath, *Iustitia Dei*, 25.

4. Ibid., 31.

5. Augustine, *The Spirit and the Letter* 10.16 (PL 44:210).

Later in the same treatise he is explicit: "What else does 'having been justified' [*justificati*] mean than 'having become/been made just' [*justi facti*], that is, by the one who justifies the ungodly, so that from being ungodly one becomes righteous [*fiat justus*]?"[6] A little later he identifies the "inscription" of the new covenant on the hearts of believers directly as *justificatio* ("justification").[7]

In the same work Augustine confirms this interpretation by showing that he takes "the righteousness of God" in Romans 1:17 to be so called because, by bestowing it, God makes people righteous (*justos facit*). Similarly in Psalm 3:8, "salvation is the Lord's" speaks of the Lord making us *salvos* ("saved").[8] Augustine repeats the point elsewhere in this text: "'the righteousness of God,' not that whereby God is righteous but that *qua induit hominem cum justificat impium* ['with which he endows a person when he justifies the ungodly']"; and again, "'the righteousness of God' by which by his gift we are made [*efficimur*] righteous. . . . This is the righteousness of God which he not only teaches through the precept of the law but also gives through the gift of the Spirit."[9]

If we turn to a later work against the Pelagians, *Grace and Free Will*, written in 426/427, Augustine appears to say the same thing concerning *justifico*: "It is necessary for a person not only that when ungodly [*impius*] he should be justified by the grace of God, that is, from being ungodly *fiat justus* ['becomes/is made just/righteous'] . . . but also, once he is already justified [*justificatus*] by faith, grace should walk with him and he lean upon it lest he fall."[10]

Is there, then, in Augustine's mind a valid sense of *justifico* that applies, in its perfect passive form, to a particular point in the believer's experience? Is this "the *event* of justification" of which McGrath speaks? If we turn back to *Various Questions*, we find Augustine emphasizing that good works do not produce grace but are produced by grace. How can someone live righteously [*juste*] who has not been justified [*fuerit justificatus*]? How can he live holily [*sancte*] who has not been made holy [*fuerit sanctificatus*]? . . . Grace justifies so that the justified person [*justificatus*] may live justly."[11]

Going on to consider Paul's testimony in 2 Timothy 4:7–8, "I have fought the good fight . . . ," Augustine comments, "How could the apostle speak presumptuously of a debt being repaid to him unless he had first

6. Ibid., 26.45 (PL 44:228).
7. Ibid., 27.48 (PL 44:230).
8. Ibid., 11.18 (PL 44:211).
9. Ibid., 9.15 (PL 44:209); 32.56 (PL 44:237).
10. Augustine, *Grace and Free Will* 6.13 (PL 44:889–90).
11. Augustine, *Various Questions to Simplician* 1.2.3 (PL 40:113).

received grace which was not due to him, grace by which having been justified [*justificatus*] he fought the good fight?"

Yet immediately the pendulum swings back again. Paul had obtained mercy, believing in the One who justifies not the godly but the ungodly in order to make him godly by justifying him. Augustine comes back to his basic sense of *justifico*, with the object variously *impium* ("ungodly") or *injustum* ("unjust, unrighteous") and the outcome *pium* ("godly") or *justum* ("just, righteous").[12]

Later on in this review of *Various Questions*, he asks, "Who can live righteously and do good works unless he has been justified [*justificatus*] by faith?"[13] Similarly he declares, "Christ died for the ungodly not that they should remain ungodly but that, having been justified [*justificati*], they should be converted from their ungodliness, believing in the one who justifies the ungodly."[14] It is consistent with Augustine's fundamental reading of Paul that he can talk of someone "beginning to be justified" and yet is also able to state repeatedly that "unless a person has been justified, he cannot do good works."[15] Does he mean any more than that a Christian cannot do good works without some partial renewal of righteousness? Or should we refer this "having been justified" to the initial remission of sins, which Augustine undoubtedly believed to be the beginning of the life of holiness?

There is some textual evidence in Augustine to confirm the latter reading. In his very late *Unfinished Work against Julian*, he contests Julian's appeal to Romans 5:1 (a verse that Augustine himself cited only infrequently) by asserting, "Justification is conferred not through remission of sins alone. . . . God justifies the ungodly not only by re-mitting a person's evil deeds but also by bestowing love [*charitatem*] so that the person may turn away from evil and do good through the Holy Spirit."[16]

In a few passages, Augustine cites the penitent tax collector who left the temple *justificatus* unlike the Pharisee. In expounding Psalm 111 (110), Augustine extols the divine *magnificentia* ("munificence," "gener-osity") of justifying the ungodly. He considers the possibility that, in the tax collector's case, a meritorious work of confession of sins preceded that divine generosity.

12. Ibid., 1.2.3 (PL 40:113).
13. Ibid., 1.2.21 (PL 40:126).
14. Ibid., 1.2.18 (PL 40:123). The translation by J. H. S. Burleigh, *Augustine: Earlier Writings*, Library of Christian Classics 6 (London: SCM, 1953), 400, fails to distinguish between the tenses, "should be justified" and "converted."
15. Augustine, *Various Questions to Simplician* 1.2.7 (PL 40:115); 1.2.5 (PL 40:114).
16. Augustine, *Unfinished Work against Julian* 2.165 (PL 45:1212).

This is the *magnificentia* of the Lord, the justification of the sinner, because "the one who humbles himself will be exalted, and the one who exalts himself will be abased." This is the *magnificentia* of the Lord, since the person who is forgiven much, loves much. This is the *magnificentia* of the Lord, since "where sin abounded, grace abounded even more." . . . For no one acts justly [*justitiam . . . operatur*] unless he has been justified.[17]

The emphasis in this section is wholly on the pardon of the sinner. A similar train of thought is evident in an important letter, *Epistle* 194, sent during 418 in the midst of the Pelagian debates, in which Augustine writes of remission of sins as grace; presents the example of the tax collector who went down *justificatus merito fidelis humilitatis* ("justified by the merit of his faithful humility"), for the person who humbles himself will be exalted (Luke 18:13–14); and then rules out the conclusion that the man's "believing humility" constituted prevenient merit, since the beginning of faith was itself the gift of God.[18]

In passages such as these, it is easy to lose sight of the normative interpretation of *justifico* assumed by Augustine. Earlier in this same letter, he asserts that the righteous/just were made so without preceding merits, for *justi . . . facti sunt cum justificati sunt* ("they were made just/righteous when they were justified"), as the apostle says, *justificati gratis per gratiam ipsius* ("justified freely through his grace") (Rom. 3:24).[19] In the late work *Rebuke and Grace*, the responsibility to bring the means of grace to everyone (since we do not know who belongs to the company of the predestined) is emphasized by Augustine so that people *justificati ex fide* ("justified from faith") may have peace with God or may begin to have peace with God—he uses both formulations.[20] Here we have one of Augustine's infrequent citations of Romans 5:1. Those schooled in Reformation theology are likely to misread Augustine in such places or at least to assume with unwarranted confidence that his meaning is plain.

Let us remind ourselves what we are engaged in so far. Since Augustine hardly ever, and never extensively, addressed the question of the different meanings of *justifico* in a systematic manner, we are looking at some of the dispersed evidence for his use of it apparently in some other sense than "make righteous." No claims are being made for an explicit coherence that may be reliably attributed to Augustine himself. For a number of reasons, he is easily read by children of the Reformation and perhaps just as easily misread. He cites Scripture at great length,

17. Augustine, *Expositions of the Psalms* 110:3 (PL 37:1464).
18. Augustine, *Epistles* 194.3.7 (PL 33:877).
19. Ibid., 194.3.6 (PL 33:876).
20. Augustine, *Rebuke and Grace* 15.46 (PL 44:944–45).

and especially the Pauline Epistles, which establish for him salvation received by grace alone—the initiative is entirely God's, who elects whom he wills—through faith apart from works performed in advance of reception, and faith itself the gift of God. That is to say, his anti-Pelagian writings in particular are replete with Pauline-inspired discussions of this kind, which do not call upon him to clarify repeatedly that *justifico* basically means "to make righteous," or to show his readers how he understands the gift of justification—of being *justificati*—in relation to this normal meaning.

We probably have sufficient evidence to demonstrate that what McGrath calls "the *event*" of justification for Augustine is essentially at least the forgiveness of sins, the pardoning of guilt. This emerges from his first major treatise against Pelagian teachings, *The Merits and Remission of Sins and Infant Baptism* of late 411 or early 412. Augustine enters into a discussion of Romans 5:16: "The judgment is from one [offense] to condemnation, but the grace is from many offenses to justification," in which the significance of "justification" contrasted with "condemnation" is not touched upon.[21] "From Christ, in whom we are all justified [*justificamur*], we obtain the remission not merely of original sin but also of the other sins we have added to it."[22] Later in the work he focuses on "the one Mediator, in whom is found [*posita est*] our propitiation and justification, by which [*per quam*] we are reconciled to God with the termination of hostilities produced by sin."[23] And again, by analogy with the serpent elevated by Moses in the desert, "whoever is conformed to the likeness of Christ's death through faith and baptism in him is freed [*liberatur*] from sin through justification and from death through resurrection."[24]

Earlier in this same anti-Pelagian treatise, Augustine spends time drawing out the controversial force of his Latin text of Romans 5:18: "As through the offense of one upon all people to condemnation, so also through the justification of one upon all people to justification of life." English translations of Augustine sometimes obscure the distinctive reading by giving "through the righteousness of one," but "through the justification of one" is useful for Augustine in ruling out imitation as the form of movement from "the one" to "the all," whether of sin or of salvation. When Paul says of Christ, "through the justification of one,"

21. Augustine, *The Merits and Remission of Sins and Infant Baptism* 1.12.15 (PL 44:117).

22. Ibid., 1.13.16 (PL 44:118). Similarly elsewhere in Augustine, *Marriage and Concupiscence* 2.27.46 (PL 44:463) and *Handbook* [*Enchiridion*] 14.50 (PL 40:256).

23. Augustine, *The Merits and Remission of Sins and Infant Baptism* 2.20.34 (PL 44:171).

24. Ibid., 1.32.61 (PL 44:145).

Augustine states that "he more expressly stated his point than if he were to say 'through the righteousness of one,'" insofar as Christ alone justifies the ungodly as alone both just and the justifier.[25]

Tracking citation and exegesis of particular verses or paragraphs of Scripture is one avenue into Augustine's theology, as also is recognition of the texts he does not use. What, for example, did he make of Romans 4:5, about the person who believes God who justifies the ungodly, to whom "faith is credited [*deputetur*] to righteousness"? Of the last clause, not very much, it seems; its infrequent occurrences never, to my knowledge, rise above simple quotation. He is much more interested in the verse's assertion of God's justification of the ungodly, which he cites very frequently.

One verse that does not occasion difficulty for Augustine is the last part of Romans 2:13, "doers of the law will be justified." In *The Spirit and the Letter* he is certain that Paul cannot have meant to contradict himself, since elsewhere Paul declares that a person is justified freely by God's grace without works of the law (cf. Rom. 3:24, 28), intending by "freely" simply that works do not precede justification. Augustine succeeds, as only he could, in demonstrating that Paul's meaning is that "justification does not subsequently accrue to them as doers of the law." The statement "The men will be liberated," so he argues, predicates liberation of existing men, whereas "The men will be created" affirms that creation will bring men into being. "The doers of the law will be honored" predicates honor accruing to those already fulfilling the law, but "doers of the law will be justified" can only mean that "the just are justified" or, if you like, "doers of the law will be created."[26]

As if sensing that he may not yet be enjoying a standing ovation, Augustine continues with this very interesting passage:

> Alternatively, the verb "will be justified" [*justificabuntur*] is used to express the meaning "will be regarded [*habebuntur*] as righteous, will be reckoned [*deputabuntur*] as righteous," as is said of a certain man, "But he, wanting to justify himself" [Luke 10:29], that is, to be regarded and reckoned as righteous. Similarly, we mean one thing by "God sanctifies his saints" and another by "Sanctified be your name" [Matt. 6:9], the former because he makes those to be saints who were not saints already, but the latter so that

---

25. Ibid., 1.14.18 (PL 44:118–19). In Augustine, *Marriage and Concupiscence* 2.27.46 (PL 44:463) and *Against Two Letters of the Pelagians* 4.4.8 (PL 44:615), the *NPNF¹* translation obscures Augustine's text, as does P. F. Landes, *Augustine on Romans* (Chico, CA: Scholars Press, 1982), 11, in translating *Exposition of Certain Propositions from the Epistle to the Romans* 29 (PL 35:2068). Later, in *Nature and Grace* 41.48 (PL 44:270) and *Handbook* 14.51 (PL 40:256), Augustine uses *justitia* instead of *justificatio*.

26. Augustine, *The Spirit and the Letter* 26.45 (PL 44:228).

what is always holy in itself might also be regarded [*habeatur*] as holy by human beings, that is, feared as holy.[27]

Augustine does not apply this alternative reading to his problem text before moving on, but presumably, by implying the meaning "doers of the law will be counted as righteous," he has secured his goal of avoiding works of law placed before and hence effecting justification. But I have found no other occurrences in Augustine of this declarative sense of justification. Luke 10:29 rarely appears elsewhere in his corpus. Yet the explanation he gives here in *The Spirit and the Letter* is sufficiently developed to suggest that it was not devised solely for this occasion. He was assiduously attentive to word usage, not solely in the service of theological sophistry.

Before focusing on justifying faith, I will summarize two rather fine passages from *The Spirit and the Letter*. The righteousness of the law is attained and fulfilled only by the person who through faith wins favor with (*concilians*) the Justifier. The work, of which it is said that he who does it will live, is done only by the justified (*justificato*). Of the faith by which justification is obtained (*impetratur*), Paul said, "If you confess with your mouth the Lord Jesus and believe in your heart that God raised him from the dead, you will be saved" (Rom. 10:9). So far as one is saved (*salvus*), thus far is one righteous (*justus*). By this faith we believe that God will raise us too from the dead, both even now in the spirit, that we may at present live sober, righteous, and godly lives, and hereafter in the resurrection of the flesh, which is earned by the spirit, which precedes it in a resurrection appropriate to itself, that is, justification. By faith in Jesus Christ, therefore, we obtain salvation, both begun in us already in reality and in perfection awaited hereafter.[28] In such a meditative exposition, justification at one point seems attained, accomplished, at another a matter of partial enjoyment. The verb is treated freely almost as a synonym of "save" and appears to possess no privileged status as a description of salvation. *Justificatio* is suggestively portrayed as the spirit's anticipation here and now of the future resurrection of the body.

The second passage insists on the partial character of righteousness experienced in this present life.

> Whatever righteousness a person has, he must not presume that he has it of himself, but from the grace of God who justifies him, and must still go on hungering and thirsting for righteousness from the one who is the liv-

27. Ibid. This passage is discussed by J. Henninger, *S. Augustinus et Doctrina de Duplici Justitia* (Mödling, Austria: St. Gabriel, 1935), 50, as evidence that Augustine here alone entertained an alternative meaning but turned away from it.

28. Augustine, *The Spirit and the Letter* 29.51 (PL 44:232–33).

ing bread and with whom is the fountain of life, who so effects [*operatur*] justification in his saints, toiling amid temptation in this life, that there is always somewhat that his generosity may add in answer to their prayer and that his mercy may pardon in response to their confession.[29]

Here with unusual clarity Augustine depicts God's continuing working in and working out of justification in God's people. Toward the end of this article I will draw out some implications of Augustine's varied presentations of the vocabulary of justification in his Latin.

How is a person justified in Augustine's eyes? To a considerable extent, the answer is given in the basic sense he assigns to justification itself. McGrath states,

> The motif of *amor Dei* ("love of God") dominates Augustine's theology of justification, just as that of *sola fide* ("by faith alone") would dominate that of one of his later interpreters. . . . It is unacceptable to summarize Augustine's doctrine of justification as *sola fide iustificamur* ("we are justified by faith alone")—if any such summary is acceptable, it is *sola caritate iustificamur* ("we are justified by love alone").[30]

If these are the only two on offer, perhaps we should decline both. We should certainly not compensate for one exaggeration by giving another.

The difficulty we face in dealing with the human response that receives justification is the reverse of our difficulty with justification itself, that is, an *embarras de richesses*. The tricky business is to strike a fair balance in an Augustine who displayed many faces, some of which theologians find vastly more congenial that others.

It is well known that Augustine influentially bequeathed to Western theology a prominent role for Galatians 5:6, "faith which is operative [*operatur*] through love." Here is one of his many considerations of this faith, from *Grace and Free Will*:

> Unthinking folk have concluded from the apostle's statement "We judge that a person is justified through faith without works of law" [Rom. 3:28] that he meant faith to suffice even for someone living badly with no good works. Heaven forbid that he should reckon such a person a "vessel of election," since after saying in one place "in Christ neither circumcision nor the lack of it has any value," he added immediately "but faith which works through love." That is the faith which separates God's faithful from impure demons—for even those, as the apostle James says, "believe and tremble" [James 2:19], but they do no good works. Therefore they do not

29. Ibid., 36.65 (PL 44:244–45).
30. McGrath, *Iustitia Dei*, 30.

possess the faith from which the righteous lives, that is, the faith which works through love, so that God grants it eternal life according to its works. But because our good works themselves come from God, from whom we have both faith and love, the self-same teacher of the Gentiles called eternal life itself grace.[31]

The phrase from Galatians 5:6 plays a pivotal role in Augustine's reconciling Paul with James on justification, in differentiating genuine faith from the mere mental assent or credence of the demons, and in coordinating scriptural teaching about rewards with his central emphasis on the gratuitous gift-character of all God's salvific blessings. He deals with this nature of justifying faith in his treatise *Faith and Works*, of 413, in one of his *Eighty-Three Various Questions*, probably in the early 390s, in *The Spirit and the Letter* at the outset of the wrangles with Pelagius and associates—and indeed throughout the literature of this sequence of controversies—and in several other works also. Let me draw out a number of points that Augustine repeatedly makes on this issue.

First, justification is received as a gift of God's gratuitous grace without preceding works or merit. Question 76 of *Eighty-Three Various Questions* deals with James 2:20: "Faith without works is useless." This passage in James shows how Paul is to be understood in declaring that people are justified without works. Both James and Paul use the example of Abraham, Paul in order to teach that "no one should suppose that it is by the merits of previous works that he has attained to the gift of justification which is in faith." Paul had in view Jewish believers offended at unqualified (i.e., uncircumcised) Gentiles being granted the grace of Christ. "For this reason the apostle Paul says that a person can be justified without works—preceding works."[32]

Later, when he cites 1 Corinthians 6:9–11—"Neither fornicators, nor idolators . . . will inherit the kingdom of God. And such indeed were you; but you have been washed, . . . you have been justified in the name of our Lord Jesus Christ and in the Spirit of our God"—Augustine comments, "By these statements he teaches quite clearly that they have not attained through past good behavior the justification of faith nor through their merits this grace which had been given them, when he says 'And such indeed were you.'"[33]

Augustine never tires of reemphasizing this cardinal refutation of Pelagians and semi-Pelagians (as later writers called those who were more accurately described as semi-Augustinians). It is basic to one of his earliest anti-Pelagian works, *The Merits and Remission of Sins and*

---

31. Augustine, *Grace and Free Will* 7.18 (PL 44:892).
32. Augustine, *Eighty-Three Various Questions* 76.1 (PL 40:88).
33. Ibid., 76.2 (PL 40:88).

Infant Baptism. Listen to *Epistle* 194 (AD 418–419), one of his weighty epistolary interventions in these debates: "It is grace which justifies the ungodly, that is, the one formerly ungodly thereby becomes just. Hence the receiving of this grace is not preceded by any merits because the ungodly merit punishment, not grace, and it would not be grace if it were awarded as something due and not freely given."[34]

At one point in this letter, Augustine toys with what seems a Pelagian argument, that there is some merit in faith if faith seeks and obtains (*impetrat*) remission of sins. The tax collector in Luke 18 went down "justified [*justificatus*] by the merit of believing humility." Nevertheless, Augustine insists, faith itself, from which all *justitia* ("justice," "righteousness") takes its beginning, is not to be attributed to human decision (*arbitrio*) or to "any preceding merits," since any good merits, such as they are, come from faith. No, faith is a free gift of God, which in turn explains why some receive it and others do not.[35] But election is not our concern on this occasion.

It follows from these texts that, should someone depart this life soon after coming to faith, justification of faith remains with him or her, obviously not because of subsequent good works, which he has had no opportunity to fulfill, but also not because of preceding good works—for he has attained justification by grace and not by good works.[36]

The second emphasis to be highlighted is that faith, which justifies without prior merit, always entails ensuing merit—the merit of good works done from faith. The passage in 1 Corinthians 6 shows that "moral conduct is required of believers from the moment of their faith," and Romans 2:13, "Not hearers . . . but doers of the law will be justified," shows that faith that fails to issue in good works is barren or dead and does not enjoy justification.[37] So, when Paul declares that a person is justified through faith without works of the law (Rom. 3:28), it is not his object that works of *justitia* be despised once one has come to profession of faith, for these works follow the person who has been justified, not qualify in advance him or her who is to be justified.[38]

This again hardly needs extensive quotation to establish in Augustine, but it is important to stress that what he is concerned to vindicate is the necessity of living, fertile faith. Hence he characteristically does not at-

---

34. Augustine, *Epistle* 194.3.7 (PL 33:877).
35. Ibid., 194.3.9 (PL 33:877).
36. Augustine, *Eighty-Three Various Questions* 76.1 (PL 40:88).
37. Ibid., 76.2 (PL 40:88).
38. Augustine, *Faith and Works* 14.21 (PL 40:211). For a fine discussion, see *Expositions of the Psalms* 31.II.3–6 (PL 36:259–62), where Augustine sets the Paul of Rom. 3:28 against the Paul of Gal. 5:6 for the purpose of clarifying the distinction in value of works before faith and after faith.

tribute justification to good works or to faith and good works. Since he is extremely careful to clarify that justification is received *sine operibus, sine ullis praecedentibus meritis* ("without works, without any preceding merits"), he seems consequently careful to avoid linking justification to works that must ensue in the justified. Hence the necessity of these works of holiness essentially attests the reality, the authenticity, of faith in the justified. This is thus one of the contexts in which Augustine speaks of justification in the perfect tense, and often in the passive. "No one works *justitiam* ['righteousness,' 'justice'] unless [already] *justificatus*: 'to believe in him who justifies the ungodly' starts from faith, so that good works do not by coming first show what a person has deserved, but by following show what he has received."[39]

Thus Augustine unmistakably preserved the distinction between faith as the free grace-gift of God and the fruitful life of good works to which it must give rise. So often one feels that his meaning would be well conveyed by the use of "alone"—faith alone without works—but the phrase *sola fide* does not occur in his corpus in this sense. It is generally deployed with a pejorative meaning, of those who perversely relied on "faith alone" while refusing to abandon their vices and pursue good works.[40]

What we have just been discussing is typically expressed by Augustine's frequent citation of Galatians 5:6, faith that *operatur* ("works") through love. This is for him a wonderfully convenient apostolic clarification of the nature of faith that receives justification. But we need carefully to fix its significance, which undoubtedly falls far short of McGrath's assertion that "we are justified *sola caritate*" ("by love alone") would be nearer to a fair summary of Augustine's doctrine than "we are justified *sola fide*."[41] Apart from anything else, "we are justified by faith" is found very frequently in his works, but to my knowledge never "justified by love." So we must forcefully insist, first of all, in making this third point, that Galatians 5:6 stands preeminently for the genuineness of faith, which is God's gift toward justification. This is nearly always the context in which this Pauline clause is cited.

The inadequate faith that Galatians 5:6 excludes may be of two kinds. On the one hand, it is mere credence, by which "even the devils believe

39. Augustine, *Expositions of the Psalms*, 110:3 (PL 37:1464).

40. See the survey by Adolar Zumkeller, "Der terminus 'sola fides' bei Augustinus," in *Christian Authority: Essays in Honour of Henry Chadwick*, ed. G. R. Evans (Oxford: Clarendon, 1988), 86–100.

41. McGrath, *Iustitia Dei*, 30. He follows G. Bavaud, "La doctrine de la justification d'après saint Augustin et la Réforme," *Revue des études augustiniennes* 5 (1959): 21–32, at 24–27, with statements such as "Aux yeux de saint Augustin, c'est la charité qui justifie le pécheur" ("In the eyes of St. Augustine, it is love that justifies the sinner") (27). Cf. also Henninger, *S. Augustinus*, 53–54.

and tremble" (James 2:19). McGrath seems to advance no further than this focus on faith as belief, "merely assent to revealed truth," "primarily . . . an adherence to the Word of God, which inevitably introduces a strongly intellectualist element into his concept of faith, thus necessitating its supplementation with *caritas* or *dilectio* (each meaning 'love, charity, affection') if it is to justify man."[42] What this approach leaves out of account is the other kind of faith found wanting by Augustine—faith that relies so heavily on grace and forgiveness as to see no need for effort and pursuit of godliness. This is certainly not merely intellectualist credence.

John Burnaby's *Amor Dei* is a surer guide to the many-layered thought of Augustine than the Oxford professor. He faces squarely the common criticism that faith, for the bishop of Hippo, fails to make contact with "the 'evangelical' faith of trusting personal relationship to God in Christ, which was as real a part of his religion as it was of St. Paul's."[43] Burnaby rounds off his paragraphs on the question by quoting another giant of Augustinian scholarship, Étienne Gilson: "The Augustinian faith in its essence is at the same time adherence of the mind to supernatural truth and humble surrender of the whole man to the grace of Christ: the mind's adherence to the authority of God implies humility, but humility in its turn implies a trust in God which is itself an act of love and charity."[44]

Augustine discussed the nature of faith, of believing, extensively, for example, in his famous pre-Anselmian dialectic of faith before, and with a view to, understanding. Here is a passage from his *Homilies on John's Gospel*, starting from John 6:29, "This is the work of God, that you believe in the one whom he has sent":

> "That you believe in him [*in eum*]," not "believe him [*ei*]." But if you believe in him, you do believe him. Yet believing him does not immediately involve believing in him. For the demons also believed him but not in him. . . . What then does it mean to believe in him? By believing to love [*amare*], by believing to love [*diligere*], by believing to go into him [*in eum ire*], and be incorporated in his members. . . .
>
> Such then is that very faith which God demands of us, and he fails to find what he demands unless he first gives what he may find. What faith, other than as the apostle defined it very fully elsewhere, "Neither circumcision

42. McGrath, *Iustitia Dei*, 30. When McGrath says of Augustine's teaching, "Faith alone is merely assent to revealed truth, itself adequate to justify," "adequate" should read "inadequate."

43. John Burnaby, *Amor Dei* (London: Hodder & Stoughton, 1938), 78.

44. Ibid., 79, citing Étienne Gilson, *Introduction à l'étude de saint Augustin* (Paris: Vrin, 1929), 36. The second edition (1943) of this work was translated by L. E. M. Lynch as *The Christian Philosophy of Saint Augustine* (London: Victor Gollancz, 1961); cf. p. 31.

nor uncircumcision counts for anything, but faith which works through love"?[45]

This faith is faith in him who justifies the ungodly, to cite another of Augustine's forms of expression in controversy. To talk of faith needing to be "supplemented" by love is misleading. Augustine, writes Burnaby, "is far from the Socratic intellectualism: to know what is good is not to do it. But he is sure that no man can have a genuine belief in the Incarnation without at least the beginnings of that humble trust in God which St. Paul meant by faith."[46]

In one of his sermons, Augustine says, after distinguishing between *credere Christum* ("believe Christ") and *credere in Christum* ("believe in Christ"):

> That person believes in Christ who also hopes in Christ and loves [*diligit*] Christ. If he has faith without hope and love, he believes Christ exists but does not believe in Christ. The one who believes Christ by believing in Christ, Christ comes into and is united into him, so to speak, and the person is made a member of his body. This cannot happen unless hope and love [*caritas*] are added.[47]

Augustine was, however, a greater theologian of love than of faith or of hope. He knew from 1 Corinthians of the superiority of love to faith and to all the gifts of God, and so it is common to find him asserting that without love faith is nothing. Here is a representative passage from the *Handbook*:

> As for love [*caritas*], which the apostle pronounced greater than faith and hope, the greater it is in any person the better that person will be. When the question is raised whether someone is a good person, it is not what he believes or hopes that is at issue but what he loves [*amet*]. For someone who loves aright [*recte*], assuredly believes and hopes aright, whereas someone who does not love believes in vain [*inaniter*], even though what he believes is true, and likewise hopes in vain . . .—unless

45. Augustine, *Homilies on John's Gospel* 29.6 (PL 35:1631). It is not easy in English to differentiate satisfactorily between Augustine's different words for "love." See also Christine Mohrmann, *Études sur le latin des chrétiens*, 2nd ed., 4 vols. (Rome: Edizioni di Storia e Letteratura, 1961), 1:197–203, on *credere in Deum* ("believe in God") in Augustine (note that this passage from the *Homilies on John* is misreferenced).

46. Burnaby, *Amor Dei*, 79–80. Burnaby cited (80, n. 2) a sermon known from its first editor as *Sermon Morin* 9.2, now since Burnaby's time regarded as inauthentic. See Pierre-Patrick Verbraken, *Études critiques sur les sermons authentiques de saint Augustin*, Instrumenta patristica 12 (Steenbrugge, St. Peter's Abbey, The Hague: Martin Nijhoff, 1976), 16, 180.

47. Augustine, *Sermon* 144.2.2 (PL 38:788). Cf. Burnaby, *Amor Dei*, 78.

what he believes and hopes is that in response to his prayer he can be granted to love.[48]

It is beyond doubt that, for Augustine, love—for which he uses a range of vocabulary, *amor, caritas, dilectio*—is the animating center of the Christian's movement in life toward God and eternity. In *Nature and Grace*, a work of the year 415 directed against Pelagius himself, he concludes, "Love [*caritas*] begun is righteousness [*justitia*] begun; love developed, righteousness developed; great love, great righteousness; perfect love, perfect righteousness—love out of a pure heart and a good conscience and faith unfeigned."[49]

But the difficulty of doing justice to all the strands in Augustine's extensive writings appears clearly in passages where it is faith that is identified with *justitia*. Psalm 32 [33] calls on the righteous in the Lord to exult. Augustine knows that his listeners may hesitate to regard themselves as *justi* ("righteous") and so chooses to question them not about their *justitia* but about their faith, since

> none will dare to say, "I'm not a *fidelis* ['believer']." I'm not yet asking you what you live but what you believe. You will reply that you believe in Christ. Have you not heard the apostle, *Justus ex fide vivit* ["the righteous lives from faith"] (Romans 1:17)? Your faith is your righteousness, because if you believe, you surely take care [*caves*], and if you take care, you make an effort, and the Lord knows your effort and sees into your will.[50]

It is almost instinctive in Augustine to use *justi* and *fideles* as synonymous (and so too *injusti* ["unrighteous"] and *infideles* ["unbelievers"]), often by the citation of *Justus ex fide vivit*.[51]

Our discussion purposely omits some strands of Augustine's teaching that bear upon his understanding of justification, such as the relationship between *justitia* and union with Christ.[52] Nor does it say much about justification and merit and reward—but listen to this one passage from the *Homilies on John's Gospel*:

48. Augustine, *Handbook* 31.117 (PL 40:286).
49. Augustine, *Nature and Grace* 70.84 (PL 44:290).
50. Augustine, *Expositions of the Psalms* 32.I.4 (PL 36:279).
51. Stanislaus J. Grabowski, *The Church: An Introduction to the Theology of St. Augustine* (St. Louis and London: B. Herder, 1957), 327, with n. 59. This book contains one of the fullest and best treatments of justification in Augustine in English.
52. McGrath, *Iustitia Dei*, 30, oversimplifies by stating that "personal union with God, which forms the basis of [man's] justification, is brought about by love, and not by faith."

What then is the meaning of "grace for grace" (John 1:16)? . . . Having obtained this grace of faith, you will be righteous by faith (for *justus ex fide vivit*), and by living by faith you will merit [*promereberis*, "deserve well of"] God, and when you have merited God by living by faith, you will receive the prize [*praemium*] of immortality and eternal life. And that is grace. Since, for what merit do you receive eternal life? For grace. For if faith is grace and if eternal life is the reward [*merces*] of faith . . . eternal life also is grace for grace.[53]

This single passage says *multum in parvo*.

I have concentrated especially on the meaning of the verb *justifico* and the noun *justitia* and on the basic role of faith in the receiving of justification. Augustine in fact teaches something close to a declarative justification by faith, perhaps even faith alone, but does so as part of a more comprehensive righteous-making that embraces what most evangelicalism has called sanctification and that hence necessitates a faith effectively operative through love and hope. The key to understanding this is to fasten on justification as both event and process, as both beginning and growth.

Sermon 158, preached against the Pelagians, expounds Romans 8:30–31, including "those whom God called, he also justified." Augustine seeks to determine which of the four divine enactments—predestination, calling, justification, glorification—we have already obtained and which we still await. Predestination happened before we existed, and we were called when we "became Christians." What about justification? Who of us will presume to call himself *justificatus*, that is, *justus* ("righteous"), which means *Peccator non sum* ("I am not a sinner")? But neither is it true that we have nothing of *justitia*. Let what we have grow, and what we do not have will be fulfilled. "Look, people have been baptized, all their sins have been pardoned, they have been justified from their sins, we cannot deny it. There remains the fight with the devil." We claim neither to have no sin (cf. 1 John 1:8) nor to have no *justitia*—for then we would be lying against the gifts of God. "For if we have nothing of righteousness, nor do we have faith; if we do not have faith, we are not Christians. But if we have faith, we already have something of *justitia*." What that something is is expressed in *Justus ex fide vivit*.

Hence this third experience *iam agitur in nobis* ["is already at work in us"]. We have been justified, but *justitia* itself grows as we progress. . . . Let each of you, already established in justification itself by having received the remission of sins through the washing of rebirth, and having received the Holy Spirit, progressing from day to day—let each of you

53. Augustine, *Homilies on John's Gospel* 3.9 (PL 35:1400).

realize where he is, let him advance, make progress and grow until he is
. . . made perfect.[54]

As the sermon proceeds, Augustine more than once reiterates that
"you already are among the predestined, the called, the justified"; "If
the faith which works through love is in you, you already belong to the
predestined, the called, the justified. Therefore let it grow in you"; "We
are sons of God, predestined, called, justified; we are sons of God, and
what we shall be has not yet been revealed."[55] But as though deliberately
to maintain the balance, on the next day the sermon, while recapping
yesterday's, which "made clear that we are justified/have been justified
according to the manner of our pilgrimage, living by faith until we enjoy
by sight," indeed speaks of Christians still imperfect as "partly justified"
(*ex parte justificatis*).[56]

From *Sermon* 158 and other passages in his works, we must extract as
one strand in Augustine's teaching on *justificatio* a declarative event that
warrants a perfect passive verb. This justification belongs at the outset
of the Christian life and includes the forgiveness of sins as its central
element. Augustine knows that "You have already been justified" can be
predicated of the baptized believer as much as "You have already been
predestined and called." Although this is a minor note in his works, it
is clearly not an isolated aberration. Augustine does not help his interpreters as much as he might to understand how event and process are
correlated in his thinking.

Nevertheless we should not lose sight of the genuine affinity between
Augustine and the sixteenth-century Reformers on justification. It is well
possible—and I have experienced this—to pass from reading extensively
in Augustine's writings of his anti-Pelagian years (which encompass
the whole latter half of his theological life as a churchman) to Calvin,
Bucer, Cranmer, Martyr, and Knox without immediately being aware
that they functioned with a different understanding of *justificatio*. What
explains this misleading impression is the extent of agreement between
Augustine's emphases in those works and the Reformers': salvation as
a gift of divine grace (cf. one of Augustine's favorite texts, "What did
you have that you did not receive?" [1 Cor. 4:7]), safeguarded by an uncompromising doctrine of election; the faith which receives the gift of
justification itself an unmerited gift of God; and a central focus on the
event aspect of justification, that is, the pardon of the guilt of original
sin and committed sins, achieved by the work of Christ.

54. Augustine, *Sermon* 158.4.4; 158.5.5 (PL 38:864–65).
55. Ibid., 158.6.6; 158.7.7 (PL 38:865–66).
56. Ibid., 159.1.1 (PL 38:367–68).

There is, as we have seen, more to be said about Augustine on justification than these salient heads. Indeed there is even something to be recorded in favor of his more inclusive doctrine than is often allowed. If it subsumes sanctification under justification, then it avoids the sharp bifurcation between the two that has characterized too much modern evangelicalism but is true neither to the New Testament nor to much Reformation theology. It has a place for merit and reward, of which there is an embarrassing abundance in the teaching of Jesus, but views them ultimately as God's grace-gifts in Christian lives. And it coordinates faith with love and with hope, which cannot fail to be a corrective, given that the two fundamental duties laid on all humanity are to love God and to love the neighbor as oneself (and Augustine even paid proper attention to "as oneself").

This chapter could have been mischievously subtitled "Can a Young Man Trust His Bible?" Not, we might conclude, if it is only a translation. I know of no evidence that Augustine ever questioned the accuracy of *justifico* and its cognates as translations of the original Greek (and Hebrew). Hence *justifico* as "make just/righteous" seemed an obvious explanation of the compound verb, and the rest is history.[57] A marginal justification of this examination of his teaching might be sought in a renewed dedication to the original languages, without knowledge of which even the greatest may go astray. Translators of Augustine today would contribute to a clearer understanding of his thought by normally translating his Latin not by "justify, justification" but by terms that obviously express the ongoing change by which the ungodly become godly.

---

57. Ibid., 292.6 (PL 38:1324). Augustine illustrates his construal of *justificare* ("to justify") as *justum facere* ("make righteous") by citing the parallels of *mortificare* ("mortify, put to death") and *vivificare* ("vivify, make alive").

4

Simul peccator et justus

Martin Luther and Justification

CARL TRUEMAN

Introduction

It is a historical truism to say that Martin Luther is the theologian of justification. No one before or since in the history of the church is so closely associated with the doctrine as he is: it dominated his own thinking, it decisively influenced the direction of his own life, and it stands at the theological heart of the great rupture in the Western church between Protestants and Catholics. In Luther's hands, it was used not only to remake soteriology but to shatter received wisdom regarding, among other things, authority, the church, the sacraments, politics, labor, the relationship of masters and servants, and all manner of cultural pursuits. The doctrine was simultaneously both the most destructive and the most creative—indeed, one might simply say "revolutionary" in the broadest sense of the word—ideological expression of the time. Given all this, any discussion of the doctrine will inevitably accord his arguments a central place, whether he is regarded as the great rediscoverer of the Pauline gospel or as the great perverter of the same.[1]

1. The literature on Luther is vast. For his life, the best work in English is that of Martin Brecht, *Martin Luther*, trans. James L. Schaaf, 3 vols. (Minneapolis: Fortress, 1993); see

Given the sheer scope of the doctrine, a comprehensive treatment of Luther's position is not possible in a single paper. My aim, therefore, is not so much to make a direct dogmatic contribution to systematic discussion of the doctrine as to offer an exposition of his theology and then raise a number of issues I believe to be of continuing relevance to modern discussions.

First, however, we need to acknowledge the significant interpretative problems that any approach to Luther's understanding of justification contains. These include the vast amount of secondary discussion of his teaching, discussion that dates from the writings, both appreciative and critical, of the sixteenth century right through to the present day, some of which I will refer to later. In addition, there is the problem of Luther's own intellectual development. The writings of a long life, one marked by important changes of mind on this and related issues, present the student with the problem of how the Luther canon itself is to be construed and read. The issues are too complex to be dealt with here, and so I will simply lay out my own approach without offering extensive defense of it, yet acknowledging that others may choose to challenge this.

I see a fairly consistent development in Luther's theology, particularly in relation to justification, from 1515 to 1520. I am also inclined in this context to relativize the significance of the "Autobiographical Fragment," with its account of the so-called tower experience for understanding Luther's theology. In addition, and perhaps more controversially, I see no major disjunction between Luther and Philipp Melanchthon on the issue of forensic justification. Again, I will not justify all of this here—it would simply take too long—but I hope that some of my reasons for adopting these positions will become clear as we proceed.

The structure of this chapter is straightforward. First it outlines the development of Luther's thinking on justification between the Romans

---

also Heiko Oberman, *Luther: Man between God and Devil*, trans. E. Walliser-Schwarzbart (New Haven: Yale University Press, 1989); Richard Marius, *Martin Luther: The Christian between God and Death* (Cambridge, MA: Belknap Press of Harvard University Press, 1999); Carl R. Trueman, "Martin Luther and the Reformation in Germany," in *The Reformation World*, ed. Andrew Pettegree (London: Routledge, 2000), 73–96. On his theology, the best one-volume account is Bernhard Lohse, *Martin Luther's Theology: Its Historical and Systematic Development* (Edinburgh: T&T Clark, 1999); still worth consulting is E. G. Rupp, *The Righteousness of God: Luther Studies* (London: Hodder & Stoughton, 1953); see also David C. Steinmetz, *Luther in Context* (Grand Rapids: Baker, 2002); Robert Kolb, *Martin Luther: Prophet, Teacher, and Hero* (Grand Rapids: Baker, 1999). On justification, an important recent systematic interaction with Luther is that of Oswald Bayer, *Living by Faith: Justification and Sanctification*, trans. Geoffrey Bromiley (Grand Rapids: Eerdmans, 2003). A recent collection of essays that gives an excellent state-of-the-art overview of work on Luther is Timothy J. Wengert, ed., *Harvesting Martin Luther's Reflections on Theology, Ethics, and the Church* (Grand Rapids: Eerdmans, 2004). For ease of reference, Luther is cited from *LW* except where no English translation is available.

lectures of 1515–1516 and *The Freedom of the Christian Man* of 1520 and highlights how this coordinates with other developments in his thinking. Then it addresses three issues of contemporary relevance to the church with respect to Luther—Luther and conversion, Luther and Melanchthon, and Luther and the cross.

The Development of Justification in Luther's Theology from 1515 to 1520

Simul peccator et justus ("at the same time sinner and righteous") is one of a number of well-known oppositions in Luther's theology. Others include law and gospel, faith and works, the hiddenness and the revelation of God. Again, that Luther's theology is full of such is no profound insight; nor should we assume that each of these pairs is simply a different way of referring to the same thing. There is a relationship between them, but it is not as simple or direct as one might assume.

The phrase is perhaps used most dramatically in a passage in Luther's lectures on Romans (1515–1516), the rediscovery of which triggered the renaissance of Luther studies under the influence of Karl Holl in the early twentieth century. Commenting on Romans 4:7, Luther has this to say:

> It is similar to the case of a sick man who believes the doctor who promises him a sure recovery and in the meantime obeys the doctor's orders in the hope of promised recovery. . . . Now, is the sick man well? The fact is that he is both sick and well at the same time. He is sick in fact, but he is well because of the sure promise of the doctor, whom he trusts and who has reckoned him as already cured, because he is sure that he will cure him; for he has already begun to cure him and no longer reckons to him a sickness unto death. In the same way, Christ, our Samaritan, has brought His half-dead man into the inn to be cared for, and He has begun to heal him, having promised him the most complete cure unto eternal life, and He does not impute his sins, that is, his wicked desires unto death, but in the meantime in the hope of the promised recovery He prohibits him from doing or omitting things by which his cure might be impeded and his sin, that is, his concupiscence, might be increased. Now, is he perfectly righteous? No, for he is at the same time both a sinner and a righteous man; a sinner in fact, but a righteous man by the sure imputation and promise of God that He will continue to deliver him from sin until He has completely cured him.[2]

2. *LW* 25:260.

Taking this as our starting point for discussion, we need to note at the outset some problems. First, the teaching of this passage is somewhat ambiguous. The believer is both justified and a sinner simultaneously, yet the precise relationship between these two is not made entirely clear or at least is not expressed with the clarity we find in Luther's later writings. There certainly appears to be a strongly proleptic dimension to what is being taught here: the believer is declared righteous now and is therefore indeed in a sense fully righteous by having Christ's righteousness imputed, on the grounds that he or she will one day actually be fully righteous; the passage stresses the promissory aspect of this, with the promise in Christ as the basis for the whole; yet Luther also seems to allow that the fact itself that the process of being made righteous has started forms at least part of the basis for this; thus he seems to allow, if you like, for justification to be based on a transformation that is not entirely projected into the future but merely perfected by such a projection.

Passages such as this led Holl to put forward the influential argument that Luther's notion of justification had a clearly sanative, transformative dimension. This had the effect of making Luther's understanding somewhat discontinuous both with the later tradition of Lutheranism as expressed confessionally in the *Book of Concord* and with the position of Melanchthon and his strongly declarative, legally expressed understanding of justification.[3]

If Holl's reading is correct and if this passage does indeed teach a form of proleptic justification, then we might add that Luther's position not only is to be differentiated from that of Melanchthon and the Lutheran confessional trajectory but also may be brought into more positive relation with Roman Catholic teaching. Differences between Roman Catholic teaching on this point and Protestantism have often been characterized as a difference between justification as process, involving the impartation of Christ's righteousness, and justification as declaration involving the imputation of Christ's righteousness. What Luther appears to be saying here embodies elements of both: it is a declaration based upon imputation, but this imputation itself is in turn based upon the known outcome of an established process, albeit one established by God's promise.

In fact, the practical ecumenical significance of such an interpretation should be minimal. Although it is true that Luther is unique in having certain of his works incorporated into the Lutheran confessional documents (the "Small Catechism," the "Large Catechism," the "Smalcald Articles"), these works in no way provide a hermeneutical framework for the explicitly confessional material and indeed are to be read in critical

3. Karl Holl, *Gesammelte Aufsätze zur Kirchengechichte*, vol. 1, *Luther* (Tübingen: Mohr, 1923).

subordination to the main body of confessional writings.[4] Further, a careful reading of Luther leads to the conclusion that the lectures on Romans are not representative of Luther's mature theology, the theology that we find, for example, in the works of 1520 or the great commentary on Galatians. Clearly, the lectures on Romans are crucial in his overall development, but they still represent a stage on the way, not the position he held by the time the Lutheran church started to define itself in terms of public confessional documents.[5] The emphasis upon humility, the emergence of the language of imputation, and the developing anti-Pelagian understanding of grace are all important markers, indicating that Luther is moving toward his later position on justification. Yet there is a clear sense that Luther's thinking continues to develop after 1516, as he himself declares later in life and as the *Book of Concord* reflects in its appreciative but critical appropriation of his writings for confessional purposes.

Moving forward in time to 1519, we find that the proleptic note in his understanding of justification has become more muted in the discussion. In his sermon "Two Kinds of Righteousness," Luther talks about Christ's righteousness as being alien to us, as coming from outside, and being infinite and perfect from the moment we come into possession of Christ by faith.[6] This righteousness, he makes clear, is the primary righteousness, the righteousness that provides the foundation for the proper righteousness that is constitutive of our actual moral transformation. In this context, Luther draws structural parallels between alien righteousness and original sin, and proper righteousness and actual sins, parallels that, as we shall see, are significant for his understanding of baptism.[7] It is against this primary background that the proleptic dimension of justification remains, evident in Luther's language of growth with respect to the alien righteousness slowly driving out the

4. See Robert Kolb and Timothy J. Wengert, eds., *The Book of Concord: The Confessions of the Evangelical Lutheran Church* (Minneapolis: Fortress, 2000), 528–29. The problem, of course, is compounded by the iconic significance of Luther within the Lutheran tradition; this lends his writings a force not possessed by those of his contemporaries; see Kolb, *Martin Luther*.

5. It is interesting that the Finnish school of Luther interpretation, in its desire to establish a basic disjunction between Luther and the *Book of Concord*, focuses its interpretation of him on his pre-1520 works; see Carl E. Braaten and Robert W. Jenson, eds., *Union with Christ: The New Finnish Interpretation of Luther* (Grand Rapids: Eerdmans, 1998); cf. Carl R. Trueman, "Is the Finnish Line a New Beginning? A Critical Assessment of the Reading of Luther Offered by the Helsinki Circle," *Westminster Theological Journal* 65 (2003): 231–44; see also Jenson, "Response to Mark Seifrid, Paul Metzger, and Carl Trueman on Finnish Luther Research," ibid., 245–50.

6. *LW* 31:298–99.

7. *LW* 31:299–300.

old man; yet it seems that Luther's thinking here, though not entirely clear, is no longer tying the initial declaration of righteousness to the anticipated eschatological perfection of righteousness but merely describing what is actually going to happen once faith (and thus Christ) is present.[8]

If we now turn to the great treatise on justification of 1520, *The Freedom of the Christian Man*, we find that just a short while after "Two Kinds of Righteousness," Luther's thinking has become much more sharply defined. The treatise famously opens with the statements that the Christian is a perfectly free lord of all and subject to none but at the same time a perfectly dutiful servant to all, subject to all.[9] The structural parallel, with its emphasis upon simultaneity of status, is reminiscent of *simul peccator et justus*, containing as it does an apparent contradiction in terms, but when we realize that Luther's language of justification is relational rather than substantial, then the problem is somewhat defused.[10] In *The Freedom of the Christian Man*, Luther constructs his argument in terms of the inner, or spiritual, and the outer, both of which are conceived in relational terms—the inner has reference to the individual before God, the outer before the world. When confronted by God's law, the individual realizes his or her helplessness and turns to the gospel. Then, by the individual's grasping Christ though faith, three things follow: the Christian possessing Christ has no need of anything else, such as works, because he or she has all that is needed through faith;[11] the Christian honors Christ by regarding him as true and trustworthy—a point that is potentially counterintuitive, as it has to do with the inner disposition of faith, not outward circumstances;[12] and finally, the union of Christ and believer, like that of groom and bride, effects the joyful exchange of sins and righteousness. Luther expresses the last point in a beautiful and important paragraph:

8. "Therefore this alien righteousness, instilled in us without our works by grace alone—while the Father, to be sure, inwardly draws us to Christ—is set opposite original sin, likewise alien, which we acquire without our works by birth alone. Christ daily drives out the old Adam more and more in accordance with the extent to which faith and knowledge of Christ grow. For alien righteousness is not instilled all at once, but it begins, makes progress, and is finally perfected at the end through death" (*LW* 31:299).

9. *LW* 31:344.

10. The importance of the language of status and relation in Luther's understanding of humanity has been noted recently by Daphne Hampson in her study of Luther in relation to possibilities for modern ecumenism; see her *Christian Contradictions: The Structures of Lutheran and Catholic Thought* (Cambridge: Cambridge University Press, 2001), esp. 9–55.

11. *LW* 31:349.

12. *LW* 31:350.

By this mystery, as the Apostle teaches, Christ and the soul become one flesh. And if they are one flesh and there is between them a true marriage—indeed, the most perfect of all marriages, since human marriages are but poor examples of this one true marriage—it follows that everything they have they hold in common, the good as well as the evil. Accordingly the believing soul can boast of and glory in whatever Christ has as though it were its own, and whatever the soul has Christ claims as his own. Let us compare these and we shall see the inestimable benefits. Christ is full of grace, life, and salvation. The soul is full of sins, death, and damnation. Now let faith come between them and sins, death, and damnation will be Christ's, while grace, life, and salvation will be the soul's; for if Christ is a bridegroom, he must take upon himself the things which are his bride's and bestow upon her the things that are his. If he gives her his body and very self, how shall he not give her all that is his? And if he takes the body of the bride, how shall he not take all that is hers?[13]

This is the classic expression of the relationship between union with Christ and the righteousness of the justified believer in the writings of Martin Luther and has therefore been part of the discussion concerning the relationship between the thinking of Luther and that of later Lutheranism, which, following in the footsteps of Melanchthon, tended to use legal language when referring to this issue and thus articulated what is often referred to as forensic justification, allowing its critics to use pejorative language such as "legal fiction" when referring to orthodox Lutheran notions of justification.[14]

Certainly, this notion of union with Christ in *The Freedom of the Christian Man* is much richer than the pejorative terminology of legal fiction seems to imply. For a start, it makes believers kings and priests with Christ, a point that, in 1520 at least, leads Luther to a highly pragmatic view of church leadership, one that he will abandon in the wake of the problems with the peasants in 1525.[15] Second, it allows us to make sense of the rather paradoxical opening statements of the treatise, for it gives a christological, and therefore crucicentric, context for understanding what Luther means in terms of the language of lordship, authority, and power. It is often forgotten in all the focus on the commonplace of universal priesthood that universal kingship is also part of Luther's

13. *LW* 31:351.

14. On Luther's use of the marriage metaphor, see Heiko A. Oberman, "*Simul gemitus et raptus*: Luther and Mysticism," in *The Dawn of the Reformation* (Edinburgh: T&T Clark, 1992), 126–54.

15. *LW* 31:354–56. On Luther's quiet abandonment of the language of universal priesthood, see Carl R. Trueman, "Reformers, Puritans, and Evangelicals: The Lay Connection," in *The Rise of the Laity in Evangelical Protestantism*, ed. Deryck W. Lovegrove (London: Routledge, 2002), 17–35.

theology and that this has a radical impact upon the way in which he envisages the Christian life. Echoing the kind of thinking we find in 1 Corinthians on the nature of Christian strength and wisdom, Luther sees the believer's life as essentially one of sacrificial service and suffering for the benefit of others, and this as contradicting human expectations in two ways: first, it is the result of God's justification, of the change of status entailed in being "in Christ"; and second, it is the precise opposite of human expectations in the way it sees lordship in terms of service and self-abnegation. Christians are therefore free in that they do not have to work for salvation and are thus no longer in servile bondage to the demands of the law; but they are servants in that they are bound, as a consequence—indeed, as a response—to Christ's great love and suffering on behalf of sinners, to serve their fellow human beings.[16]

In this context, Luther can still in 1520 speak of growth in actual righteousness, yet here the discussion is not pitched in the same manner as we saw earlier, where the transformation of the believer viewed proleptically seemed to form part of the basis for justification. Now Luther is emphatic that transformation is no part of justification but, rather, a consequence of it. The proleptic dimension of his thinking on justification, apparent in 1516, is now entirely absent. To understand why this has come about, we need to set the development of this doctrine within the context of his wider theology. As the central doctrine of the Christian faith, it inevitably stands in relation to other issues, such as his doctrine of God, his understanding of baptism, and his view of sin, all of which are significant for the development of his thinking. It is to these we must now turn.

Parallel Developments in Luther's Theology

One of the most obvious aspects of Luther's theology of justification is the increasing prominence of the notion of status and relation rather than substance and transformation in his thought. This is strongly hinted at in his language of *simul peccator et justus* and comes dramatically

---

16. *LW* 31:358. For a discussion of Luther's ethics, including the ticklish issue of his relationship to the so-called third use of the law, see the following: Paul Althaus, *The Ethics of Martin Luther*, trans. R. C. Schultz (Philadelphia: Fortress, 1972); H. Bornkamm, *Luther and the Old Testament*, trans. E. W. Gritsch and R. C. Gritsch (Philadelphia: Fortress, 1969); David F. Wright, "The Ethical Use of the Old Testament in Luther and Calvin: A Comparison," *Scottish Journal of Theology* 36 (1983): 463–85; also the essays by Karlfried Froehlich, Carter Lindberg, Ricardo Willy Rieth, and Scott Hendrix in Wengert, *Harvesting Martin Luther's Reflections*. Again, from a systematic perspective, the work of Bayer is helpful; see his *Living by Faith*.

to the fore in the opening couplet of *The Freedom of the Christian Man*. Its origins are found in Luther's eclectic relationship to his medieval background, his theology of baptism, and his radical understanding of the cross.

From the time of Joseph Lortz, scholars have recognized the absurdity of seeing Luther's theology as a clean break with the past. Instead scholars such as Heiko Oberman and David Steinmetz have offered an increasingly nuanced understanding of Luther's relationship to the theology of his medieval teachers. I suggest that this change in the understanding of how human beings are to be understood in terms of status rather than substance is positively connected to developments within late medieval Catholicism.[17]

The crucial connection between Luther and medieval theology is the tradition in which he himself was schooled, that of the *via moderna* of Gabriel Biel and company, which stressed the decisive role of the divine will in justification. This voluntarism had a deep and critical impact upon Catholic thought. First, by emphasizing that the basis of and criteria for justification were those established by God's will rather than those imposed by some necessary ontology, the necessity for infused habits of grace in justification was undermined. They were still necessary, but the accent was on the establishment of the divine *pactum* ("covenant"), with its condition whereby God would not deny grace to those who did what was in them (i.e., their best). In other words, there was a shift in the *via moderna* toward a focus not on intrinsic qualities in the sinner but on the relationship between God and sinners that the divine *fiat* established. That is, the transformation of the believer was seen to take place within the context of a change of status rather than vice versa.[18]

The relationship of this idea to Luther's mature thinking on justification has generally been seen as a balance sheet. Negatively, it is well known that Luther came to reject entirely the assumption that human

---

17. See Joseph Lortz, *The Reformation in Germany*, 2 vols. (London: Darton, Longman and Todd, 1968). Lortz's work, originally published in German in 1939, argues for a positive connection between Luther and late medieval nominalism but retains much of the old partisan approach by regarding nominalism as itself a decadent and debased form of Catholic theology. Oberman did much to help overthrow both this understanding of nominalism and the unhelpful theological dogmatism that undergirded earlier studies of Luther, both Catholic and Protestant; see Heiko Oberman, *The Harvest of Medieval Theology*, 3rd ed. (Durham, NC: Labyrinth, 1983); also Steinmetz, *Luther in Context*.

18. See Oberman, *Harvest*; also William J. Courtenay, "Nominalism in Late Medieval Religion," in *The Pursuit of Holiness in Late Medieval and Renaissance Religion*, ed. Charles E. Trinkaus and Heiko A. Oberman (Leiden: Brill, 1974), 26–59; Courtenay, *Covenant and Causality in Medieval Thought: Studies in Philosophy, Theology, and Economic Practice* (London: Variorum Reprints, 1984); Courtenay, *Capacity and Volition: A History of the Distinction of Absolute and Ordained Power* (Bergamo, Italy: P. Lubrina, 1990).

beings were able to achieve even the most minimal acts of righteousness outside union with Christ, although the identification of the human requirement with humility helped to pave the way to his later understanding of justification by faith. Luther's increasingly radical understanding of the nature of sin as rendering human beings utterly impotent for any move toward God effectively destroyed the usefulness of this kind of *pactum* theology. In short, Luther's anti-Pelagianism prevented him from allowing that doing the most minimal of good works was even a hypothetical possibility. Further, and connected to this, it appears (if we are to trust the "Autobiographical Fragment" of 1545) that this theology was a constitutive element in the epistemological problems that led to Luther's own doubt and despair. After all, how could one ever know that one has done what is in oneself? One could always, surely, have performed Mass with a little more devotion, or confessed just a few more sins if one had really thought hard about it.[19]

On the positive side, however, Luther developed the voluntarism of the *via moderna* in a way that safeguarded, if it did not in fact magnify, the need for revelation as the only source of reliable knowledge of God. By stressing the importance of God's will in the constitution of all reality, it undermined the kind of ontologism proposed by the Thomistic tradition, and God became, in himself, a mystery outside any specific revelation of his attitude and actions toward creation. And most important, Luther also carried over into his mature theology the idea of justification as including, at a most foundational level, a divine decision, and he did so in a way that maintained and indeed intensified the *via moderna*'s rejection of the notion of condign merit as a basis for initial acceptance by God.[20]

There are other significant points of interest, however, beyond these two. The whole weakening of the ontological nature of salvation as proposed by the *via moderna* points toward precisely the kind of shift in understanding of humanity that we see coming through in Luther. The crucial question in salvation is no longer an ontological one—is the individual undergoing the necessary transformation through the system of sacramental grace?—but, rather, the following: where does this

19. For a more detailed discussion of Luther's relation to medieval theology, particularly as mediated through his relationship with Johannes von Staupitz, see David C. Steinmetz, *Misericordia Dei: The Theology of Johannes von Staupitz in Its Late Medieval Setting* (Leiden: Brill, 1968); Steinmetz, *Luther and Staupitz: An Essay in the Intellectual Origins of the Reformation* (Durham, NC: Labyrinth, 1980).

20. These themes are evident in a number of the controversial disputations and proposals of 1517 and 1518; see "The Disputation against Scholastic Theology"; "The Ninety Five Theses against Indulgences"; "The Heidelberg Disputation"; and "The Explanations of the Ninety-Five Theses" in *LW* 31.

person stand regarding the divine decision? It is this which makes the difference between being justified and not justified, and it is this which accents the relational nature of justification, of humanity, and of God in a way that bears such significant fruit in the thought of Luther. Human identity before God is primarily a question of status: is one justified in relation to the divine decision, or not? So we can conclude by saying that, yes, the *via moderna* provided a context for Luther's theology that undercut human assumptions about God and stressed the centrality of revelation; yes, its concepts constituted the personal crisis of Luther's own faith; yes, it opened the way for a focus on the divine decision. But we must also remember that it paved the way for a revision of the way humanity itself was understood.[21]

Alongside the significance of the doctrine of God, we must also place Luther's developing understanding of baptism (and the correlative doctrine of sin) during this period. The medieval theology in which Luther had been schooled regarded sin as a *fomes*, a piece of kindling wood, with the potential of setting the whole human being on moral fire, so to speak. Baptism countered this by dampening it, making it weaker and thus less of a danger. Baptism and the justification that followed it were therefore processes consisting of a pilgrimage from a state of sin to a state of perfection constituted by the slow but sure healing of the sinful nature.[22]

As Luther's thinking developed, however, his increasingly radical understanding of the impact of sin led him to revise his understanding of the significance of baptism. In this context, the parallel between alien righteousness and original sin that we noted earlier in the sermon on the two kinds of righteousness is important. Both alien righteousness and original sin, after all, are acquired irrespective of any works of the individual concerned: the former through the faith relation to Christ, the latter through solidarity with Adam. This is a clear indication that Luther's thinking on justification cannot be isolated from wider theological concerns, particularly those relating to baptism.

21. Cf. the comment of Hampson: "Luther speaks of the person not as derived 'being,' but in terms of his modes and relations—as one who fears, is undermined, loves, finds security, and is set free. One sees how profound was the break—and hence how difficult ecumenical conversation unless Catholics should come to conceive of the person in a different way" (*Christian Contradictions*, 35).

22. Luther sees different understandings of baptism as lying at the heart of his differences with Catholic contemporaries over justification; see his comments in "Against Latomus" (1521): "Paul calls that which remains after baptism, sin; the fathers call it a weakness and imperfection rather than sin. Here we stand at the parting of the ways. I follow Paul and you the fathers—with the exception of Augustine, who generally calls it by the blunt names of fault and iniquity" (*LW* 32:220).

Luther was already decisively moving in this direction by the time of the lectures on Romans, preferring instead to frame his discussions of baptism in terms of the Pauline language of death and life, language that he uses to connect baptism to justification and thence to the process of renewal:

> But we must note that it is not necessary for all men to be found immediately in this state of perfection [of being dead to sin], as soon as they have been baptized into a death of this kind. For they are baptized "into death," that is, toward death, which is to say, they have begun to live in such a way that they are pursuing this kind of death and reach out toward their goal. For although they are baptized unto eternal life and the kingdom of heaven, yet they do not all at once possess this goal fully, but they have begun to act in such a way that they may attain it—for baptism was established to direct us toward death and through this death to life—therefore it is necessary that we come to it in the order which has been prescribed.[23]

Here the proleptic nature of justification in the Romans lectures is reflected in the proleptic nature of baptism—it is a reaching out toward death, a move, if you like, in the right direction. This language of death and resurrection, however, will become intensified over the next five years and find its culmination in *The Babylonian Captivity of the Church* in 1520, where it becomes a metaphor for the whole of the Christian life:

> Baptism, then, signifies two things—death and resurrection, that is, full and complete justification. When the minister immerses the child in the water it signifies death, and when he draws it forth again, it signifies life. Thus Paul expounds it in Romans 6. . . . This death and resurrection we call the new creation, regeneration, and spiritual birth. This should not be understood only allegorically as the death of sin and the life of grace, as many understand it, but as actual death and resurrection. For baptism is not a false sign. Neither does sin completely die, nor grace completely rise, until the sinful body that we carry about in this life is destroyed. . . . For as long as we are in the flesh, the desires of the flesh stir and are stirred. For this reason, as soon as we begin to believe, we also begin to die to this world and to live to God in the life to come; so that faith is truly a death and a resurrection, that is, it is that spiritual baptism into which we are submerged and from which we rise.[24]

Luther then proceeds to attack those who make baptism simply a start to the Christian life and who then see the other sacraments as taking

---

23. *LW* 25:312.
24. *LW* 36:67–68; on the significance of Rom. 6, baptism, and justification in the later Luther, see Robert Kolb, "God Kills to Make Alive: Romans 6 and Luther's Understanding of Justification (1535)," *Lutheran Quarterly* 12 (1998): 33–56.

over the process, so to speak, and bringing it to completion. For Luther, this makes baptism little more than a false start.[25]

Various elements combine to allow Luther to speak in this way. Most notable is surely the increasingly radical understanding of sin. Sin is not simply something akin to a wound or a tendency that twists or misdirects human moral agency. It is, rather, something all-encompassing that dominates and controls all of human life. Thus it is not healing that the sinner needs; rather, it is death and resurrection, for only these radical steps can address the truly radical nature of sin itself as involving primarily a certain status before God.[26]

At the heart of Luther's mature understanding of baptism, then, as with his mature understanding of justification, is a notion of humanity that sees human beings primarily in terms of relation and status. This is often summed up in studies of Luther's thought with reference to his *totus homo*, or "whole human being," anthropology. This is a concept of vital relevance to any discussion of his understanding of justification and, given the centrality of justification to his theology as a whole, to any coherent understanding of Luther's theological contribution to the West. What Luther offers is not a view of human nature primarily in terms of an ontology or a substance whereby terms such as *justus* and *peccator* are applied to the individual in terms of some basic part of their being, coordinated by a process of transformation; rather, he uses this language to talk in terms of the believer's status and relations with respect to God and the world, the two basic contexts for understanding human existence.

In the medieval Catholic view, building on the thought of Augustine, justification was primarily a process whereby the individual steadily became more and more righteous through the impartation of Christ's righteousness.[27] This process had itself been closely linked to the sacramental system of the church and to the notions of infusions of grace via the sacraments and the importance of created habits of grace.[28] In other

25. *LW* 36:69.

26. Cf. Luther's comments on Rom. 5:12: "[Original sin] is not only a lack of light in the mind or of power in the memory, but particularly it is a total lack of uprightness and of the power of all faculties both of body and soul and of the whole inner and outer man" (*LW* 25:299).

27. For detailed discussion of the history of justification, see Albrecht Ritschl, *The Christian Doctrine of Justification and Reconciliation: The Positive Development of the Doctrine*, eds. H. R. Mackintosh and A. B. Macaulay (Edinburgh: T&T Clark, 1900); Alister E. McGrath, *Iustitia Dei: A History of the Christian Doctrine of Justification* (Cambridge: Cambridge University Press, 1998); on Luther in this context, see Heiko Oberman, "'Iustitia Christi' and 'iustitia Dei': Luther and the Scholastic Doctrines of Justification," in *The Dawn of the Reformation*, 104–25.

28. Oberman, *Harvest*, 160–84.

words, justification was rooted in an understanding of human nature that took very seriously ontological questions of substance, process, and being as the starting point for individual salvation. This is not to deny that such an approach ruled out all considerations of status; clearly, the commonplace Catholic language of "being in a state of grace" or "a state of mortal sin" is indicative of a notion of humanity and of salvation that gives room for status or relational language. It is merely to assert that the primary accent in the discussion of salvation was on change in being, with change in status being defined in the light of this.

In Luther, however, it is arguable that the concept and language of status have increasing priority over the concept and language of transformation. For Luther, everyone, believer and unbeliever, is *simul peccator et justus*: the unbeliever is righteous before the world but unrighteous before God; the believer is unrighteous before the world but righteous before God, a point that, as we shall see below, is connected to Luther's understanding of the cross.[29] This relational understanding of sinfulness and righteousness is also very clear in Luther's understanding of baptism and its relationship to the Christian life. Yes, baptism marks the start of the Christian life, but it also expresses the whole content of the Christian life from birth to death as well. It is not primarily the start of a process to be carried on by other sacraments; it is, rather, the sign of all that the Christian life is about—dying to sin and self and rising to Christ—and it confers this status upon its subject. This is why Luther can use such paradoxical language as that of *simul peccator et justus* and that of the Christian being both free and a slave: once these are understood as relational categories, they cease to be paradoxical.

This understanding of the primary importance of status is something that, as we noted above, Luther derived in part from the medieval doctrine of God as developed by the theologians of the *via moderna*. This was also reinforced by the biblical text. While the Latin term *reputare* ("to reckon" or "to count") and its cognates, with their relevance to theologies that emphasized the divine decision, were part and parcel of Occamist discussions of justification with which Luther would have been familiar, the Vulgate too translated the Greek λογίζεσται ("to reckon") as *reputatur*, and so Luther would have been familiar with this usage in a more narrowly biblical context as well and would no doubt have ap-

---

29. See Luther's comment on thesis 63 of the 95 Theses: "But this treasure [the gospel] is naturally most odious, for it makes the first to be last. . . . The gospel destroys those things which exist, it confounds the strong, it confounds the wise and reduces them to nothingness, to weakness, to foolishness, because it teaches humility and a cross. . . . Therefore it is not surprising that this saying of Christ is most odious to those who desire to be something, who want to be wise and mighty in their own eyes and before men, and who consider themselves to be 'the first'" (*LW* 31:232).

proached the Greek text with this semantic baggage in tow. Luther's use of the word nonetheless did not represent a straightforward adoption of the Occamist usage but was, rather, something of a development and departure from the Occamist tradition in that he focused its meaning very much on the acquittal of the guilty and the promise of the grace of God. In so doing, he again pressed the conventional language into the service of a more explicitly status-oriented theology than the previous tradition and paved the way for imputation, rather than impartation, to be the basis of Lutheran understandings of justification.[30]

The final development of the years 1516 to 1520 is the theology of the cross, which, though not directly related to a discussion of status, yet represents an important auxiliary part of such theology in that both the language of status and the theology of the cross form part of what is essentially a theology of the Christian life, which is contrary to all human expectations. The most famous example is the theology of the cross as articulated at the Heidelberg disputation in 1517, where Luther pressed the need for theologians to understand God according to God's revelation, not according to human expectations. Thus God's power, holiness, glory, and so forth, are to be conceived in terms of the suffering, shame, and death of the cross and not in terms of some human criterion. For to do the latter would be to create a theology of glory, not of the cross.[31] Luther regards the cross, however, as more than just a point of epistemological relevance; it is also a paradigm for understanding salvation and the Christian life. In "The Heidelberg Disputation," the theses on the theology of the cross are framed by theses that talk of the need for human beings to despair of their own efforts to please God and then to put their faith in Christ. What Luther does here is decisively shift the emphasis away from ethics to the paradoxical action of God in the event of the cross; he shatters any notion that ethical behavior forms part of the road to justification. Again, this is part and parcel of his status language.[32] Yet the theology of the cross is also so much more than the mere dethronement of received moral theory. It is also a paradigm of the Christian life, the existential expression of what baptism symbolizes in terms of the horizons of

---

30. See Lohse, *Martin Luther's Theology*, 261.

31. The key theses are 19–22: see *LW* 31:40–41. On Luther's theology of the cross, see Walther von Loewenich, *Luther's Theology of the Cross*, trans. H. J. A. Bouman (Minneapolis: Augsburg, 1976); Alister E. McGrath, *Luther's Theology of the Cross* (Oxford, UK: Blackwell, 1985).

32. The theological theses, which are an explicit attack on the theology of the *pactum* theology of the *via moderna*, are followed by twelve philosophical theses attacking Aristotle. Although Aristotle's understanding of ethics and virtue are not mentioned explicitly, the antithesis between his moral theory and that of the cross is implicit both in the theological theses and thesis 29 in the philosophical section. See *LW* 31:41–42.

expectation regarding Christian experience: the way to life is through death, the way to eternal bliss is through temporal suffering. The whole of the Christian life is, if you like, to be contrary to all human expectations of what the blessed life should be like—a point that is embodied in Luther's teaching on baptism and that is picked up in his major treatise on justification, *The Freedom of the Christian Man*. Freedom in this treatise only makes sense if we understand that at root this is a freedom determined by status, not a freedom being steadily acquired by substantial or ontological change.

To summarize thus far: Luther's theology from 1515 to 1520 undergoes development that places increasing emphasis upon the language of status and relation to emphasize the role of the divine decision and of Christ's alien righteousness in justification; this development builds selectively upon Luther's medieval background in the *via moderna* and is evident not only in his understanding of justification and of righteousness but also in his views of sin, baptism, and the role of the cross in the Christian life. All of this serves to distinguish him somewhat from the medieval tradition not only on the issue of his anti-Pelagian understanding of God's salvific activity but also on the issue of the nature of justification itself, which is seen primarily as a change in status, not a change in substance or a process.

After this straightforward exposition of Luther's thinking on justification, we conclude by discussing three issues of significance to contemporary understanding of Luther's thought.

Luther and Melanchthon

From the time of the Reformation onward, attempts have been repeatedly made to separate the thinking of Martin Luther from that of his younger colleague, Philipp Melanchthon. Critics have seen fundamental differences between the two men on a variety of issues, from their understandings of the human will to their views of the Eucharist. As far as justification is concerned, this difference has focused on the question of forensic justification: is the forensic notion of justification, as formulated by Melanchthon, consistent with the teaching of Luther? This question has frequently been answered in the negative, though not always for the same reasons. Karl Holl, for example, argued for a distinction between the two men in a manner that allowed him to emphasize what he saw as the ethical nature of justification in Luther, effectively bringing his theology into line with the concerns of the post-Kantian, antimetaphysical Ritschlian line of thinking to which Holl himself belonged.[33] In contrast, Lowell Green has argued that Melanchthon in fact helped Luther to discover the gospel, particularly through his clarification of forensic concepts in Paul and his impact upon Luther's first series of lectures on Galatians.[34] More recently, Tuomo Mannermaa and the Finnish school of Luther interpretation have offered yet another appraisal of the relationship, arguing that Holl's approach is completely wrongheaded; they have instead posited a basic disjunction between Luther and Melanchthon from an avowedly metaphysical/ontological standpoint, claiming that Luther's understanding of justification is very close to that of the Eastern notions of *theōsis*.[35] The existence of any fundamental disjunction between Luther and Melanchthon has massive implications for understanding the Lutheran confessions and thus for any ecumenical encounters that involve the Lutheran church, for Lutheran self-identity, and for the iconic use of Luther for arguments in battles raging about forensic justification.

Although space prevents detailed examination of either Holl or the Finnish school, a number of observations lead me to conclude that the differences between Luther and Melanchthon are more ones of emphasis and terminology than of real substance. It is true that Melanchthon uses metaphors that set justification within a specifically legal context whereas Luther prefers the marriage image, but this does not require that the two positions be contradictory or mutually exclusive.

First, we have seen that, between 1515 and 1520, Luther's thinking on justification moves away from a proleptic concept of righteousness as part of its content toward a much greater emphasis upon the extrinsic divine decision. Parallel to this is the increasingly clear distinction Luther draws between two kinds of righteousness, the active and the passive. Given the precision with which the Luther of, for instance, 1519 onward will make this distinction, it is perhaps not at all surprising that the interpretations of Holl and the Finnish school disproportionately depend upon the earlier writings of Luther, since clearly the writings from 1520 onward are simply not as susceptible to any understanding of

33. Holl, *Luther*, 111–54. For a recent defense of Holl's overall approach to Luther, see James M. Stayer, *Martin Luther, German Saviour: German Evangelical Theological Factions and the Interpretation of Luther, 1917–1933* (Montreal and Kingston, Ont.: McGill-Queen's University Press, 2000). An alternative reading of the Luther-Melanchthon relationship is offered by Lowell Green, *How Melanchthon Helped Luther Discover the Gospel: The Doctrine of Justification in the Reformation* (Fallbrook, CA: Verdict, 1980). Cf. Timothy J. Wengert, *Law and Gospel: Philip Melanchthon's Debate with John Agricola of Eisleben over Poenitentia* (Grand Rapids: Baker, 1997); "Melanchthon and Luther / Luther and Melanchthon," *Lutherjahrbuch* 66 (1999): 55–88; Bengt Hägglund, "Melanchthon versus Luther: The Contemporary Struggle," *Concordia Theological Quarterly* 44 (1980): 123–33.

34. Green, *How Melanchthon Helped Luther*.

35. See the essays in Braaten and Jenson, *Union with Christ*.

justification that places transformative notions at its center. Rather, the Luther of 1520 onward emphasizes the absolute priority of the extrinsic divine decision and the passive righteousness received by faith, and thus he exhibits an important area of mutual concern with Melanchthon's forensic approach.[36]

Second, the nature of theological inquiry at Wittenberg was decidedly communal. To think of separate theologies for Luther, for Melanchthon, for Bugenhagen, and so forth, is possible only when they are seen purely in terms of the production of individual books. In fact, these books were the result of constant social and intellectual interaction between the various Wittenberg players and were thus not, in a deep sense, the product of a single author but of the theological ferment of Wittenberg as a whole. The communal activity of drinking beer in the alehouse was as crucial, in its way, to Wittenberg theology as the individual study of books in the library. This fact should automatically temper any discussion that seeks to sharpen authorial differences and juxtapose texts from different works in a manner that sets them at odds with each other.

Third, we know that Luther had great admiration for Melanchthon's exegesis, especially his commentary work on Romans from 1532 and his scholia on Colossians from 1534. Indeed, the *Table Talk* is full of lavish praise for the work on Romans, with Luther at one point indicating that it would have pleased Augustine but infuriated Jerome.[37] Though an argument from silence is not conclusive, we might have expected tensions or problems between the two over justification to have emerged in such a context; in fact, there is no indication that Luther is not very happy with Melanchthon's work in this area.[38]

Fourth, any breach between Melanchthon and Luther on justification would also involve a breach between Luther and the confessional documents of the Lutheran church. Given that the church produced a number of documents in Luther's lifetime over which both he and Melanchthon agreed (the "Augsburg Confession" of 1530 and the "Smalcald Articles"

---

36. See Trueman, "Is the Finnish Line a New Beginning?"; see also the comments of Paul Althaus, *The Theology of Martin Luther*, trans. R. C. Schultz (Philadelphia: Fortress, 1966), 241–42; Rupp, *Righteousness*, 30–31. The crucial importance of the distinctions Luther makes regarding righteousness is made clear by Robert Kolb, "Luther on the Two Kinds of Righteousness," in Wengert, *Harvesting Martin Luther's Reflections*, 38–55. In terms of the contemporary significance of this, Kolb draws attention to the absence of the distinction between the two righteousnesses in the Lutheran–Roman Catholic "Joint Declaration on the Doctrine of Justification" (ibid., 38, n. 1). The necessity of ignoring such a distinction in a Lutheran–Roman Catholic agreement on justification is symptomatic of precisely the differences in ontology that Daphne Hampson sees as lying at the heart of the disagreement between the two communions; see Hampson, *Christian Contradictions*.

37. WA.Tr 1, 130, 1–4 (316).

38. Cf. WA.Tr 2, 235, 19–22; 4, 610, 18–19.

of 1537, to name but two), the positing of any disagreement between the two men has to deal with the question of how such confessional agreement between them was able to exist.[39]

Finally, there is the crucial evidence of the letter to Johannes Brenz that Melanchthon wrote on May 12, 1531, articulating his notion of forensic justification.[40] Here Melanchthon opposes Brenz's notion that justification is primarily transformation by the Holy Spirit; instead Melanchthon argues that it is the declaration of God in the court of the conscience, based on the promise of God.[41] What is significant about this letter, and what scholars have missed on occasion, is that on the very paper of this letter, Luther himself in his own hand wrote a postscript where he both expresses his satisfaction with the approach of Melanchthon and offers his own account of justification. The differences between the two men are clear—Melanchthon emphasizes the promise whereas Luther emphasizes Christ—but there is no hint of a disagreement about anything of substance between them. Indeed Luther explicitly regards any differences as being primarily those of emphasis and choice of language.[42]

The significance is obvious: from an interpretive point of view, any approach that drives a wedge between Luther and Melanchthon on justification by ignoring the wider material conditions of theological work in Wittenberg, or that isolates texts from the larger context, or that overemphasizes the importance of Luther's early work by failing to take account of internal developments within Luther's own thinking between 1515 and 1520, or that ignores Luther's own comments relative to the work of Melanchthon must be found wanting at a simple methodologi-

39. For the texts of these two, see Kolb and Wengert, *The Book of Concord*, 30–105, 297–328.

40. WA.Br 6, 98–101.

41. WA.Br 6, 100, 25–29, 38–40.

42. WA.Br 6, 100, 49–101. Luther's opening remarks are particularly clear (49–55): "Et ego soleo, mi Brenti, ut hanc melius capiam, sic imaginari, quasi nulla sit in corde meo qualitas, quae fides vel charitas vocetur, sed in loco ipsorum pono Iesum Christum, et dico: Haec est iustitia mea, ipse est qualitas et formalis (ut vocant) iustitia mea, ut sic me liberem et expediam ab intuitu legis et operum, imo et ab intuitu obiectivi illius Christi, qui vel doctor vel donator intelligitur. Sed volo ipsum mihi esse donum vel doctrinam per se, ut omnia in ipso habeam." ("I myself, Brenz, usually take it thus: I imagine that there is no quality in my heart which is called either faith or love, but I put in their place Jesus Christ, as I say: This is my righteousness, he himself is my status and my formal righteousness (so-called). In this way I free myself and escape from the sight of the law and of works,—further, I even escape from that objective Christ who is understood either as teacher of doctrine or as the giver of a gift. On the contrary, I want him to be himself both my gift and my doctrine, so that I might have everything in him.") Clearly, Luther sees his explanation as an alternative way of expressing the same doctrine as that offered by Melanchthon.

cal level, at the very least because such an approach cannot account for important aspects of Luther's life. From the ecumenical point of view, this then raises the obvious question of whether an ecumenism that proceeds on the basis of isolating Luther from his own confessional trajectory is of any real use whatsoever. Such segregation is, I suggest, both historically flawed and ecumenically irrelevant: as an ecclesiastical movement, ecumenism must place at its center the confessional documents of the churches involved, not a few isolated texts by single individuals, even when those individuals, such as Luther, have their writings explicitly cited in the confessional material. Therefore neither the Luther of Holl nor the Luther of the Finns is of much use in this regard, however amenable their versions of his thinking might be to certain other streams of theology.

Luther and Conversion

The second issue is that of Luther and conversion. There is little doubt that Luther's writings have had a profound impact on evangelical understandings of conversion in relation to justification, primarily, I suspect, through the work of John Bunyan, who appropriated Lutheran ideas for many of his writings, most notably in his account of Christian in the *Pilgrim's Progress*, and through the famous experience of John Wesley, when his heart was strangely warmed, in part, through the reading of Luther. Still, from what I have said so far, it should be clear that the appropriation of Luther for later evangelical conversionism is not an unproblematic move.[43]

First, the only account we have of any such "conversion" is the "Autobiographical Fragment," which is found in the preface to the edition of Luther's works published in 1545. Whether this is a conversion is unclear, as Luther's writings seem to indicate that what it describes happened somewhat earlier than 1519, the date he himself supplies, and thus predates points at which, in the same document, he declares himself to have been an insane follower of the Pope. Further, whatever Luther is describing here appears to have had no functional importance in his public ministry: we hear this story only in 1545, a year before Luther's death.[44]

43. For a more detailed discussion of the issues, see Carl R. Trueman, "Was Luther an Evangelical?" in *The Practical Calvinist*, ed. Peter Lillback (Fearn, UK: Christian Focus, 2002), 131–48.

44. The full texts of the "Preface to the Complete Edition of Luther's Latin Writings" (1545) is in *LW* 34:323–38; the passage referring to the "tower experience" is found on pp. 336–37.

Second, Luther has, as we have seen, a very high view of baptism that is closely connected to his view of justification. As in the Lord's Supper, to reduce the sacrament to symbolism would be to divest it of its salvific power, which, for Luther, inevitably includes the giving of the incarnate Christ to the recipient of the sacrament. This is why—in significant contrast, I would guess, to modern evangelicals—when Luther was tempted by the devil, his response was to point the devil to his baptism as the sign that he belonged to Christ, not to some experience of what we might today call conversion. Now, although the efficacy of the sacrament can be grasped only by faith, there is a sense in which baptism itself engrafts the believer into the body of Christ and thus creates the context where the great battle takes place between God and Satan as to who will rule over the individual.[45] This ties in with Luther's reading of Romans 7 in his commentary. Here the kind of struggles, or *Anfechtungen* (in which he was assailed by doubts), of which Luther (as a Christian, of course) will later complain are ascribed specifically to the *Christian believer* and not to an individual in the throes of some kind of preconversion torment. Indeed Luther gives no less than twelve reasons from within the chapter itself for reading it in this way.[46] Again, the argument essentially revolves around the kind of inner/outer distinction and contrast that will be so important in Luther's theology. Only spiritual persons can truly understand their carnality, their unworthiness before God, their obnoxiousness in themselves to God.[47]

This all makes perfect sense in the context of the overall direction of Luther's theological development: the outwardly righteous individual, who stands confident before God that he or she is worthy of his favor, is the one who is inwardly foul and obnoxious to God—who is, if you like, *simul justus* (outwardly) *et peccator* (inwardly). The Christian, however, is *simul justus* (inwardly) precisely because of being *peccator* in his or her own eyes and, given the theology of the cross, in the eyes of the world. Given, then, the power of baptism and the fact that the struggles of law and gospel are the struggles of the believer, not the unbeliever (who is, after all, content in his or her own righteousness), it is arguable that, for Luther, the preaching of law and gospel is not to be understood in, for instance, quite the straightforward conversionist sense that underlies the narrative of Christian in *Pilgrim's Progress* but more in terms of

---

45. See Luther's comment: "But Satan, though he could not quench the power of baptism in little children, nevertheless succeeded in quenching it in all adults, so that now there are scarcely any who call to mind their own baptism, and still fewer who glory in it; so many other ways have been discovered for remitting sins and getting to heaven" (*LW* 36:57–58).

46. *LW* 25:328–36.

47. *LW* 25:328.

the perennial battle that goes on within baptized believers throughout their lives. This is why Luther regards the preaching of the law and of the gospel as two sides of the same coin, a coin that never ceases to be relevant.[48]

How does this, then, impact on our reading of Luther on justification today? First, discussion of Luther's understanding of justification must take into account the ecclesiological and sacramental dimension of his breakthrough. Justification is linked to baptism, just as the shifts in thinking about justification find their counterparts in shifts in thinking about baptism. Thus reflection upon justification should necessarily entail reflection upon issues relating to the doctrine of the sacraments and of the church. This is something that, like Luther's understanding of the human person in terms of relation and status, has been lost in many of the discussions raging on about Luther and justification in various circles today. The blame for radical individualism, whether of the evangelical or the Bultmannian kind, cannot easily be laid at the door of Luther's teaching on justification unless this teaching is itself ripped from its historical and theological context. Luther's own approach, as we would expect from a man educated in what was, by and large, a medieval context, placed more emphasis upon the corporate dimensions of Christianity than is often supposed.

Second and following on from the first point, politically, this approach should serve to undercut much of the "Here I stand!" rhetoric that one often finds in Protestant circles regarding Luther and justification. The close connection of justification in Luther's mind not simply with faith but also with baptism means that any appropriation of Luther as an icon of justification by later evangelical Protestantism has to be done with a critical awareness that there are aspects even of his very theology of justification with which much of later Protestantism would be very uncomfortable. Luther's sacramental theology, as a whole, is not that of contemporary evangelicalism, which is often Zwinglian at best on the Lord's Supper and, more often than not, Baptist regarding baptism. It is not my place here to discuss either of these options but simply to point out that the relationship between sacraments and justification in Luther's thinking is not incidental and that discussions of justification that use fidelity to Luther and the Reformation as part of the rhetorical, if not theological, argument need to take this into account.

48. This thinking is reflected in thesis 1 of the 95 Theses: "When our Lord and Master Jesus Christ said, 'Repent,' he willed the entire life of believers to be one of repentance" (*LW* 31:25).

Justification and the Theology of the Cross

The third point about contemporary discussion relates to the connection, mentioned earlier, between Luther's understanding of justification and his theology of the cross. The paradoxical nature of justification (that God does everything, I do nothing; that only as I realize my own unrighteousness do I become righteous before God) parallels Luther's reflections on the cross: it is only as Christ makes himself a sinful, weak, defeated man in terms of outward appearance that God is revealed as gracious and righteous and powerful. Luther then taps this rich theological vein in *The Freedom of the Christian Man*, where true freedom is manifested in the service of others, turning on its head all received notions of freedom. Indeed, Luther's theology goes further: if true theology is theology of the cross, then the outworking of justification inevitably entails suffering and sacrifice as the means by which believers both demonstrate their vital union with Christ and point the world to the kind of God they worship.

It is here that Luther's theology of justification is of particular relevance in the present day. One of the issues theologians must face is that of power and manipulation, and it must be acknowledged that theology and doctrine, not least the doctrine of justification, lend themselves to precisely the kind of manipulative behavior and abusive bullying that stands as a contradiction of what doctrine, conceived in terms of the cross, should be. As with the issue of baptism, the abstraction of Luther's understanding of faith and imputation from the context of God as revealed in Christ dying on the cross leads to distortion, moral and doctrinal. If, however, justification is seen within the context of the cross, then it surely becomes a contradiction of the doctrine to use it as a means of power, exploitation, or self-promotion because, in the very act of so doing, one contradicts a vital part of what justification is for Luther.

The applications of this are surely obvious. First, those who critique the Lutheran understanding of justification need to acknowledge that the doctrine involves much more than a certain reading of Romans. It also involves engagement with Paul's teaching in 1 Corinthians about the nature of the Christian gospel relative to human expectations of what God is like and what should be expected of the Christian life. One should not, for example, lambaste Luther for too individualistic a view of justification in terms of an excessive emphasis upon the *coram Deo* ("before the face of God") aspect of the doctrine. In fact, justification establishes a relationship of servanthood between the believer and any who cross his or her path. It is, in other words, a socially transformative doctrine.

Second, Luther's theology provides Christian theologians with a resource that allows them to begin tackling many of the awkward questions that thinkers, since at least the time of Thomas Hobbes, have asked about the coercive nature of religion. For example, the Marxian critique of religion, which sees it as essentially a deceptive palliative used by the dominant class to defuse class tensions, becomes somewhat less compelling when it is realized that the doctrine of justification does not involve the manipulation of others so much as the necessary involvement of the one articulating the doctrine in suffering and self-giving. I cannot believe that I am justified by the crucified God unless I myself come to believe that the total freedom that this gives me is realized in my total bondage to service of, and suffering for, others. Of course, this then opens the Christian up to the Nietzschean objection that Christian morality is itself a slave morality, a morality of weakness and defeat. This too is true but is in fact the whole point, and dare one say it, Friedrich Nietzsche had an insight here, though he sadly chose to judge it in the light of an atheology of glory, not a theology of the cross: the message of the cross for Luther is that Christ is empowered precisely at this moment of total disempowerment, and this is also the message of justification—humans are empowered, liberated, at precisely the point when they realize they themselves are powerless and bound. The implications for a response to the Marxian and Nietzschean critiques are therefore obvious: we should glory in the fact that Christianity renders us weak and powerless in the world's eyes because it is in this weakness and powerlessness that we become powerful in relation to God—powerful, if you like, in our true humanity.[49]

Third, in giving horizons of expectation that look to suffering and servitude as providing Christian authenticity, Luther's theology also provides material for a deep critique of modern Western consumerism, where the very excess of goods and comfort generates boredom, acquisitiveness, an obsession with alleviating even the slightest discomfort, and a church that, at least in the materially more prosperous Christian suburbs of America, is often indistinguishable in attitude and posture from the wider culture to which it belongs—a cultural Protestantism of the kind that serves the purpose of baptizing the political and social aspirations of the West rather as the church of Luther's day sanctioned

49. Orthodox theologians have already done significant work in this area; see Miroslav Volf, *Exclusion and Embrace* (London: Abingdon, 1996); Anthony C. Thiselton, *Interpreting God and the Postmodern Self* (Edinburgh: T&T Clark, 1995); Kevin Vanhoozer, "The Trials of Truth: Mission, Martyrdom, and the Epistemology of the Cross," in *First Theology* (Downers Grove, IL: InterVarsity, 2002), 337–73; Graham Tomlin, *The Power of the Cross* (Carlisle, UK: Paternoster, 1999); Tomlin, "The Theology of the Cross: Subversive Theology for the Postmodern World?" *Themelios* 23, no. 1 (1997): 59–73.

its own institutional greed by turning grace itself into a commodity. By placing the cross back at the center of authentic Christianity, Luther points an accusing finger at those who make too easy a marriage between the empowering ambitions of the societies in which we live and the true empowerment of Christ.[50]

Conclusion

The topic of Luther on justification is a vast one. Given that this doctrine was at the center of Luther's reconstruction of the whole of theological rationality and thus of his understanding of the world, a presentation such as this can barely skim the surface. But to summarize its argument, the following points are significant:

(1) Luther's theology undergoes significant development in the years 1516–1520, and attempts, such as those by Holl and Mannermaa, to construct proposals on the basis of an excessive emphasis on the earlier works are flawed precisely because they fail to take into account this development.

(2) Luther's use of the language of status and relation is basic to understanding what he is saying and, as it ties in with his views of sin, of baptism, and of ethics, must be taken into account in any ecumenical use of his writings.

(3) Ecumenical discussion must take seriously the substantial identity between Luther's mature theology (1519 onward) and the confessional documents contained in the *Book of Concord*. The historical and theological problems driving a major wedge between them are inseparable.

(4) The relationship between Luther and later evangelicalism on justification, particularly in terms of conversionism and baptism, is far more problematic than is often acknowledged.

(5) In the theology of the cross, Luther has left a legacy for modern theology that, through its insights into Paul's teaching in 1 Corinthians, is a crucial resource for responding to some of the more difficult contemporary challenges; it is a theology we abandon to our cost.

---

50. At the risk of introducing a personal axe to grind, I might add that the kind of song sung in church is both reflective and constitutive of the expectations of the people. It is therefore significant that the habit of psalm singing, with its emphasis upon lament and suffering, has all but died out in evangelical churches—a sign perhaps that the horizons of expectation that psalm singing embodies have also died out.

5

Calvin's Doctrine of Justification

Variations on a Lutheran Theme

Karla Wübbenhorst

In most historical surveys of the doctrine of justification, John Calvin may not merit even a mention. The party lines are usually drawn as "Luther versus the Vatican." Regensburg, Trent, and the "Joint Declaration" of 1999 have all conceived of the problem in this way. Thus any consideration of Calvin's doctrine of justification will inevitably be against the background of the Lutheran/Catholic divide. The initial question becomes this: Is Calvin's doctrine Lutheran? Is it a turn of the wheel back toward something recognizably Catholic? Or is it a turn forward into something distinct and unanticipated, which we might call "Calvinistic" or "Reformed"?

As I see it, Calvin's doctrine answers, to some extent, to all three descriptions. Calvin is undoubtedly a disciple of the Lutheran evangelical movement. This might be said of Calvin generally, notwithstanding his departures from Lutheran understandings of sacrament and Scripture, but it can be said particularly of the teaching on justification. For Lutherans, the doctrine of justification by grace through faith alone is "the article by which the church stands or falls."[1] Calvin calls it "the main hinge upon

---

1. Alister McGrath points to "precursors of [this] phrase . . . in the writings of Luther himself: e.g., WA 40 III.352.3, 'quia isto articulo stante stat Ecclesia, ruente ruit Ecclesia'"

which religion turns."[2] There is agreement, then, that this doctrine is at the very heart of the evangelical program, which the Reformation is contending for. But as Brian Gerrish points out, Calvin defines discipleship as a creative continuation in the trajectory of the master.[3] True imitators, as opposed to apes, possess the freedom to stand critically within a tradition, to correct it, and to develop it. Calvin's doctrine of justification corrects the Lutheran doctrine or, rather, protects it in the face of certain Catholic objections and, in so doing, develops that doctrine in a more neonomian and realistic direction. The neonomian emphasis is shared by Reformed thinkers before Calvin and becomes characteristic of later Calvinism. Calvin's realism is also shared by the Calvinists to the extent that they, too, complement the evangelical perspective with a more scholastic one and place justification within the context of an *ordo salutis*.

This article attempts a roughly chronological sketch of Calvin's ideas on justification as they develop in dialogue with Luther and other influences from 1536 through 1559. Since there is scant room here to trawl Calvin's complete corpus, it concentrates on three landmarks: the first *Institutes* of 1536, the commentary on Romans published in 1539, and the final *Institutes* of 1559. The general outline of the teaching on justification is in place by 1539 and changes little. What does change is the position of this doctrine in the *Institutes* and, as this would imply, the ideological relation of it to other doctrines.

The Wittenberg Teaching

Calvin's doctrine of justification was deeply indebted to that which had been developed at Wittenberg. In his lectures on Romans from 1515 and 1516, Luther taught that justifying righteousness is the "alien righteousness of Christ." This represented a departure from the Augustinian understanding, in which justifying righteousness, albeit completely the

---

("for if this article stands, the Church stands; if it falls, the Church falls"), but notes that the earliest currency of the exact words "articulus stantis et cadentis ecclesiae" ("the article by which the church stands or falls") seems to be in the Lutheran *and Reformed* milieu of the early seventeenth century. This is contra Loofs, who associates it with Lutheran theologians of the eighteenth century. See Alister E. McGrath, *Iustitia Dei: A History of the Christian Doctrine of Justification*, 2 vols. (Cambridge: Cambridge University Press, 1986), 2:193, n. 3.

2. "Praecipuum esse sustinendae religionis cardinem." See John Calvin, *Institutes* III.xi.1 (John Calvin, *Werke*, ed. Guilielmus Baum, Eduardus Cunitz, and Eduardus Reuss, 59 vols. in 49, Corpus Reformatorum [Brunswick, Ger.: C. A. Schwetschke et Filium, 1863–1900], 2:533).

3. B. A. Gerrish, "John Calvin on Luther," in *Interpreters of Luther*, ed. Jaroslav Pelikan (Philadelphia: Fortress, 1968).

gift of God, was something that inhered in the human subject. The implications of this departure were far reaching. Not only did it abstract righteousness from the believer, making it possible for Luther to affirm that the Christian was *simul justus et peccator*,[4] it also abstracted the scene of justification, as it were, from the face of the earth. Justification took place not before the eyes of one's neighbors but *coram Deo* ("before the face of God," or "in the presence of God") or, as Melanchthon would put it, *in foro divino* ("in the divine forum," or "before the divine tribunal").[5] A parallel shift occurred in the understanding of grace, which was not only abstracting but also dynamizing. Grace became a word for the attitude of divine favor, not for a kind of holy substance that came from God and took root in the Christian. Philipp Melanchthon articulated this view of grace as *favor Dei* in his *Loci Communes* of 1521.

It was Melanchthon who worked out a language of imputation and contrasted the divine act of "declaring" sinners righteous, based on the extrinsic righteousness of Christ, with the Augustinian idea of God's "making" them righteous by a conversion of their wills.[6] Part of the development toward this forensic idea of justification was the increasing focus on the objective substitutionary work of Christ rather than on the subjective influence of his person.[7]

Calvin in 1536

In the *Institutes* of 1536, Calvin speaks of justification at the end of his chapter on the law. After establishing the principle that accurate human self-knowledge must needs be in a theistic frame of reference, he goes on to announce the fall of Adam and the subsequent condemnation of all his progeny by the standard of God's law. Although we are thus God's enemies, God's love for us has provided a remedy in Christ. There follow an exposition of the Ten Commandments and then the section on justification, which contrasts the impossibility of a legal, works-based righteousness to the happy possibility of a righteousness grasped through faith in Christ. The works route to divine approbation is vain because we can never make up what we have lost in Adam. Fur-

4. WA 56.270.9–11; 343.16–23.

5. Philipp Melanchthon, *Opera Quae Supersunt Omnia*, ed. Carolus Gottlieb Bretschneider, 28 vols., Corpus Reformatorum (Halle, Ger.: C. A. Schwetschke et Filium, 1834–1860), 21:421.

6. Melanchthon, "Apology of the Augsburg Confession" (1530), art. 4, par. 252.

7. McGrath, *Iustitia Dei*, 2:23: Melanchthon's early emphasis on the person of Christ "contrasts significantly with his later emphasis [post-1530] upon the more abstract concept of the *work* of Christ associated with his doctrine of forensic justification."

thermore, once we embark on that course, we must keep the whole of the law, which no one can do. We cannot offer any form of satisfaction that God will regard positively, let alone works of supererogation, and Calvin scoffs at the trifling character of the works that human beings name so proudly—things which have been added by human invention to what Scripture commands. On the other hand,

> certain indeed is that faith which rests upon God's mercy alone. . . . We must . . . recognize that our salvation consists in God's mercy alone . . . not in any worth of ours, or in anything coming from us. . . . For never will we have enough confidence in God unless we become deeply distrustful of ourselves. . . . When all our confidence is utterly cast down yet we still rely on his goodness, we grasp and obtain God's grace, and (as Augustine says) forgetting our merits, we embrace Christ's gifts. . . . [For] no one can attain this assurance except through Christ, by whose blessing alone we are freed from the law's curse. The curse was decreed and declared for us all, since, on account of the weakness inherited from our father Adam, we could not fulfill the law by our own works, as was required of those who desired to obtain therefrom righteousness for themselves. By Christ's righteousness then are we made righteous and become fulfillers of the law. This righteousness we put on as our own, and surely God accepts it as ours, reckoning us holy, pure, and innocent. Thus is fulfilled Paul's statement: "Christ was made righteousness, sanctification and redemption for us" [1 Cor. 1:30]. For our merciful Lord first indeed kindly received us into grace according to his own goodness and freely-given will, forgiving . . . our sins, which deserved wrath and eternal death [Rom. 5:11; 6:22]. Then through the gifts of his Holy Spirit he dwells and reigns in us and through him the lusts of our flesh are each day mortified more and more. We are indeed sanctified, that is, consecrated to the Lord in complete purity of life, our hearts formed to obedience to the law. Then lastly, even while we walk in the Lord's ways . . . something imperfect remains in us . . . to teach us always to shift all trust from ourselves to him [Rom. 7:23]. Accordingly those works also which are done by us while we rush along the Lord's way . . . cannot of themselves render us acceptable . . . to God. But Christ's righteousness, which alone can bear the sight of God because it alone is perfect, must appear in court on our behalf, and stand surety for us in judgment [Heb. 11:6; Rom. 8:34]. Received from God, this righteousness is brought to us and imputed to us, just as if it were ours. Thus in faith we continually and constantly obtain forgiveness of sins; none of the filth or uncleanness of our imperfection is imputed to us, but is covered over by that purity and perfection of Christ.[8]

After itemizing the uses of the law (which even at this early stage are three, in contradistinction to Luther's two), Calvin elaborates on the third

---

8. Calvin, 1536 *Institutes*, I.31–32 (Battles, 34–35); *Werke*, 1:48–49.

use and revisits the theme of works. Good works are the content of the Christian life, but they have no competency as a cause of justification. Justification is the gift of free forgiveness, but if a holy life does not follow upon it, the blood of Christ, which purchased the gift, is despised—for it is shed, Calvin says, "as often as [we] sin."[9] The works we perform following justification have no more power to satisfy for sin than works before justification. Still, concludes Calvin,

> it will be nothing amiss for us to regard holiness of life to be the way, not indeed that leads, but by which those chosen by their God are led, into the glory of the Heavenly Kingdom. For it is God's good pleasure to glorify those whom he has sanctified [Rom. 8:30]. For this reason, observances of commandments are sometimes called "righteousness" of the Lord: not those by which the Lord justifies, that is, holds and regards as righteous; but by which he trains his own to be righteous, whom he previously justified by his grace. But if anyone attributes even the slightest portion to works, he perverts and corrupts the whole of Scripture, which assigns complete credit to the divine goodness.[10]

The 1536 *Institutes* are quite Lutheran, not only for the fact that their structure reflects that of Luther's catechism but also in their content, perhaps particularly in the teaching on justification, which is little anticipated by the thought of the Swiss Reformers. The sections just quoted reflect Luther's insistence that the basis of justification is the "alien righteousness of Christ," to whom we cling by faith. Although faith is thus the necessary condition of justification, it does not challenge Christ's righteousness as its sole cause. Calvin will later make this point by using the different Aristotelian types of causality. In 1536 he sounds more Luther-like in speaking of the "gospel promises, which our merciful Lord freely offers to us, not by reason of any worth or good deed of ours, but out of his fatherly goodness, imposing on us no other condition than that we embrace wholeheartedly the very great gift of his good pleasure."[11] The inverse proportion that Calvin draws between faith and works at every stage of the story—the stark contrast between the proud, self-reliant legalist and the humble believer trusting to Christ—is also reminiscent of the paradoxical strain in Luther's theology.

In the 1559 *Institutes*, Calvin will summarize the meaning of Christ's mediatorship under the figure of the *mirifica communicatio*—the "wonderful exchange."[12] Although one thinks of patristic sources (Irenaeus's

9. Ibid., I.36 (Battles, 39); *Werke*, 1:53.
10. Ibid., I.38 (Battles, 41); *Werke*, 1:55.
11. Ibid., I.31 (Battles, 34); *Werke*, 1:48.
12. Calvin, *Institutes* IV.xvii.2; *Werke*, 2:1003.

"He became man in order that we might be made gods" or Athanasius's "who, through his immense love became what we are, that He might bring us to be even what He is Himself"),[13] Luther's similar idea of the *commercium admirabile* ("the wonderful exchange") may have provided more proximate inspiration.[14] In any case, we meet, in another Luther-like moment of the first *Institutes*, an early version of the material that Calvin will later collect under the figure of "the wonderful exchange":

> This is our assurance, that Christ the Son of God is ours and has been given to us, so that in him we may also be sons of God. . . . We experience such participation in him that, although we are sinners, he is our righteousness; while we are unclean, he is our purity; while we are weak, while we are unarmed and exposed to Satan, yet ours is that power . . . given him . . . to crush Satan; while we still bear about with us the body of death, he is yet our life. In brief, because all his things are ours and we have all things in him, in us there is nothing.[15]

Also evident, however, is Melanchthon's language of imputation, and his forensic metaphor is observed when Calvin says, "Christ's righteousness . . . must appear in court on our behalf, and stand surety for us in judgment. Received from God, this righteousness is brought to us and imputed to us, just as if it were ours."[16] That "as if" is what the Lutheran confessing tradition insists upon. The believer's righteousness is a counterfactual judgment, declared over us because of God's mercy and for the sake of Christ. On the other hand, Calvin cites Augustine in this section with approval and even says, "By Christ's righteousness then, we are made righteous," before adding that "God accepts [this righteousness] as ours, reckoning us . . . innocent."[17] The latter sentence clarifies that we are righteous only by divine consent, but it is interesting that it does not seem to bother Calvin to use the Augustinian phrase "made righteous," which Melanchthon has identified as alternative to his own view.

In the 1536 *Institutes*, we see Calvin definitely embracing the developed Protestant doctrine of forensic justification together with its underlying concern that any refusal of *this* form of justification will imply necessarily a vain and ungrateful belief in the possibility of *self*-justification. At the same time, however, we see him struggling to work out a view of the place of the law and of actual righteousness, a view that will eventu-

---

13. Irenaeus, *Against Heresies* 5, preface; Athanasius, *On the Incarnation of the Word* 54.
14. WA 5.608.16.
15. Calvin, 1536 *Institutes*, I.33–34 (Battles, 36–37); *Werke*, 1:51.
16. Ibid., I.32 (Battles, 35); *Werke*, 1:49.
17. Ibid., I.32 (Battles, 34); *Werke*, 1:48–49.

ally distinguish him from the Lutheran voice. In his 1536 treatment of justification, Calvin uses the term "sanctification" and declares, in what must be a conscious misquotation of Romans 8:30, that God "glorif[ies] those whom he has *sanctified*."[18] But Calvin has not, at this point, drawn out very carefully the relation between justification and sanctification or their place in the *ordo salutis*, although he does seem to see them as successive. He notices a certain order in the verse "Christ was made righteousness, sanctification and redemption for us,"[19] which he glosses as follows: "Our merciful Lord *first* indeed kindly received us into grace according to his own goodness and freely-given will, forgiving . . . our sins. . . . *Then* through the gifts of his Holy Spirit he dwells and reigns in us. . . . We are indeed sanctified. *Then lastly*" (I paraphrase Calvin here) Christ's perfection will stand surety for us and cover the imperfection that remains in both our members and our works so that they may not be judged until that final day, when our "old man" is destroyed and with incorruptible bodies we are glorified.[20] If I am correct in reading this whole section as a gloss of the terms "righteousness," "sanctification," and "redemption," plucked from 1 Corinthians 1:30, then Calvin in 1536 is contemplating a successive relation among justification, sanctification, and redemption. The first he considers as free forgiveness (nothing is yet said of imputed righteousness, which he will say later is also involved); the second as a mortification of the flesh and a vivification to good works; the third as a nonimputation of our lingering sin while we are being sanctified and as a completion of that work, attested by a bodily renewal. Perhaps the term "redemption" does not serve him as well as he would like for the third phase, and at a later point he refers to "glorification," from Romans 8:30, as "sanctification's" successor.

Calvin in 1539

In 1539 Calvin publishes his commentary on Romans and the second edition of the *Institutes*. From this version onward, perhaps because of what he has learned in working closely with the text of Romans, the section on justification expands and moves about, arguably with the effect that it becomes more important. It is now that Calvin begins to

18. Ibid., I.38 (Battles, 41); *Werke*, 1:55. Emphasis added. Calvin does not include a parenthetical reference to Rom. 8 here, which he probably would do if he thought he was quoting the text exactly.

19. It is strange that Calvin also misquotes this verse (1 Cor. 1:30), leaving out "wisdom," the first term used of Christ in the fourfold list.

20. Calvin, 1536 *Institutes*, I.32 (Battles, 34–35); *Werke*, 1:49. "Primum . . . Deinde . . . Tum postremo." Emphasis added.

refer to justification as "the main hinge upon which religion turns."[21]
All the *Institutes* prior to the final version of 1559 work with a law,
then a faith, structure. In 1536 the section on justification concludes
the law section. In 1539 it is moved, so that it comes under "faith" and
follows the exposition of the Creed. It maintains this place until the
final version. In 1559 the law/faith structure is abandoned in favor of
a new structuring principle, the *duplex cognitio Dei*—the knowledge
of God as Creator and as Redeemer.[22] The exposition of *both* the law
and the faith (or at least the law and the *gospel*, as it is contained in
the bulky *second* article of the Creed) is then placed in book 2—the
knowledge of God the Redeemer—but justification is removed to the
third book. After the knowledge of God is outlined in books 1 and 2,
there is a shift to the subjective, as we might expect from the principle
laid down in the opening line of the *Institutes*. Justification is now
placed so as to fall in this more subjective realm, which is at once both
pneumatological and concerned with the *beneficia Christi* ("benefits
of Christ").[23]

From 1539 onward, repentance is brought forward, so that it is discussed before justification; the discussion of the Christian life, however,
stands as the very last chapter of the *Institutes* from 1539 to 1550, at a
great distance from both repentance and justification. The 1559 order
inserts the discussion of the Christian life between repentance and justification and heads up the whole section with a discussion of the Holy
Spirit and faith, his principle work.[24] The effect, I suggest, is to confound
the supposed causal successions of repentance and justification, justification and the Christian life. Calvin's mature insight is that everything flows
from the Holy Spirit, who brings us all the benefits of Christ, through
the primary gift of faith—but as Calvin might say, we "pass over" this
now to say more on it "in its proper place."[25]

21. Calvin, 1539 *Institutes*, VI.1: "principuum esse sustinendae religionis cardinem"
(identical with 1559) (*Werke*, 1:737). See also Calvin's comments on Rom. 1:17: "We have
now the principle point or the main hinge of the first part of the Epistle,—that we are
justified by faith through the mercy of God alone" (John Calvin, *Commentaries on Romans*
[Owen, 66]); *Werke*, 49:21–22.

22. Edward A. Dowey Jr. makes a persuasive case for this view of the final *Institutes'*
structure in *The Knowledge of God in Calvin's Theology*, expanded ed. (Grand Rapids:
Eerdmans, 1994).

23. The title of the final edition's third book is "The Mode of Obtaining the Grace of
Christ, the Benefits It Confers and the Effects Resulting from It."

24. F. L. Battles presents these shifts in a helpful diagrammatic form in *Analysis of
the Institutes of the Christian Religion of John Calvin* (Phillipsburg, NJ: P & R, 1980), 15.
His chart is especially useful in conjunction with the "Synopsis Editionum Institutionis
Calvinianae" in Calvin, *Werke*, 1:li–lviii.

25. See below.

1539—Calvin's Lutheran Allegiance Strengthens

In the Romans commentary of 1539, several ideas emerge that exert a lasting influence on Calvin's understanding of justifying righteousness and begin to distinguish it. His allegiance to forensic justification, however, is unwavering. Grace is understood extrinsically as *favor Dei*; justifying righteousness is understood as properly Christ's and improperly ours—that is, not only by imputation but by a declaration that is contrary to fact. And "God's tribunal" (*tribunal Dei*) is a favorite figure for the forum in which self-reliant, socially approved legalists are condemned and faithful, socially despised dependents find mercy. The polemic continues to be aimed at those who would regard works as in any way meritorious, whether or not in conjunction with faith.

In the Romans commentary, Calvin seems more aware of certain enemy positions and defines his own position more carefully in order to leave no handle for theirs. In so doing, he pronounces even more of the Lutheran shibboleths. He defends, for example, the unscriptural addition of the word "alone" to the phrase "justification by faith" because he perceives its power to clarify the Protestant position over against those who attempt "to blend faith with the merits of works. They indeed allow that man is justified by faith; but not by faith alone; yea, they place the efficacy of justification in love, though in words they ascribe it to faith."[26] Although Calvin has contemporary "schoolmen" in mind here, he recognizes that his own revered Augustine is the fountainhead of the error. In 1536 Calvin may have been reticent about differences between the Protestants and the father whose teaching on grace had so inspired them all, but now he becomes explicit about these differences, as Melanchthon before him had been. In his comments on Romans 3:21 and 5:5, Calvin explicitly rejects Augustinian exegesis. Romans 5:5 speaks of the love of God being shed abroad in our hearts by the Holy Spirit. Augustine interprets "the love of God" in the "active sense"—as *human beings' love for God*. Calvin remarks that "Augustine . . . is mistaken in his view" and that "love is . . . to be taken here in . . . a passive sense"[27]—as *God's love for human beings*—a wonderful truth of which Christians become more and more convinced as the Holy Spirit increases their faith. Augustine is one of those of whom Calvin says, "They place the efficacy of justification in love, though in words they ascribe it to faith."[28]

So, what is at stake here? To place the efficacy of justification in love rather than faith means that a person is understanding justification to

26. Calvin, *Commentaries on Romans*, at 3:28; *Werke*, 49:65.
27. Ibid., at 5:51; *Werke*, 49:92.
28. Ibid., at 3:28; *Werke*, 49:65.

include the regenerating work of the Holy Spirit. This is Augustine's understanding, but Calvin argues that it is not Paul's and, moreover, that it is not compatible with the gospel of justification based on God's gratuitous mercy alone. Faith, as Calvin sees it, is a wholly receptive faculty—it recumbs on the mercy of God, the promises attested in Christ. Love, on the other hand, is a more positive, deed-filled concern—in the love of God and neighbor are summarized all the works of the law! If works of the law, under the name of love, are smuggled into the concept of justification—even if they are, as Augustine allows, worked in us by the Holy Spirit—then what of the "righteousness of God without the law" that Romans 3:21 joyfully announces? And Calvin's phrase about tranquilizing the consciences of men is important. It reveals that Calvin is very aware of the pastoral consequences of bad theology built on faulty exegesis. The principle is simple: whatever *Christ* does we can be sure is done perfectly—if that is imputed to us, we have no cause to worry, but whatever *we* do is only partial and leaves plenty of room for anxiety in the conscience.

Calvin's comment on that important verse, Romans 3:21, may be excerpted as follows:

> The righteousness of God, which we obtain by faith . . . has been revealed, [Paul] says, *without the law*, that is, without the aid of the law; and the law is to be understood as meaning works. . . . We ought then to know, that the merits of works are excluded. We also see that he blends not works with the mercy of God; but . . . sets up mercy alone. It is not unknown to me, that *Augustine* gives a different explanation; for he thinks that the righteousness of God is the grace of regeneration; and this grace he allows to be free, because God renews us, when unworthy, by his Spirit; and from this he excludes the works of the law, that is, those works, by which men of themselves endeavor, without renovation, to render God indebted to them. . . . But that the Apostle includes all works without exception, even those which the Lord produces in his own people, is evident from the context. . . . [Some] think that these two things well agree,—that man is justified by faith through the grace of Christ,—and that he is yet justified by the works, which proceed from spiritual regeneration. . . . But Paul takes up a very different principle,—that the consciences of men will never be tranquillized until they recumb on the mercy of God alone. . . . Hence also is their sophistry confuted, who falsely accuse us of asserting, that according to Scripture we are justified by faith only, while the exclusive word *only*, is nowhere to be found in Scripture. But if justification depends not either on the law, or on ourselves, why should it not be ascribed to mercy alone? and if it be from mercy only, it is then by faith only.[29]

29. Ibid., at 3:21 (p. 136); *Werke*, 49:57–59.

Augustine and the Catholic conciliar documents that enshrine his thought know nothing of the cherished Reformed distinction between justification and sanctification, but we see here in the commentary on Romans the logical process by which Calvin becomes convinced that this was a distinction worth contending for. Justification by faith alone and the connected idea of justification as something distinct from newness of life (and thus something narrower than the Catholic definition) hereafter become fixed principles in Calvin's teaching on the doctrine. At 3.11, the beginning of the section on justification by faith in the final version of the *Institutes*, Calvin begins by asserting the "double grace" of justification and sanctification, and in section 6 he upbraids Osiander for not properly distinguishing them. Section 19 contends for the usage "through faith alone."[30]

1539—Calvin's Distinctive Voice Emerges

Besides causing him to back Luther's *sola fide* and second Melanchthon's dissatisfaction with Augustine, some of the insights Calvin gains from his close look at Romans take him in a rather less Lutheran direction. Luther disliked Aristotle, but in his comment on Romans 3:22, Calvin invokes some of Aristotle's causes to distinguish the role of faith from the role of Christ's righteousness and again from God's provident mercy. God's mercy is said to be the efficient cause, Christ's righteousness the material cause, and the word with faith the instrumental cause.[31] This is even more precise than calling faith the condition but not the cause of justification, which is the language of Luther and of the 1536 edition of the *Institutes*. The idea of multivalent causality survives into the 1559 edition of the *Institutes*.[32]

The Romans commentary also seems to be where Calvin comes to realize the vital importance of Christ's human obedience to the work of mediation. In his comments on Romans 3:24 and 4:25, he clearly teaches that the content of Christ's righteousness is his obedience. But I suspect it is in the course of his careful study of that extended inverse typology in Romans 5 between Christ and Adam that Calvin fully recognizes the potential of the obedience theme to unify the whole story of salvation history. In the final *Institutes*, Calvin writes, "Now someone asks, How has Christ abolished sin, banished the separation between us and God,

---

30. *Werke*, 2:533, 537–38, 548–49.

31. Calvin, *Commentaries on Romans*, at 3:22: "When therefore we are justified, the efficient cause is the mercy of God, the meritorious is Christ, the instrumental is the word in connection with faith" (Owen, 138); *Werke*, 49:60.

32. Calvin, *Institutes* III.xiv.17, 21; *Werke*, 2:575, 578.

and acquired righteousness to render God favorable and kindly toward us? To this we can in general reply that he has achieved this for us by the whole course of his obedience."[33] Calvin supports the statement with a reference to Romans 5:19: "As by one man's disobedience many were made sinners, so by one man's obedience we are made righteous." If the Romans commentary does inaugurate Calvin's interest in the concept of Christ's obedience, it is a concept that develops somewhat thereafter. In 1539 Calvin seems to be focusing obedience more narrowly, on Christ's death, whereas later it becomes a wider concept, encompassing the whole of the metaphorical cross-bearing that Jesus does throughout his earthly life.

That Calvin emphasizes this idiom of Christ's obedience in his theology may distinguish him but does not necessarily oppose him to Luther. This focus on the human obedience, however, leads to a peculiar theology of mediation that brings him into open conflict with Lutheran views. I think particularly of the difference over the extent to which attributes of the individual natures may be communicated and the Lutherans' derision at what they call the *extra Calvinisticum*. The striking thing about Calvin's doctrine of mediation is that it places such emphasis on the human nature of Christ. Although this appears to have been the case from the beginning and may have originally taken its cue from the second paragraph of the Creed, the understanding of justification as taking place in virtue of Christ's human obedience no doubt encouraged any leanings this way. To be sure, Calvin avows that neither nature can accomplish mediation on its own;[34] it is just that there is a definite asymmetry in the work he appropriates to the respective natures. Perhaps he would have done better to say that it is *redemption* that is orchestrated by the triune God and *mediation* that particularly required that Christ be human. On the whole, Calvinist Christology is periodic and asymmetrical, but Lutheran Christology is more fully communicative. So, what follows if Jesus, while incarnate, did not have complete access to all the prerogatives of his divine nature? When we see such a Christ faithful, when we see him obedient, working out a righteousness for us, then we realize he must be obtaining his faith from the same source we do, the Holy Spirit.

One of the things that makes Calvin's mature doctrine of justification distinctive is this role he gives to the Spirit. Not only sanctification but also justification in the 1559 *Institutes* is unquestionably pneumatological. It is moved to the third book; it is dependent on the faith that the Holy Spirit creates and on the fellowship of righteousness, the bond

33. Ibid. II.xvi.5; *Werke*, 2:370–71.
34. Ibid. II.xiv.3; *Werke*, 2:354–55.

of mystical union that the Spirit establishes between the believer and Christ. This pneumatological element in, or indeed the move outward from (though never away from), the Christ-personalism that characterizes Luther and toward other persons of the Trinity may be partially explained by the particular kind of Mediator theology Calvin expresses. On the other hand, the structure of the Epistle to the Romans itself and some of the content, for example, the magisterial eighth chapter, *would* prompt one to seek connections between justification, as it is exposed in the third chapter, and the more pneumatological territory into which the argument progresses. It would probably, however, encourage one to see them successively.

From 1539 to 1559 (Calvin's *simul*)

Another idea, and perhaps his most profound, that can be seen in Calvin's commentary on Romans and that remains a feature of his theology to the end is expressed in his comment on Romans 8:9: "That gratuitous remission of sins can never be separated from the Spirit of regeneration; for this would be as it were to rend Christ asunder."[35] The 1559 *Institutes* declares that if you wish "to attain righteousness in Christ [you] must first possess Christ; but you cannot possess him without being made partaker in his sanctification, because he cannot be divided into pieces."[36] This is more than a piece of enduring diction. Having concluded, contra Augustine, that there is no place, under justification proper, for newness of life, Calvin must now relate newness of life to justification. There is nothing particularly new in that; it is just the old problem, which Luther also faced, of how to exclude the antinomian charge. But the answer we see Calvin developing *is* somewhat new. In contrast to the *successive* language of 1536 ("Our Lord *first* . . . received us into grace according to his own goodness, forgiving . . . our sins . . . *then* through the gifts of his Holy Spirit he dwells and reigns in us"), we now hear the language of *inseparability*, based on this Christ in whom we have some participation and who must remain whole. Inseparability is not yet the language of *simultaneity*, and indeed the Letter to the Romans is unlikely to prompt such a thought.[37] In the 1546 commentary on 1 Corinthians, however, Calvin makes a slight adjustment to his earlier remark on Romans:

35. Calvin, *Werke*, 49:144.
36. Calvin, *Institutes* III.xvi.1; *Werke*, 2:586.
37. Romans itself deals *successively* with justification (chs. 3 and 4), engrafting into Christ (chs. 5 and 6), and sanctification (chs. 7 and 8).

We cannot be justified freely through faith alone without *at the same time* living holily. For these fruits of grace are connected together, as it were, by an indissoluble tie, so that he who attempts to sever them does in a manner tear Christ in pieces. Let therefore the man who seeks to be justified through Christ, by God's unmerited goodness, consider that this cannot be attained without his taking him *at the same time* for sanctification, or, in other words, being renewed to innocence and purity of life.[38]

This teaching that the distinct graces of justification and sanctification not only are inseparable but also are established in us *at the same time* because, in Christ, we possess their common source is, as it were, Calvin's great *simul*.[39] The passage from the 1559 *Institutes*, quoted above, incorporates this insight when it adds, "Since, therefore, it is solely by expending himself that the Lord gives us these benefits to enjoy, he bestows both of them *at the same time*, the one never without the other."[40]

The force of Calvin's *simul* is to improve Luther's and Melanchthon's teachings to the extent that they are made more resistant to charges of antinomianism and antirealism. The antinomian feel to Luther's thought goes back perhaps to his strongly dualistic and supersessionistic presentation of the law versus the gospel—his dread of making Christ into a second Moses.[41] Good works in the gospel era are not so much a fulfillment of the law as a transcendence of it. Christians perform them not in deference to the Decalogue but from a love of neighbor that takes its cue from Christ's self-giving love for them.[42] Melanchthon is much more keen on the law than is Luther. He does see good works in the gospel era as a fulfillment of the law, but he perhaps concentrates on this in a way that is reductive and mechanical, and too statically causal. For him, the law is the proximate cause, albeit a negative one, of both repentance and faith. Faith, in turn, accesses justification, and justification gains for Christians the power to keep the law spontaneously.[43] Whereas, in Luther, law is the cause of faith in the sense that the stricken conscience is impelled toward Christ, in Melanchthon, faith is the cause of works of the law in that justification by faith is what gives Christians the ability to do them.

38. John Calvin, *Commentary on 1 Corinthians*, at 1:30; *Werke*, 49:331. Emphasis added.

39. Luther's great *simul* being *simul justus et peccator*.

40. Calvin, *Institutes* III.xvi.1; *Werke*, 2:586. Emphasis added.

41. WA 40–1.207, 250; *LW* 35:17–24.

42. *LW* 31:333–77.

43. Philipp Melanchthon, *Annotationes in Evangelium Matthaei* (StA 4:153–54); *Loci Communes 1521* (StA 2:148.22–24; 2:149.19–21); *Articuli de Quibus Egerunt per Visitatores* (1527), cited in McGrath, *Iustitia Dei*, 2:27, 201, nn. 38–40.

Calvin starts from quite a different point—the revelation of God in Christ. All God's grace and goodness are found in Christ, and it is only when we begin to have faith in him that we are stricken in conscience. Randall Zachman suggests that this sense of faith's priority over contrition developed gradually in Calvin because of his reflection on Psalm 130:4: "But there is forgiveness with you, so that you may be revered" (NRSV).[44] The effect of this insight is to refute any sort of causal relation between justification and sanctification, between gospel and works that satisfy the law, and instead to make the revelation of God in Christ the simultaneous cause of both.

Luther is not far from this conclusion himself. "Although the bulk of [Luther's theology] set[s] forth [the order of first law, then gospel], Luther . . . can speak not only of *simul* law and gospel, but also of the gospel itself as revealing both the condemnation of sin and our redemption from it."[45] Moreover, it is a personalist, Christ-mystical reason that Luther gives for the justified, in fact, going on to perform good works. It is because justification "marries" the Christian to Christ.[46] Melanchthon's reason for the justified going on to perform good works is more deontological. The ability to do works that fulfill the law is mediated not by Christ personally but by a more mechanistic chain of causality, the most proximate term being the decree of justification itself. It is this move from personalism into a more forensic abstraction that opens Melanchthon's doctrine to the charge of antirealism.

This is a standard Catholic complaint, and I must admit, I have some sympathy with it. Does it not make God a liar to declare someone righteous when the declaration is contrary to fact? To declare someone acquitted is one thing, but *righteous*? Would that not be to use the word "righteousness" in a singular and equivocal sense? Luther's theology as a whole, because it is cast as a theology of the cross—a theology where truth is not known in a straightforward fashion but *sub contraria specie* ("under the condition of contradiction")—is much more tolerant of equivocation than Calvin's theology is. For example, Luther believes that the only works that can be called good are those performed in faith. Calvin, on the other hand, acknowledges a more straightforward definition of "goodness" when he says that there is a realistic difference between a Camillus and a Catiline, a virtuous pagan and a villain.[47] No works outside faith can endure judgment, and even

44. Randall C. Zachman, *The Assurance of Faith: Conscience in the Theology of Martin Luther and John Calvin* (Minneapolis: Fortress, 1993), 155.

45. Ibid., 73.

46. WA 56.382.26–27.

47. Calvin, *Institutes* II.iii.4; *Werke*, 2:212–13. See also *Institutes* II.ii.13, 14, 17, 22, 24; *Werke*, 2:196–205.

works performed with faith must themselves be justified before they are truly acceptable; never are they meritorious. Nonetheless, Calvin's refusal to bend the straightforward meaning of "goodness" like a wax nose is a signal that the antirealist charge was more worrisome to him than it was to Luther.

The way in which Calvin's *simul* speaks to the antirealist complaint is that it pictures a temporal sanctification being worked out *within* a justification that is complete and unassailable *coram Deo*. This is quite different from justification *followed by* sanctification, for it means that there is no moment at which persons can be right with God at which they are not also engaged upon fulfilling the sainted identity that has been imputed to them. The *simul* is buttressed by Calvin's personalistic starting point. Those baptized into Christ have a share in his death and resurrection. Calvin associates these particular moments in the life of the Mediator with two distinct aspects of justification: Christ's death brings the remission of sins because, in the atoning death, God accepts Christ's righteousness as a propitiation. The innocent One is punished, and, "as if" we were the innocent ones, we are acquitted. Christ's resurrection brings God's gracious acceptance of us; it earns us life, the promised reward of righteousness, but this reward is extended to us "as if" we were righteous.[48] So, according to Calvin, justification has these two parts: one in which God acts negatively, desisting from imputing our sins to us and forbearing to exact their punishment, and another in which God acts positively, imputing Christ's righteousness to us and including us in its reward. Both the negative and the positive actions, we note, are imputative.

The point of discerning these two parts is to assure believers that justification is complete. If God only desisted from imputing our original and past sins to us, it would be conceivable that the future may still be conditional upon our perfect keeping of the law or, if we cannot, upon some works-based system of self-propitiation (e.g., the sacramental economy of the medieval Catholic Church). Calvin is anxious to exclude these alternatives in the commentary on Romans 5. With the second aspect of justification, however, Calvin makes clear that nothing is conditional because Christ has earned for us not only the remission but also the reward. It is within this secure context, then, that we strive and struggle to realize, under the governance of the Holy Spirit, the identity that is already ours.

48. Calvin works out this distinction in the course of his commentary on Romans (at 3:25; 4:25; 6:4) and states it again clearly in his *Commentary on 1 Corinthians*, at 1:30, and in the 1559 *Institutes*, though in the latter with no connection to Christ's death and resurrection.

Calvin in 1559

Concerning the doctrine of justification, in the final version of the *Institutes* the basic affirmations of imputed righteousness and faith in the mercy of God rather than trust of self in works of the law are the same as we have seen throughout. Doctrines—such as the *simul* and the multivalent causality, allowing for the recognition that the Trinity, and not just Christ, is the agent of salvation—that are emergent in the commentary on Romans mature in the final *Institutes*. Calvin speaks here of a mystical union with Christ, wrought by the Holy Spirit, the Author of faith, the Creator of this community of righteousness, and from this union arises a double grace: justification and sanctification. They are simultaneous, and although they can be distinguished, they cannot be separated. The death and resurrection of Christ, which we saw provided the basis for a distinction within justification itself, effect a similar distinction within sanctification. The normative role of the death and resurrection of Christ should not be surprising perhaps, as justification and sanctification are both described as *beneficia Christi*—benefits that flow from Christ. The main content of sanctification, then, is repentance, and repentance consists of a putting to death of the flesh as a sharing in the death of Christ (*mortificatio*) and a quickening in the Spirit as a sharing in his resurrection (*vivificatio*). Calvin refuses to distribute the work of justification to Christ and the work of sanctification to the Spirit. Rather, he regards Christ as the *material content* of *both* the righteousness imputed to us in justification *and* the repentance inspired in us in sanctification. Similarly, the Spirit is the *energy* involved when sinners gain the power to believe *both* that their sins are forgiven *and* that God is graciously disposed toward them.

Through Andreas Osiander, the Lutheran Reformer in Nuremberg, Calvin arrived at a better understanding of the difference between matter and energy or, as he says elsewhere, essence and quality. The critique of Osiander, who in 1550 published a book advancing a certain view of justification, is extended and supplies to the 1559 edition new content that swells the familiar treatment of our doctrine. Osiander believed that we are justified not by Christ's human obedience but by an inflowing of Christ's essential righteousness. Justifying righteousness is, in this view, not something Christ has earned but an essential property that he has in virtue of his divinity. McGrath remarks that Osiander's view represents an interesting case where there is no problem about the righteousness being alien—it is *Christ's*, but it is essentially imparted, not forensically imputed.[49] The fact that Calvin reacted so strongly against Osiander's

49. McGrath, *Iustitia Dei*, 2:3.

proposal, even though no kind of Pelagianism was at issue, reaffirmed his allegiance and that of the Reformed party to forensic justification.

Calvin's commentary on 1 Corinthians 15 (1546) takes up the same Christ/Adam typology as Romans 5, only now Calvin's list of enemies are different. Both texts, says Calvin, are about spiritual regeneration, and in both, the apostle's main point is that Christ excels Adam, but the evaluation of the Adamic nature is much more nuanced in the 1546 commentary than in 1539. Calvin's new set of enemies are the Manichees and Servetus and those who believe in a heavenly flesh theory, as Apollinaris was supposed to have done, instead of semi-Pelagians who wish to account their works for merit and advocate free will. Some of Osiander's views seem to place him quite close to the heavenly flesh people. He believes that Christ's incarnation is such an eternal reality that even if humankind had not fallen, the Son of God would have appeared as a man. Further, he believes that Adam was created in the physical image of the incarnate Christ.[50] In the commentary on Romans 5, it is hard to separate the essential Adamic nature from its accidental corruption. In the commentary on 1 Corinthians 15, Calvin notes a distinction between our *essential* nature, which does not need to be made righteous by any physicalistic infusion of heavenly substance, and our *qualitative* nature, which is what the Holy Spirit reforms by its influence.

This drawing of fine distinctions instead of declaring, as Calvin does in the commentary on Romans, that humanity is nothing but a mass of sin is typical of what I understand as a move in Calvin's more mature writing from a purely evangelical theological outlook to an evangelical one that also shows signs of scholastic interests. Otto Pesch sets up two very helpful categories: the scholastic or sapiential, and the evangelical or existential species of theology.[51] Evangelical theology is "zoomed in" on personal concerns. Objective truths must be owned *pro nobis* ("by us"). We seek to know God not as God is in himself but as God is in relation to us. Knowledge of God is participatory knowledge. The scholastic perspective is "zoomed out." It comprehends the evangelical perspective, but it also seeks relations between this and other parts of wisdom. It asks questions about things that are, not necessarily the questions that are burning "for me." If it is true that the *Institutes* has evolved from an entirely evangelical first edition to bear some traits, in its final edi-

---

50. Calvin, *Institutes* I.xv.3; *Werke*, 2:136–37.

51. Otto Pesch, "Existential and Sapiential Theology—the Theological Confrontation between Luther and Thomas Aquinas," in *Catholic Scholars Dialogue with Luther*, ed. Jared Wicks (Chicago: Loyola University Press, 1970), 61–193. This essay distills Pesch's more exhaustive treatment of the subject in his dissertation *Theologie der Rechtfertigung bei Martin Luther und Thomas von Aquin* (Mainz: Matthias Grünewald, 1967).

tion, of scholastic theology,[52] then the otherwise mysterious move that Calvin makes in reversing the order of sanctification and justification in his 1559 treatment would be more understandable.[53] Calvin is trying to answer the big, zoomed-out question of what God is after with human beings, and he is answering it in terms of a people for God's name, a band of adopted children, all bearing the family likeness. It is only from a perspective of the individual conscience that justification can become an independent or a final concern instead of a larger process of working out God's ends and the telos of creation.

Justification, for Calvin, remains through to the final edition "the main hinge upon which religion turns," and in what Calvin says about it, he is still very zealous for, and true to, the standard evangelical platform. But those, such as Barth, who contrast Luther and Calvin as respectively the theologians of justification and regeneration are quite right. And those,

52. With my description of scholastic theology above, I hope to be clear that this is a *type* or *style* of theology, not to be confused with any of the doctrinal content of particular scholastic theologies, e.g., Calvinism. In claiming that Calvin's theology takes a turn to the scholastic, I am not declaring an opinion on how closely Calvin's theology can be identified with that of the Calvinists, but only suggesting that it begins to concern itself with different kinds of questions.

53. Calvin's decision to treat regeneration first, then justification, in book 3 has occasioned much scholarly speculation. Paul Wernle and Wilhelm Niesel (cited in François Wendel, *Calvin: The Origins and Development of His Religious Thought*, trans. Philip Mairet [London: Collins, 1963], 233) argue that his reason for inverting the more accustomed order may have been in answer to the Catholic charge of antinomianism. Paul Van Buren, *Christ in Our Place: The Substitutionary Character of Calvin's Doctrine of Reconciliation* (London: Oliver and Boyd, 1957), 107–8, suggests that "since sanctification is only partial . . . Calvin may have treated it first to make sure that the reader would not consider it of lesser importance." Wendel himself seems to think there is a "didactic" logic to approaching the matter in the way that Calvin does (233), although he is careful to add that this is no "causal" logic (234). Joseph McLelland, "Renaissance in Theology: Calvin's 1536 *Institutio*—Fresh Start or False?" in *Papers from the 1986 International Calvin Symposium* (Montreal: McGill University Press, 1987), 154–74, suggests that "the significant reversal of the usual order of justification and sanctification . . . in Book Three . . . repeats [Calvin's fundamental] insight about the inseparability of humanity and divinity," which is first expressed in the opening word of the *Institutes* and which provides "the new architectonic of Calvin's mature theology" (168). All these proposals are vaguely unsatisfying (although the basic interpretation, elaborated here, of Calvin's development is shared with McLelland). During the 2003 Edinburgh Dogmatics Conference, Bruce McCormack suggested that regeneration comes first because of Calvin's convictions about infant baptism; I hope that his contribution to this volume of papers will elaborate further on this intriguing proposal. I think that, whatever the reason, it must have to do with a shift of interest rather than of belief. Calvin's understanding of the economy of justification and sanctification is consistent from fairly early on. It is always possible that only in 1559 did he discipline his structure to a true expression of his belief, but it is likelier that 1559 marked a shift in what Calvin wanted to do with his *Institutes* as a whole and that the new book 3 took shape according to new interests that had come to characterize Calvin's theological project.

such as Zachman, who say that justification is not even the main metaphor for reconciliation in Calvin are right. He much prefers adoption,[54] where God is pictured as a bountiful Father, to the justification image of the just and merciful Judge. Lutheran scholars tend to regard this prioritizing of regeneration as a regression from Luther's pure insights; danger lurks whenever consciences are referred, as they see it, back to their own piety for assurance rather than to the free mercy of God in Christ.[55] The debate will no doubt continue about whether this creative disciple of Luther's has enhanced or defaced his forerunners' legacy. His modifications have been subtle but significant, rendering the doctrine in Calvin's hands more pneumatological, more trinitarian, more realistic, more nomian, and more integrated with God's desire and action toward the world entire.

54. Zachman, *Assurance of Faith*, 11, distinguishes Luther and Calvin when he says that the former is focused on a theology of the cross whereas the latter "sets his discussion of salvation within the context of the Fatherhood of God." Zachman does not use this distinction to dissociate the two Reformers, nor does he wish to set up adoption as *another* understanding, which those who dislike the priestly and objective overtones of justification can alternatively embrace:

> The grace of justification is the foundation and basis of our adoption by God; for God can only regard us as God's children if God forgives us our sins and reckons us as righteous. However, the grace of sanctification is the purpose and goal of our adoption, for God adopts us so that we might actually become God's gratefully obedient children. Thus with regard to the basis of our adoption, Calvin is in complete agreement with Luther: God can only regard us as God's children on the basis of the forgiveness of sins. In this context, the grace of sanctification is necessarily subordinated to the grace of justification. However, given Calvin's emphasis on adoption over and above the theology of the cross (which is also found in his theology), Calvin can also speak of the necessary subordination of justification to sanctification when he speaks of the purpose of our adoption, something that Luther's emphasis on *theologia crucis* would not allow him to do. (11)

See also B. A. Gerrish, *Grace and Gratitude: The Eucharistic Theology of John Calvin* (Edinburgh: T&T Clark, 1993), 27. Gerrish identifies two prevailing images for God in Calvin, the "fountain" and the "father."

55. Zachman, *Assurance of Faith*, 3.

6

A Tale of Two Imperial Cities

Justification at Regensburg (1541) and Trent (1546–1547)

ANTHONY N. S. LANE

Introduction

This contribution expounds and contrasts two very different statements on justification from the 1540s.[1] In 1541 leading Protestant and Roman Catholic theologians meeting at the Regensburg Colloquy produced an agreed-upon statement on the doctrine. A few years later the Council of Trent defined the doctrine in a deliberately anti-Protestant manner, rejecting the position agreed at Regensburg.

During the early years of the Reformation, the doctrine of justification was subjected to considerable scrutiny. It was one of the major emphases of the Reformers in their protest against late medieval Roman Catholicism. The latter had well-defined positions on many doctrines, such as the Eucharist, that left little or no room for maneuver when these doctrines were challenged by the Reformers. It was different with justification. The Reformers presented the doctrine in a new light, pos-

---

1. The first part, on Regensburg, develops further some of the material in A. N. S. Lane, *Justification by Faith in Catholic-Protestant Dialogue: An Evangelical Assessment* (Edinburgh and New York: T&T Clark, 2002), 46–60.

ing new and hitherto unanswered questions. This created a problem for their opponents, as there was no consensus in the Catholic Church on the doctrine of justification and, more important, there had been no authoritative pronouncements.[2] Individual Roman Catholic theologians were free to develop their doctrines in different ways, and these varied from uncompromising hostility to the Protestant doctrine to almost complete agreement with it. Genuine dialogue was possible between the two sides, as the Roman response to the Protestant doctrine was not predetermined.

Among those most sympathetic to Luther's doctrine in the Roman Catholic Church was an Erasmian reforming group in Italy known as the *spirituali*, which included leading cardinals.[3] One of these, Gasparo Contarini, in 1511 underwent a conversion experience that he described in a private letter later that year and that has affinities with Luther's (later) "tower experience."[4] There are different assessments of Contarini's doctrine of justification, but I have argued elsewhere that he eventually came to accept the key points of the Protestant doctrine.[5] In Germany also there was a significant group of Catholic humanists seeking reform within the Roman Catholic system. Noteworthy among these was Johann Gropper, who in 1538 published his highly influential *Enchiridion*, a handbook for reform of the diocese of Cologne.[6] Among such Catholic humanists there was widespread sympathy for the Protestant idea that Christ's righteousness is imputed or reckoned to us. A key motive behind this development was the belief that "the converted Christian still needs to throw himself on the mercy of God."[7] In many ways these reforming humanist Catholics shared a similar spiritual background to the Reformers.

2. For a brief survey of Catholic opinion in the early years of the Reformation, see H. Jedin, *A History of the Council of Trent*, 2 vols. (London: Thomas Nelson, 1957–1961), 2:167–71.

3. *Spirituali* was a contemporary term. Twentieth-century scholarship introduced the confusing term "evangelism" for this movement. E. G. Gleason, "On the Nature of Sixteenth-Century Italian Evangelism: Scholarship, 1953–1978," *Sixteenth Century Journal* 9, no. 3 (1978): 3–25.

4. For the text of the letter, see E. G. Gleason, ed., *Reform Thought in Sixteenth-Century Italy* (Chico, CA: Scholars Press, 1981), 24–28. On the letter and the parallels and differences between Contarini's experience and Luther's, see H. Jedin, "Ein 'Turmerlebnis' des jungen Contarinis," in *Kirche des Glaubens, Kirche der Geschichte*, 2 vols. (Freiburg im Breisgau: Herder, 1966), 1:167–80.

5. A. N. S. Lane, "Cardinal Contarini and Article 5 of the Regensburg Colloquy (1541)," in *Grenzgänge der Theologie*, ed. Otmar Meuffels and Jürgen Bründl (Münster: Lit, 2004), 163–95.

6. On Gropper's doctrine of justification, see R. Braunisch, *Die Theologie der Rechtfertigung im "Enchiridion" (1538) des Johannes Gropper* (Münster: Aschendorff, 1974).

7. The different doctrines are set out by E. Yarnold, "*Duplex iustitia*: The Sixteenth Century and the Twentieth," in *Christian Authority*, ed. G. R. Evans (Oxford: Oxford Uni-

Regensburg Colloquy and Article 5

The Colloquy

From 1530 there was a series of colloquies aimed at reconciling the two sides in Germany—to avert civil war and to enable a common front against the Turkish threat. The greatest chance of success came in three gatherings that were held in 1540 and 1541.[8] These began with a colloquy at Hagenau in June and July 1540, but some of those expected failed to appear and the two sides could not agree on how to proceed. The colloquy was adjourned to Worms, where it met in November, this time with a good lineup of theologians. After long delays, discussion of original sin began in January, and agreement was reached in a few days.[9] At this point Nicholas Granvella, the imperial chancellor, adjourned the debate to the coming diet at Regensburg.[10] Meanwhile at Worms secret discussions had been taking place between Martin Bucer and Wolfgang Capito on the Protestant side and the humanist Catholics Gropper and Gerard Veltwyck (Granvella's secretary).[11] Gropper, with Bucer's cooperation, went on to draw up the "Regensburg Book," which was to be used as a basis for further discussion.[12]

---

versity Press, 1988), 207–13; quotation from 213. See also J. Rivière, "Justification," in *Dictionnaire de théologie catholique*, ed. A. Vacant, E. Mangenot, and E. Amman, 15 vols. (Paris: Letouzey et Ané, 1903–1950), 8:2159–64; R. B. Ives, "An Early Effort toward Protestant-Catholic Conciliation: The Doctrine of Double Justification in the Sixteenth Century," *Gordon Review* 11 (1968/1970): 99–110.

8. On the colloquies in general, see Jedin, *History of the Council of Trent*, 1:372–91; C. Augustijn, *De Godsdienstgesprekken tussen Rooms-katholieken en Protestanten van 1538 tot 1541* (Haarlem, Neth.: De Erven F. Bohn, 1967); V. Pfnür, "Die Einigung bei den Religionsgesprächen von Worms und Regensburg 1540/41 eine Täuschung?" in *Die Religionsgespräche der Reformationszeit*, ed. Gerhard Müller (Gütersloh: Mohn, 1980), 55–88; B. Hall, *Humanists and Protestants, 1500–1900* (Edinburgh: T&T Clark, 1990), 142–70.

9. For the debates on original sin, see Philipp Melanchthon, *Opera Quae Supersunt Omnia*, ed. Carolus Gottlieb Bretschneider, 28 vols., Corpus Reformatorum (Halle, Ger.: C. A. Schwetschke et Filium, 1834–1860), 4:33–78; H. Mackensen, "The Debate between Eck and Melanchthon on Original Sin at the Colloquy of Worms," *Lutheran Quarterly* 11 (1959): 42–56. For the formula, see Melanchthon, *Opera*, 4:32–33.

10. For Regensburg, see P. Matheson, *Cardinal Contarini at Regensburg* (Oxford: Oxford University Press, 1972); E. G. Gleason, *Gasparo Contarini* (Berkeley and Oxford: University of California Press, 1993), 186–256.

11. See C. Augustijn, "De Gesprekken tussen Bucer en Gropper tijdens het Godsdienstgesprek te Worms in December 1540," *Nederlands Archief voor Kerkgeschiedenis* 47 (1965/1966): 208–30.

12. On its origins, see H. Eells, "The Origin of the Regensburg Book," *Princeton Theological Review* 26 (1928): 355–72; R. Stupperich, "Der Ursprung des 'Regensburger Buches' von 1541 und seine Rechtfertigungslehre," *Archiv für Reformationsgeschichte* 36 (1939):

Contarini was appointed papal legate for the final colloquy, which took place at the Regensburg Diet. The diet was opened on April 5, 1541.[13] On April 21, the emperor selected as the debaters Philipp Melanchthon, Bucer, and Johann Pistorius the Elder on the Protestant side and Gropper, Julius Pflug, and Johann Eck on the Roman Catholic side, and the colloquy was able to begin. Calvin and Albert Pighius were also present, but not as debaters.[14] The "Regensburg Book," whose origin was a closely guarded secret, became the basis for discussion. On April 27 the first four articles, on human innocence before the fall, free choice, the cause of sin, and original sin, were quickly agreed upon, building on the Worms agreement.[15] The fifth article, on justification, was discussed from April 28 to May 2.[16] Eck and Melanchthon both found it too imprecise, and it was agreed that a new article should be drawn up. Gropper drew up a shorter version.[17] Draft and counterdraft were discussed until eventually, on May 2, the Protestants were allowed to amend a Catholic draft to their own satisfaction.[18] All the parties gave their consent to the final draft, a translation of which is found at the

88–116; R. Braunisch, "Die 'Artikell' der 'Wahrhaftigen Antwort' (1545) des Johannes Gropper: Zur Verfasserfrage des Worms-Regensburger Buches (1540/41)," in *Von Konstanz nach Trient*, ed. R. Bäumer (Munich: Ferdinand Schöningh, 1972), 519–45. For the text, see G. Pfeilschifter, ed., *Acta Reformationis Catholicae* (Regensburg: F. Pustet, 1959–), 6:21–88. The "Regensburg Book" went through four drafts (not all of which survive) and Pfeilschifter gives textual critical apparatus.

13. The acts of the colloquy were published by various participants. In 1541 Bucer and Melanchthon produced Latin and German editions, and Calvin produced an edition in French (John Calvin, *Opera Quae Supersunt Omnia*, ed. Gulielmus Baum, Eduardus Cunitz, and Eduardus Reuss, 59 vols. [Brunswick, Ger.: C. A. Schwetschke et Filium, 1863–1900], 5:509–684). An abridged English translation of Bucer's edition is found in D. J. Ziegler, ed., *Great Debates of the Reformation* (New York: Random House, 1969), 143–77.

14. On Calvin's role in the colloquies, see W. H. Neuser, "Calvins Beitrag zu den Religionsgesprächen von Hagenau, Worms, und Regensburg (1540/41)," in *Studien zur Geschichte und Theologie der Reformation*, ed. L. Abramowski and J. F. G. Goeters (Neukirchen: Neukirchener Verlag, 1969), 213–37.

15. On the Worms and Regensburg articles on original sin, see A. Vanneste, "La préhistoire du décret du concile de Trente sur le péché originel," *Nouvelle revue théologique* 86 (1964): 500–510. For a summary of the first four articles, see J. Raitt, "From Augsburg to Trent," in *Justification by Faith*, ed. H. G. Anderson, T. A. Murphy, and J. A. Burgess, Lutherans and Catholics in Dialogue 7 (Minneapolis: Augsburg, 1985), 210–11.

16. For the text, see Pfeilschifter, *Acta Reformationis Catholicae*, 6:30–44. The full title was "De Restitutione Regenerationis et Justificatione Hominis Gratia et Merito, Fide et Operibus."

17. For the text, see Pfeilschifter, *Acta Reformationis Catholicae*, 6:44–52.

18. For the text, see ibid., 6:52–54. The new title was "De Justificatione Hominis." D. Hampson, *Christian Contradictions: The Structures of Lutheran and Catholic Thought* (Cambridge: Cambridge University Press, 2001), 64–65, has a translation of parts of the article. She seems to have confused the opening paragraphs of art. 5 with the four articles that were agreed upon earlier (compare pp. 63–64 with 291–92).

end of this paper. Granvella and Contarini were jubilant; Eck needed some persuasion to sign.

The colloquy itself failed in due course, but this was because of differences on other doctrines, such as the Eucharist and the underlying issue of the authority of the church,[19] not because of shortcomings in the statement on justification. On May 22 the colloquy came to a close, the article on justification being its only significant achievement. Even during the colloquy there were those on both sides who were unwilling to accept the article; after the failure of the colloquy, there was even less interest in supporting it. The Regensburg Diet was not to end for another two months, on July 29.

Reactions to Article 5

From the outset there were two contrasting Protestant reactions to the agreed-upon article on justification. The first was that it was compatible with the Protestant position and represented a significant concession on the Roman Catholic side. The second was that it was a compromising patchwork of two incompatible positions, blighted by ambiguity.

John Calvin expresses well the first reaction in a letter written to William Farel a few days after agreement had been reached. There he expresses astonishment that their opponents conceded so much. The article, he claims, preserved the substance of true doctrine and contained nothing not to be found in "our writings"—although he admits that it could have been stated more clearly.[20]

On this article in particular, see F. Dittrich, *Gasparo Contarini, 1483–1542* (1885; repr., Nieuwkoop, Neth.: De Graaf, 1972), 651–700; W. von Loewenich, *Duplex Iustitia: Luthers Stellung zu einer Unionsformel des 16. Jahrhunderts* (Wiesbaden: Franz Steiner, 1972), 34–38; Matheson, *Cardinal Contarini at Regensburg*, 104–13; K.-H. zur Mühlen, "Die Einigung über den Rechtfertigungsartikel auf dem Regensburger Religionsgespräch von 1541—eine verpaßte Chance?" *Zeitschrift für Theologie und Kirche* 76 (1979): 331–59; Gleason, *Gasparo Contarini*, 227–35, 240–56; C. S. Smith, "Calvin's Doctrine of Justification in Relation to the Sense of Sin and the Dialogue with Rome" (M.Phil. thesis, London Bible College, 1993), 128–48; A. Lexutt, *Rechtfertigung im Gespräch: Das Rechtfertigungsverständnis in den Religionsgesprächen von Hagenau, Worms, und Regensburg, 1540/41* (Göttingen: Vandenhoeck & Ruprecht, 1996), 250–60.

19. This was the issue on which all the colloquies failed (H. Jedin, "An welchen Gegensätzen sind die vortridentinischen Religionsgespräche zwischen Katholiken und Protestanten gescheitert?" *Theologie und Glaube* 48 [1958]: 50–55).

20. John Calvin to Guillaume Farel, May 11, 1541, in *Letters of John Calvin*, trans. David Constable, 4 vols. (Philadelphia: Presbyterian Board of Publication, 1858), 1:260. Calvin, *Opera*, 11:215–16; A. L. Herminjard, *Correspondance des Reformateurs dans les pays de langue française*, 9 vols. (Geneva: H. Georg; Paris: M. Levy, 1866–1897), 7:111; in a letter to Pierre Viret of August 3 or 13, 1541, Calvin was negative about the colloquy as a whole (*Letters of John Calvin*, 1:279; Calvin, *Opera*, 11:262; Herminjard, *Correspondance*

Luther, who was not himself present at the colloquy, consistently expresses the second reaction.[21] In an initial letter on May 10/11, he brands it "patched and all-embracing." He claims that the two ideas—of justification by faith alone without works, and faith working through love—were "thrown together and glued together"; whereas one refers to becoming righteous, the other refers to the life of the righteous. "So they are right, and so are we." This is like sewing a new patch onto an old garment.[22]

Kaspar Cruciger began by emphasizing the conformity of the article with Lutheran doctrine, but two weeks later he was more aware of its ambiguities.[23] Initial enthusiasm followed by reservations marks much of the Protestant response to article 5. There were two prime reasons for this. The first was the failure to reach agreement on other articles. The enthusiasm that greeted article 5 was enthusiasm for the prospect of agreement across the board, not enthusiasm for the idea of agreeing in one point only. Events were soon to prove how unrealistic this was. The second reason was the way in which some on the Roman side were interpreting the article and the awareness of its ambiguities. But although failure to agree on other articles dramatically undermined the value of article 5 at the time, it does not of itself indicate that the agreement on justification was not genuine. Regarding the interpretations given to the article, we must distinguish between unfounded claims made about its teaching and genuine ambiguities that lie in the text itself.[24] Although the former were a matter of concern for the Protestant party at the time, only the latter need detain us as we examine its teaching today.

---

des Reformateurs, 7:218). On Calvin's view, see W. H. Neuser, "Calvins Urteil über den Rechtfertigungsartikel des Regensburger Buches," in Reformation und Humanismus, ed. M. Greschat and J. F. G. Goeters (Witten: Luther-Verlag, 1969), 176–94.

21. For Luther's view, see von Loewenich, Duplex Iustitia, 29–34, 48–55 (cf. 26–29), where the weakness of Luther's arguments is spelled out. See also Pfnür, "Die Einigung bei den Religionsgesprächen von Worms und Regensburg 1540/41," 64–68.

22. Martin Luther to Johann Friedrich, May 10 or 11, 1541, in WA.Br. 9:406–9, no. 3616. It has rightly been observed that the objections of both Rome and Wittenberg concerned not so much the content of art. 5 as fear of how the other side would exploit it. Unlike the participants at Regensburg, neither Luther nor the Vatican was willing to settle for anything short of total victory (Gleason, Gasparo Contarini, 244).

23. Kaspar Cruciger to Johann Bugenhagen, May [5], 1541, (Melanchthon, Opera, 4:252–53). Cruciger also shared Burckhard's skepticism regarding the prospects for agreement on the other articles. Cf. Cruciger to Justus Menius, May 5, 1541, (ibid., 4:259), where he stated that the article "quae etsi non est a nostris composita, sed utrinque consarcinata, tamen a nostra doctrina, quod discrepet, nihil habet" (Cruciger to Bugenhagen, May 19, 1541, [ibid., 4:304]).

24. By unfounded claims, I am thinking especially of the claim that it teaches that we are accepted by God sola dilectione, reported by both Melanchthon (Opera, 4:430, 485, 499) and Pistorius (ibid., 4:445).

Regensburg did not have a good press. The prevailing judgment was negative.[25] But with the shift from a polemical to an ecumenical approach in recent years, this judgment has been reconsidered.[26] Also, it is important to distinguish between the colloquy in general, which clearly failed, and article 5, which did produce agreement. Matheson's pithy (and exaggerated) judgment on the colloquy is often cited: "The dialogue between Protestantism and Catholicism at the Diet of Regensburg in 1541 did not fail. It never took place."[27] But his judgment on article 5 is far more positive, and he calls it "a finely balanced piece of conciliation" that "exhibits an integrity all its own" and "takes up a clear line."[28] Not all are convinced. McGrath concurs with Dermot Fenlon's judgment that article 5 was a "scissors and paste job," describing it as "a mere juxtaposition of the Catholic and Protestant positions, with a purely superficial engagement with the serious theological issues at stake."[29] Gleason likewise states that "both style and content make it obvious that article 5 was the work of a committee. The modern reader will search in vain for logical consistency, since the essence of the agreed-upon text was a compromise between two basically incompatible positions."[30] But the present discussion will come to a more favorable assessment.[31]

The Teaching of Article 5

What does article 5 in fact teach? Underlying the entire article is the idea of *duplex justitia*, or twofold righteousness—that conversion brings both inherent and imputed righteousness. The term *duplex justitia* is not itself found in the article, but the article is built on the idea that there

25. Hall, *Humanists and Protestants*, 143, documents this, especially on the Catholic side.

26. See Anderson, Murphy, and Burgess, *Justification by Faith*, §§45–48, pp. 32–33, which concludes that Regensburg indicates that "the two ways of explaining justification are not necessarily exclusive."

27. Matheson, *Cardinal Contarini at Regensburg*, 181, the final words of the book.

28. Ibid., 107–8. Pfnür, "Die Einigung bei den Religionsgesprächen," 76–77, states that the article is not delusion but thoroughly pertinent.

29. Alister E. McGrath, *Iustitia Dei: A History of the Christian Doctrine of Justification*, 2 vols. (Cambridge: Cambridge University Press, 1986), 2:60–61. This judgment is softened in the third edition (Cambridge: Cambridge University Press, 2005), 315–16. D. Fenlon, *Heresy and Obedience in Tridentine Italy: Cardinal Pole and Counter Reformation* (Cambridge: Cambridge University Press, 1972), 55.

30. Gleason, *Gasparo Contarini*, 227–28.

31. I will be arguing this in a forthcoming book, provisionally titled *Compromising Patchwork or Ecumenical Breakthrough? The Regensburg Article on Justification (1541)— Introduction, Text, and Commentary*.

are these different "righteousnesses" (inherent and imputed), which are clearly set out.

What is the significance of this idea of twofold righteousness? Catholics and Protestants were offering two contrasting models of justification. The Protestant teaching was that God accepts us as righteous (what Protestants understand by justification) because Christ's righteousness is reckoned or imputed to our account. That is, we are acceptable to God not because of anything that we have done, nor indeed because of the change that God brings about within us, but because of what Christ has done for us on the cross. We are acceptable not for what we are or do (which remains imperfect) but in Christ. The Catholic teaching, by contrast, was that justification is about God changing us by the Holy Spirit and thus making us acceptable to himself. At baptism/conversion we are transformed within by the grace of God, by *gratia gratum faciens*, grace that makes us pleasing or acceptable, which brings about within us an inherent righteousness. Thus we have the contrast between the Protestant view that we become acceptable on the basis of *imputed* righteousness (the righteousness of Christ reckoned to our account) and the Catholic view that we become righteous through Christ's righteousness being imparted to us or infused in us, through an inner change that gives us an *inherent* righteousness. The key contribution of Regensburg was to insist that with conversion we receive *both* of these: inherent *and* imputed righteousness.

How does Regensburg develop this idea? The teaching of the article can be summarized in a few points:

(1) The term "justification" is understood in the Protestant sense of being accepted and reckoned righteous by God (§§4.1, 6; 5.2), although it is noted that the early fathers understood it differently to refer to inherent righteousness (5.1).

(2) This justification or reckoning righteous is on account of Christ and his merit (§§4.1, 2; 5.2), on the basis of imputed righteousness (§§3.6; 4.4, 6). It is not on the basis of inherent righteousness or the righteousness of works (§§4.6; 5.1–5.2). Protestant concerns are effectively met by the clear and unambiguous insistence that acceptance is on the basis of imputed and not inherent righteousness. But it is also true that we are called righteous because of the good deeds that flow from inherent righteousness (§5.3).

(3) Although God accepts us on the basis of imputed righteousness, he also at the same time (§4.3–4.4) gives us his Holy Spirit (§§3.6; 4.4), through which we become partakers in the divine nature (§2), are renewed (§§6; 8.1), have inherent righteousness (§§5.1, 3), receive the infusion of love (§§4.3–4.4), and begin to do good works (§§5.3; 8.2–8.3, 9, 10) and fulfill the law (§4.3). We should grow in virtues (§6) and in the

renewal that we have received (§8.1). This growth comes through good works (§8.2). The Catholic concern for love and good works is clearly and unambiguously met by the insistence on the simultaneous gift of the Holy Spirit and love leading to good works.

Sanctification is not presented as merely a consequence (whether desirable or inevitable) of justification but as a parallel and inseparable gift.

(4) Justification and the gift of the Spirit are received by faith (§3.6). The faith that justifies is a living faith (§§4.1, 4), and it is by the Holy Spirit that we are moved to this faith (§§3.5; 4.2). In particular, this faith is efficacious through love (§§4.1, 5), although the function of faith is to appropriate God's gifts (§§3.6; 4.2, 4, 6). Faith not only believes all that God has revealed but also in particular assents to and acquires confidence from God's promises (§3.5). It is all right to teach justification by faith alone so long as this is not to the exclusion of teaching about repentance and good works (§§10.1–2).

(5) Coming to faith involves hating sin in mind and will (§3.1) and repenting (§§3.2–5; 4.2, 10), which occur through the prevenient movement of the Spirit (§3.1).[32] Our free choice has a role to play concurring in good works (§8.3).

(6) Although we are renewed by the Holy Spirit, this renewal is imperfect, and it is not on this that we should rely but only on Christ's gift of righteousness (§5.1), his role as mediator (§6), and his promises (§7).

(7) Nonetheless, God has promised to reward our good works in this life and the next (§§8.2–8.3, 9). Eternal life is an inheritance based on promise, but works are rewarded to the extent that they are done in faith and from the Spirit (§8.3).

I have argued elsewhere that Calvin was right to claim that there is nothing here that cannot be paralleled in the writings of the Reformers (indeed, in his own writings) and that the other side had conceded a great deal.[33] He was also right to admit that it was not perhaps as clearly stated as the Reformers would have wished, but this is a very minor complaint given that this was a document that had been accepted by some of the leading Roman Catholic theologians of the day. It is noteworthy that the evolving Protestant criticism of article 5 complained about its ambiguities and the manner in which the "other side" was interpreting it, but did not concede that it was incompatible with either

32. Gleason, *Gasparo Contarini*, 228, observes that "the relative importance of the prevenient motion of the Holy Spirit and the response of the human intellect and will is left unclear." This is true, but it is a problem only if one supposes that the article has to resolve all theological issues. Article 2 has more to say on the topic.

33. See A. N. S. Lane, "Calvin and Article 5 of the Regensburg Colloquy," in *Calvinus Praeceptor Ecclesiae*, ed. H. Selderhuis (Geneva: Droz, 2004), 233–63.

the "Augsburg Confession" or Melanchthon's "Apology of the Augsburg Confession."

What were these ambiguities and misinterpretations? Two key points recurred.[34] The first concerned the status of good works. The article affirms that sin remains after conversion,[35] but it needs to teach more clearly that the regenerate can never satisfy the law of God in this life and that God is nevertheless pleased with our imperfect obedience. Clarification is also needed on the distinction between the sins which do and those which do not cause us to lose grace and the Holy Spirit.

Second, there was considerable concern about the statement that the faith that justifies is a faith that is effectual through love (*efficax per caritatem*). The article states that we are justified or accepted as righteous on the basis of a living and efficacious faith (§4.1). Again, justification does not happen without the infusion of love, and the faith that justifies is effectual through love (§4.3, 5). What is the problem here? None of the Reformers wanted to state that it was possible to have saving faith without love. That saving faith is a living faith accompanied by love leading to good works was not controversial. But the (separated) statements that we are justified on the basis of *efficacious* faith and that faith is effectual through love *could* be taken to mean that justification is on the basis not of faith alone but (to use the Catholic formula) of "faith formed by love." Thus it was claimed by some Roman Catholics at Regensburg that the article taught justification by *love* alone.[36] Such an interpretation is clearly excluded by the article itself—but the fact that it could be claimed (however unreasonably) made the Protestants suspicious of the ambiguity of the formula.[37]

Twofold Righteousness

Having clarified the teaching of the article, let us return again to the doctrine of twofold righteousness. Is this not evidence that the article is a mere patchwork of incompatible views? Or is it in fact a consistent statement, albeit making terminological concessions to both sides? At first

34. E.g., in Melanchthon's comments in *Opera*, 4:413–19, 419–31, 479–91.

35. The renewal brought by the Holy Spirit is imperfect (§6), and we are therefore to depend not upon our inherent righteousness but upon Christ's righteousness given to us as a gift (5.1).

36. Melanchthon, *Opera*, 4:430, 445, 485, 499.

37. The statement that justifying faith is *efficax per caritatem* is immediately followed in the article by the affirmation that this faith justifies by appropriating mercy and imputed righteousness and that this righteousness is not imputed on account of any imparted worthiness or perfection (§§4.5–4.6). Acceptance on the basis of inherent righteousness (such as love) is very carefully excluded.

sight the patchwork charge appears to be self-evidently true. Catholics spoke of an inherent, imparted righteousness, the inner transformation of sinners by the gracious act of the Holy Spirit so that they actually *become* righteous, so that God accepts them as righteous because they really are. Protestants spoke of an imputed righteousness, of Christ's righteousness being *reckoned* to our account, so that, unworthy as we are, we are accepted by God on account of Christ. Regensburg links these two together and affirms that in conversion we receive *both* types of righteousness. Surely Luther was right to summarize this mockingly as the claim that "so they are right, and so are we"? Or was he? The doctrine of twofold righteousness needs to be explored a little more carefully.

The first point to note is that what Regensburg calls "inherent righteousness" corresponds to what Protestant theologians called (and call) "sanctification." The Reformers all but universally agreed that conversion brings both justification and sanctification. The only concession that Regensburg demanded of them was terminological—to use the term "inherent righteousness" of sanctification. This was not much of a concession, since many of them (such as Bucer and Calvin) were already accustomed to use the word "righteousness" at least sometimes when referring to sanctification.[38] On the Catholic side, a rather bigger concession was demanded. They had to admit the validity of imputed righteousness. This was a significant step. Contarini appears to have been innocent of the idea before Regensburg. Gropper's *Enchiridion* contains some references to imputation, but the idea is not nearly as clear as in the Regensburg article.[39] Contarini was required to accept a new idea; Gropper, to develop an existing idea. They both did so wholeheartedly and went on to expound and defend the theme of imputed righteousness in their later writings.[40] Both were to attract the attention of the Inquisition as a result and, together with other cardinals, were suspected of Protestant tendencies because of their support for article 5.[41]

38. E.g., M. Bucer, *Metaphrases et Enarrationes Perpetuae Epistolarum D. Pauli Apostoli* (Strassburg: W. Rihel, 1536), preface, 11–14; Bucer, *Metaphrasis et Enarratio in Epist. D. Pauli Apostoli ad Romanos* (Basel: P. Pern, 1562), 11–14; D. F. Wright, ed., *Common Places of Martin Bucer* (Abingdon, UK: Sutton Courtenay, 1972), 160–67; Calvin, *Institutio* 3.3.8–3.3.9.

39. Johann Gropper, *Enchiridion Christianae Institutionis* (Cologne: Peter Quentel, 1538), fols. 129b, 130b, 132a–133a.

40. Gasparo Contarini, *Epistola de Justificatione*, in *Gegenreformatorische Schriften (1530 c.–1542)*, ed. F. Hünermann, Corpus Catholicorum 7 (Münster: W. Aschendorff, 1923), 27–31; Johann Gropper, *Antididagma, seu, Christianae et Catholicae Religionis . . . Propugnatio* (Cologne: Jaspar Gennepaeus, 1544), fols. 11b, 13b, 14a.

41. P. Simoncelli, "Vom Humanismus zur Gegenreformation—das Schicksal des Regensburger Buches in Italien: Versuch einer Rekonstruktion," in *Pflugiana: Studien über Julius Pflug (1499–1564)*, ed. E. Neuss and J. V. Pollet (Münster: Aschendorff, 1990), 111–12.

Second, Regensburg does not simply place imputed and inherent righteousness side by side as unreconciled and conflicting concepts. The reason the Reformers insisted on imputed righteousness was that both our own inherent righteousness and the righteousness of our works remain imperfect and it is not on that basis that we can stand before God. It is on the basis of imputed righteousness, Christ's righteousness reckoned to our account, that we are accepted by God. Article 5 makes precisely this point. We are accepted by God on the basis of imputed righteousness, on account of Christ, not on the basis of "the worthiness or perfection imparted to us in Christ" (§4.5). The believer depends not on inherent righteousness but only on the gift of Christ's righteousness (§5.1). Ambiguity and patchwork are not the appropriate terms to describe this. Contarini was a good learner at this point. In a letter written to defend article 5, he places heavy emphasis on the need to rely not on inherent but on imputed righteousness *alone* because of the imperfection of the former.[42]

Article 5 taught that we receive both inherent and imputed righteousness. It also taught that we should rely on the latter (imputed) righteousness and not on our inherent righteousness. The Council of Trent was to take a very different line on both points.

The Council of Trent

The Origins of the Tridentine Decree on Justification

The breakdown of the Regensburg Colloquy revealed the irreconcilable nature of the split between the two sides. Conciliation and negotiation had failed. The need now was for clear lines of demarcation. It was with this in mind that the Council of Trent (1545–1563) was called.[43] It set out to define Roman Catholic dogma in a firmly anti-Protestant manner, as in the Decree on Justification (1547).[44] A number of the delegates were

42. Contarini, *Epistola de Justificatione*, 29–30.

43. Much of the material on Trent is taken from Lane, *Justification by Faith in Catholic-Protestant Dialogue*, 60–85.

44. Latin and English texts in N. P. Tanner, ed., *Decrees of the Ecumenical Councils*, 2 vols. (London: Sheed & Ward; Washington, DC: Georgetown University Press, 1990), 2:671–81; English translation in J. H. Leith, ed., *Creeds of the Churches*, 3rd ed. (Atlanta: John Knox, 1982), 408–24. These both avoid words such as "righteous[ness]," instead keeping to words from the "just" root ("just[ice]"). This is more consistent and more closely reflects the Latin, but since I have used the words "righteous[ness]" throughout, there is no virtue in translating Trent differently. Accordingly, quotations from the decree are my own translation, always made with reference to these two translations and at times drawing closely upon them.

more or less favorable to Luther's teaching on justification,[45] but the eventual decree was firmly anti-Lutheran. The debate opened on June 21, 1546, and the final version of the decree was promulgated on January 13 of the following year.

Two questions proved to be especially contentious at the council. The second of these concerned the certitude of being in a state of grace, an issue that will not detain us here.[46] The first question relates to the doctrine of twofold righteousness.[47] This doctrine was put forward by Cardinal Girolamo Seripando, who shared with the other *spirituali* the belief in the Christian's ongoing need for mercy. He held that the "imperfect justice which the just man is able to attain deserves to be rewarded with eternal life only when it is complemented by Christ's justice."[48] Therefore the Christian at the last judgment should "appeal to God's mercy and put his trust in the merits of Christ."[49] His was a doctrine of twofold righteousness according to which inherent righteousness is insufficient and needs to be complemented by imputed righteousness. This imperfection was due to the effects of concupiscence.[50] In drawing up the second draft of the decree, submitted in August 1546, Seripando

---

On the Tridentine decree on justification, see Jedin, *History of the Council of Trent*, 2:166–96, 234–35, 239–61, 283–316; also H. Rückert, *Die Rechtfertigungslehre auf dem tridentinischen Konzil* (Bonn: A. Marcus und E. Weber, 1925). I have not managed to consult E. Stakemeier, *Glaube und Rechtfertigung: Die Verhandlungen und Lehrbestimmungen des Trienter Konzils über den Glauben als Anfang, Fundament, und Wurzel aller Rechtfertigung* (Freiburg im Breisgau: Herder, 1937).

45. See Jedin, *History of the Council of Trent*, 2:172–73, 177, 180–81, 187–93, 279–80, 290–91.

46. For discussions of this at Trent, see ibid., 2:249–53, 285–86, 288–90, 297–98; also Rückert, *Die Rechtfertigungslehre*, 191–216; E. Stakemeier, *Das Konzil von Trient über die Heilsgewißheit* (Heidelberg: F. H. Kerle, 1947), esp. 171–87 on the final outcome.

47. For discussions of this at Trent, see esp. Jedin, *History of the Council of Trent*, 2:241–49, 253–58, 284–85, 286–88, 308. Also S. Ehses, "Johannes Groppers Rechtfertigungslehre auf dem Konzil von Trient," *Römische Quartalschrift* 20, no. 2 (1906): 175–88; Rückert, *Die Rechtfertigungslehre*, 217–56; H. Jedin, *Papal Legate at the Council of Trent: Cardinal Seripando* (London and St. Louis: B. Herder, 1947), 348–92; P. Pas, "La doctrine de la double justice au concile de Trente," *Ephemerides theologicae lovanienses* 30 (1954): 5–53; J. F. McCue, "Double Justification at the Council of Trent: Piety and Theology in Sixteenth Century Roman Catholicism," in *Piety, Politics, and Ethics: Reformation Studies in Honor of George Wolfgang Forell*, ed. C. Lindberg (Kirksville, MO: Sixteenth Century Journal, 1984), 39–56 (which qualifies the arguments of Pas); Yarnold, *"Duplex iustitia,"* 213–22. For a study that concentrates more on Seripando's doctrine, cf. E. Stakemeier, *Der Kampf um Augustin auf dem Tridentinum* (Paderborn: Bonifacius, 1937), 130–82, 209–22.

48. Jedin, *Papal Legate at the Council of Trent*, 335. Cf. Yarnold, *"Duplex iustitia,"* 214, 223.

49. Jedin, *History of the Council of Trent*, 2:284.

50. Jedin, *Papal Legate at the Council of Trent*, 315–25.

included a chapter "on twofold righteousness."[51] A committee radically revised this draft before it was submitted to the council the following month. The "twofold righteousness" was expressly rejected in favor of "one righteousness": "There are not two righteousnesses, which are given us, God's and Christ's, but one righteousness of God through Jesus Christ, that is love or grace, by which the justified are not merely reputed, but truly called and are righteous." But the draft earlier states that when we are justified, his righteousness is "communicated and imputed to us, as if it were our own."[52] Jedin refers to this second passage as the "Achilles heel of the September draft."[53]

Seripando raised the issue again in October, questioning the rejection of the doctrine of twofold righteousness, which was held by Catholic theologians in Italy and Germany, such as Contarini and Gropper.[54] The legates put this issue to the council as follows: Has the justified Christian who perseveres to the end in good works "so completely met the claims of divine justice that when he appears before the judgment-seat of Christ he obtains eternal life on account of his own merits"? Or "is he in need, in addition to his own inherent justice, of the mercy and justice of Christ, that is, of the merits of His Passion, in order to supplement what is wanting in his own personal justice?"[55] These questions were discussed in October. There was some sympathy for Seripando at the level of practical piety, but his view was felt to be defective theologically.[56] Some spoke of demanding eternal life as a right at the last judgment,[57] although others thought that to boast there of good works

51. Jedin, *History of the Council of Trent*, 2:241, 243; *CT* 5:829. For the two forms of this draft, see *CT* 5:821–33.

52. *CT* 5:423.

53. Jedin, *Papal Legate at the Council of Trent*, 355. Cf. Jedin, *History of the Council of Trent*, 2:243. For the text of this draft, see *CT* 5:420–27.

54. Jedin, *History of the Council of Trent*, 2:247–48; *CT* 5:486–88. Elsewhere Seripando spelled this out at greater length, appealing to Pighius, Gropper, and Contarini (*CT* 12:664–71).

55. Jedin, *History of the Council of Trent*, 2:249; *CT* 5:523.

56. McCue, "Double Justification at the Council of Trent," argues that the doctrine of double justification exposed the tension between piety and theology in sixteenth-century Catholicism. Jedin, who does not sympathize with Seripando's theology, acknowledges the strength of his appeal to the need for mercy at the last judgment (*Papal Legate at the Council of Trent*, 363–64).

57. E.g., the Franciscan Ludovicus Vitriarius: "When the justified man appears before God's judgement seat, God asks him 'What is your request?' He responds: 'I demand eternal life.' 'On what grounds?' 'Because you are obliged to give it to me.' 'By what law?' 'Yours, because it says in your law that you will reward each according to what they have done [Psalm 62:12]'" (*CT* 5:569). Pas, "La doctrine de la double justice," 23, 35, gives examples of those holding that eternal life may be demanded as a debt.

was to be a Pharisee.[58] Diego Lainez branded twofold righteousness a Lutheran novelty and warned against turning the throne of justice into a throne of mercy.[59]

Seripando was faced with the thankless task of producing the next draft, which he concluded with a further reference to the ongoing need for mercy: "Because no one should judge himself, lest he fall into the devil's snare, the righteous should not cease to call on God's mercy for their sins, offences and negligencies and to trust in the merits of our Lord Jesus Christ." This is because we will be judged by the secret judgment of God at the end and ought not to judge ourselves before then.[60] This draft was revised as a result of the council debates. The inscrutability of God's judgment remained, but the opposite conclusion was drawn. Instead of the exhortation to call on mercy or to trust Christ's merits, there is the statement that "nothing more is needed for the justified to be said (provided they have worked with that affection of love which is required in this mortal life) to have fully satisfied God's law and, as it were sprinkled everywhere with divine grace, to have truly merited eternal life."[61] This statement of the adequacy of works was repeated, with minor changes, in the final decree (ch. 16). Seripando felt betrayed and wrote in the margin that the whole passage was the work of someone who does not know what he is talking about or who is afraid of falling into Lutheran error.[62]

In November, feeling hard done by, Seripando gave an impassioned speech, which spanned two days, defending his orthodoxy.[63] Here he proposed two further additions to the text of the decree in an attempt to retain the idea of the need for ongoing mercy. The first was a statement that those who know that their love is inadequate should "call upon God's mercy for the sake of the merits of Christ's Passion."[64] The second was that where it was stated that the Christian should "keep before his eyes the strict judgment of God," there should be added that this should lead

---

58. E.g., Richard of Le Mans (*CT* 5:536).

59. Jedin, *History of the Council of Trent*, 2:253–58. For these and Lainez's ten other arguments against twofold righteousness, see C. E. Maxcey, "Double Justice, Diego Laynez, and the Council of Trent," *Church History* 48 (1979): 269–78. For the text of Lainez's speech, see *CT* 5:612–29.

60. *CT* 5:515; Jedin, *Papal Legate at the Council of Trent*, 377. For the text of this draft, see *CT* 5:510–17.

61. *CT* 5:639; Jedin, *Papal Legate at the Council of Trent*, 378. For the text of this draft, see *CT* 5:634–41.

62. *CT* 5:663, n. 2; Jedin, *Papal Legate at the Council of Trent*, 378; Yarnold, "*Duplex iustitia*," 219.

63. *CT* 5:666–76.

64. Jedin, *History of the Council of Trent*, 2:287–88; *Papal Legate at the Council of Trent*, 386; *CT* 5:671–72, to be added to the draft at *CT* vol. 5, p. 639, lines 33–35.

to "fleeing to the mercy of God through the merits of Christ with the sorrow of penitence."[65] These proposals were both rejected.[66]

Seripando was thwarted at every point. His doctrine of twofold righteousness was rejected, though not formally condemned.[67] His belief in the need for ongoing mercy was rejected. "No place is made [in the Tridentine decree] for the statement for which Seripando had fought so valiantly, namely that the just man must continue to have recourse to the merit of Christ's passion for the mercy he needs."[68] Instead the sufficiency of inherent righteousness is affirmed.[69] These two key points of the Regensburg article—the insufficiency of our inherent righteousness and the consequent need for imputed righteousness upon which to rely—were clearly rejected by the Tridentine fathers.

The final form of the decree was based on three stages in the process of justification: first, the conversion of an adult unbeliever to the faith, a rare event in sixteenth-century Europe; second, the means by which justified and baptized Christians preserve their justification, progress in it, and attain to eternal glory; and third, the way in which those who fall from grace can recover their forfeited justification.[70] The final decree broadly, but not totally, follows this basic structure. In expounding the decree, we will follow these three headings and add a fourth: certitude of being in a state of grace.

The decree begins with a positive exposition of the doctrine in sixteen chapters and concludes with thirty-three canons, each anathematizing a heretical statement. In what follows, we will expound the positive doctrine of the sixteen chapters. Where the canons relate to the teaching of the chapters, this will be indicated in footnotes. The council fathers were especially interested in opposing Luther, Melanchthon, and the "Augsburg Confession" and paid very little attention to the Reformed theologians at

65. *CT* 5:672, to be added to the draft at *CT* 5:640:1–2; Jedin, *History of the Council of Trent*, 2:288.

66. Jedin, *Papal Legate at the Council of Trent*, 386–87; *History of the Council of Trent*, 2:292.

67. Whereas the September draft spoke of *one* righteousness, the final decree speaks of the righteousness of God as the sole formal cause of justification. The change in position of the one/sole removes the direct contradiction of Seripando's doctrine (Pas, "La doctrine de la double justice," 45–46).

68. Yarnold, "*Duplex iustitia*," 222.

69. It has been noted, however, that Seripando fails to make a distinction between imparted or infused righteousness and the righteousness of works. It is the shortcomings of the latter that he accentuates (Jedin, *History of the Council of Trent*, 2:253; Yarnold, "*Duplex iustitia*," 216, 220). This does not entirely resolve the issue, however. For the *spirituali*, the problem was not just the failings of their works but the weakness of their love. Also, the Tridentine decree states that eternal life is merited by *works*.

70. Jedin, *History of the Council of Trent*, 2:181–82.

this stage.[71] But how well did they know the views of their opponents? This is an important question, as the council condemned not the persons of the Reformers but only their teaching—contrary to the practice of some earlier councils.[72] There is good evidence that the council fathers relied mainly on second- or thirdhand compilations of quotations from the Reformers. These were mostly drawn from the years up to 1526 and reflected some views that were later rejected or modified.[73]

The purpose of the council in general, and of this decree in particular, was to define Roman Catholic theology in opposition to Protestantism, not to decide between legitimate schools of Catholic theology.[74] Thus in places there is a vagueness in the language with this specific intent, as with the statements on the certitude of grace.

Stage 1: Initial Justification of Adults (Chapters 1–8)

All people have lost their innocence in Adam's sin and are children of wrath (Eph. 2:3). Neither Gentiles nor Jews could by their own efforts escape from their bondage to sin,[75] but God sent his Son as a propitiator for our sins and those of the whole world (chs. 1–2). Just as their unrighteousness stems from our birth in Adam, they need to be born again in Christ, that is, to move from their fallen state in Adam to a state of grace and adoption in order to be justified. This move cannot take place without baptism or the desire for it (chs. 3–4). With adults the first move is taken by God's predisposing grace, a call that comes from God without any merits on their part. They then have the free choice on whether to assent to this grace and cooperate with it or to reject it. It is wrong to suppose either that we do nothing or that we can turn to God of our own free will without grace (ch. 5).[76]

Cooperating with grace leads to a series of events that prepare us for justification.[77] By hearing, we come to believe that God justifies the

71. Ibid., 2:307.

72. H. Jedin, "The Council of Trent and Reunion: Historical Notes," *Heythrop Journal* 3 (1962): 7–8.

73. T. Freudenberger, "Zur Benützung des reformatorischen Schrifttums im Konzil von Trient," in *Von Konstanz nach Trient*, ed. R. Bäumer (Munich: Ferdinand Schöningh, 1972), 577–601; V. Pfnür, "Zur Verurteilung der reformatorischen Rechtfertigungslehre auf dem Konzil von Trient," *Annuarium historiae conciliorum* 8 (1976): 407–28; E. Iserloh, "Luther and the Council of Trent," in *Justification by Faith: Do the Sixteenth-Century Condemnations Still Apply?* ed. K. Lehmann (New York: Continuum, 1997), 164–67. Cf. H. Jedin, "Das Konzil von Trient und der Protestantismus," *Catholica* 3 (1934): 137–56.

74. Jedin, "The Council of Trent and Reunion," 8–10.

75. See cans. 1–2.

76. See cans. 3–5.

77. See can. 9.

ungodly by his grace. Recognizing that we ourselves are sinners and considering God's mercy, we turn from fear of divine justice to hope in God's mercy, trusting that God will be favorable to us for Christ's sake. We then begin to love God, the source of righteousness, and are thus moved to hate sin and repent of it. We then resolve to receive baptism, begin a new life, and keep the commandments (ch. 6).

This process of preparation comes before justification itself, "which is not only the forgiveness of sins but also the sanctification and renewal of the inner person," whereby we change from being unrighteous to righteous, an enemy of God to his friend. Five different causes of justification are given. Although these distinctions originated with Aristotle, Trent does not use them in a strictly Aristotelian manner, in keeping with the policy of the council to avoid scholastic and technical language.[78] The definition of each cause, given in parentheses, is my own based on a number of different accounts.[79] The *final* cause (the end or purpose for which a change is produced) is "the glory of God and Christ and eternal life." The *efficient* cause (the agent producing the change) is the merciful God, who freely washes and sanctifies us, sealing and anointing us with the Spirit. The *meritorious* cause (an intermediate cause that contributes to a change by making it worthy of taking place) is the Lord Jesus Christ, who merited our justification by his passion, making satisfaction for us to the Father.[80] The *instrumental* cause (the means used to bring about a change) is "the sacrament of baptism, which is the sacrament of faith, without which [faith] no one was ever justified." Lastly, "the sole *formal* cause [that which makes something to be what it is] is the righteousness of God: not that by which he himself is righteous, but that by which he makes us righteous." It is noteworthy that of these five causes, four refer to God's action and only one to human activity.[81] Since at the time of Trent the overwhelming majority of Catholics were baptized as infants, although the instrumental cause refers to human activity, it involved mere passivity on the part of the one justified.

78. See G. Philips, "La justification luthérienne et le concile de Trente," *Ephemerides theologicae lovanienses* 47 (1971): 354.

79. Aristotle, *Physics* 2.3 (trans. Philip H. Wicksteed and Francis M. Cornford, Loeb Classical Library [Cambridge: Harvard University Press, 1968–], 1:128–31); T. Mautner, *A Dictionary of Philosophy* (Oxford: Blackwell, 1996), 68; R. A. Muller, *Dictionary of Latin and Greek Theological Terms* (Grand Rapids: Baker, 1985), 61–63. My definitions assume that it is causes of a *change* that are being described. M. Hocutt, "Aristotle's Four Becauses," *Philosophy* 49 (1974): 385–99, argues that Aristotle's four causes are better understood as four different answers to the question "why?"—i.e., as "four becauses."

80. See can. 10.

81. A point made by G. Vandevelde, "Justification between Scripture and Tradition," *Evangelical Review of Theology* 21 (1997): 139.

"Endowed by him with this righteousness we are renewed in the spirit of our mind and are not only considered to be righteous but are truly called and are righteous, each receiving righteousness within ourselves." To be justified, we need to receive the merits of Christ's passion, but this involves the love of God being poured out in our hearts by the Holy Spirit and abiding in us. In justification we receive not just the forgiveness of sins but also the infusion of faith, hope, and love.[82] Faith without the addition of hope and love does not unite us with Christ, and faith without works is dead. Newly baptized believers are summoned to keep the commandments in order to preserve their new righteousness spotless for the final judgment (ch. 7).

How are we to understand Paul's teaching that we are justified by faith and freely? This means that faith is "the beginning of human salvation, the foundation and root of all justification." Justification is a free gift because it is not merited by anything that precedes it, whether faith or works (ch. 8).

There are some points to note. Words have different meanings from those found in Protestant theology. Faith is "head belief" in doctrine whereas hope is a personal trust, described in words remarkably similar to Calvin's definition of saving faith.[83] The word "justification" is used to refer to both forgiveness and renewal. But beyond these linguistic differences lies a serious doctrinal issue. Trent affirms that at conversion two things happen: we are inwardly renewed and we are accounted righteous by God. The Reformers also agreed that the same two things happen, although this was not always appreciated at Trent.[84] But on what *grounds* are we accounted righteous? For the Reformers, this is clear—we are accounted righteous because of the righteousness of Christ, which is reckoned to our account, imputed to us. At conversion we are indeed changed and renewed, but the ground for our acceptance by God is not this inward renewal but the "alien" righteousness of Christ reckoned to us. What is the Tridentine position? It is widely held that Trent teaches that we are accepted by God on the basis of the righteousness that he has implanted in us—this being the implication of the fact that the sole formal cause of justification is "the righteousness of God: not that by which he himself is righteous, but that by which he makes us righteous" (ch. 7). The difference over the formal cause of justification

---

82. See can. 11.

83. "A firm and certain knowledge of God's benevolence toward us, founded upon the truth of the freely given promise in Christ, both revealed to our minds and sealed upon our hearts through the Holy Spirit" (John Calvin, *Institutes* III.ii.7).

84. McGrath, *Iustitia Dei*, 2:72, gives an example from *CT* 5:266.

has traditionally been identified as the fundamental difference between the two sides.[85]

But is it true that Trent teaches that God accepts us on the basis of inherent righteousness? This is not explicitly stated. In chapter 7 we read that the formal cause is "the righteousness of God . . . by which he makes us righteous." This righteousness is not defined more precisely, although the second half of canon 10 encourages the view that this refers to inherent righteousness.[86] The decree proceeds to state that "endowed by him with this righteousness we are renewed in the spirit of our mind and are not only considered to be righteous but are truly called and are righteous, each receiving righteousness within ourselves." This certainly affirms the simultaneity of the renewal and the reckoning as righteous, but there is no statement that the latter is the consequence of the former.[87] There is an ongoing Catholic tradition, found in Bellarmine, Newman, and Küng, that in initial justification God declares us righteous and that his declaration is effective, making us righteous, giving us inherent righteousness.[88] In this understanding, inherent righteousness is the consequence of God's declaration of righteousness. But although Trent can be read this way where *initial* justification is concerned, there is no doubt that once we are inwardly renewed, it is this renewal that makes us acceptable to God. This is the clear implication both of the rest of chapter 7 and of the remainder of the decree. Trent is reluctant

85. C. F. Allison, *The Rise of Moralism: The Proclamation of the Gospel from Hooker to Baxter* (London: SPCK, 1966), x, 2–3, 6–10, 178–80 (looking at Catholic-Protestant controversy at the end of the sixteenth and beginning of the seventeenth centuries); Alister E. McGrath, *ARCIC II and Justification: An Evangelical Anglican Assessment of "Salvation and the Church"* (Oxford, UK: Latimer House, 1987), 21–23, 27–29; Yarnold, *"Duplex iustitia,"* 222. Cf. Robert Bellarmine, *De Justificatione* 2.2, in *Disputationes de Controversiis Christianae Fidei adversus Huius Temporis Haereticos*, 4 vols. (Cologne: B. Gualtherus, 1619) 4:895: "The whole controversy can be reduced to this simple question: whether or not the formal cause of absolute justification is the righteousness inherent in us."

86. On the interpretation of this canon, see Stakemeier, *Der Kampf um Augustin*, 209–10; Jedin, *Papal Legate at the Council of Trent*, 389–90, cf. 370–72; M. Schmaus, *Katholische Dogmatik*, 5th ed., 5 vols. in 8 (Munich: Max Hueber, 1953–1958), 3/2:96–97; W. Joest, "Die tridentinische Rechtfertigungslehre," *Kerygma und Dogma* 9 (1963): 48–50.

87. M. Schmaus, *Dogma*, vol. 6, *Justification and the Last Things* (Kansas City and London: Sheed & Ward, 1977), 73–74, argues that the council "left open the question of the connection between the forgiveness of sins and the inner renewal" (73–74). Citing the beginning of ch. 7 of the decree, he claims, "The council's definition implies that the man justified by God is declared just (DS 1528), but that this declaration at the same time creates the state of justification. God's declaration is not a result of the preceding justification, but rather its foundation" (64). (This work is the English translation of the work cited in the previous note, and as such is both more recent and considerably abridged.)

88. Bellarmine, *De Justificatione* 2.3, in *Disputationes*, 4:898; J. H. Newman, *Lectures on Justification* (London: J. G. and F. Rivington; Oxford: J. H. Parker, 1838), 70–91; H. Küng, *Justification* (London: Burns & Oates, 1964), 202–4, 206, 210–11, 294–95.

to concede the existence of sin in the justified, an issue that has been seen as fundamental to the dispute.[89] Thus, although there may be ambiguity regarding the relation between *initial* acceptance and renewal, there is no doubt that *subsequent* acceptance is on the basis of inherent righteousness.

Stage 2: Progression in Justification (Chapters 7, 10–11, 16)

The decree does not stop with the acquisition of justification. At conversion we receive a true and Christian righteousness, and we need to keep the commandments and preserve our righteousness spotless for the day of judgment and thus gain eternal life (ch. 7). Having been justified, we then need (through faith and works) to grow in the righteousness that we have received through Christ's grace, increasing in justification.[90] This comes through day-to-day discipleship and obedience to the commandments of God and the church (ch. 10). Justification does not exempt us from keeping the commandments,[91] and we should not say that they are impossible to observe, with God's help.[92] We do not cease to be righteous through committing everyday venial sins, for God will not abandon us unless we first abandon God. We should not boast in faith alone as if that will enable us to gain our inheritance and glory without first suffering with Christ. We are to seek God's glory and also to look for a reward (ch. 11).

God will reward the works of the faithful Christian.[93] Eternal life at the end is both a grace promised in mercy and a reward given to good works and merits. It is indeed a gift of grace in that it is only by God's help that we can achieve it. It is only because, as head to the body and the vine to its branches, Christ strengthens us that we are able to perform meritorious works that please God. But at the same time, "nothing more is needed for the justified to be considered, by the works which they have done in God, to have fully satisfied God's law (according to the state of this life) and to have truly merited eternal life."[94] This happens

89. Allison, *Rise of Moralism*, 182–83.
90. See can. 24.
91. See cans. 19–21.
92. See can. 18.
93. See can. 26. Richard Hooker delightfully summarizes the twofold role of reward for Trent: "In meriting, our actions do work with two hands: with the one, they get their morning stipend, the increase of grace; with the other, their evening hire, the everlasting crown of glory" ("A Learned Discourse of Justification, Works, and How the Foundation of Faith Is Overthrown" [*Sermons* 2.33], in *The Works of That Learned and Judicious Divine, Mr. Richard Hooker*, ed. John Keble, 7th ed., 3 vols. [Oxford: Oxford University Press, 1888], 3:539).
94. See can. 32.

only because of God's grace at work within us. Our righteousness is our own, but it does not originate from us. "Our" righteousness is the same righteousness that is imparted to us by God through Christ's merit. God has promised a reward for our works, but we must remember that our merits are his gifts, and trust and glory in him, not in ourselves. Because of our proneness to offend, we should keep in mind God's severity and judgment as much as his mercy and goodness and not presume to judge ourselves (ch. 16).

Stage 3: Loss and Recovery of Justification (Chapters 13–15)

It is those who persevere to the end who will be saved, and we need to be vigilant lest we fall (ch. 13). If by sin we do fall away from the grace of justification, it is possible to regain it through the sacrament of penance, the "second plank after shipwreck."[95] This repentance of a Christian after falling is very different from that at baptism. It requires not only a change of heart but also the sacramental confession of one's sins (at least in desire), priestly absolution, and making satisfaction. God remits the eternal punishment due our sin, but there remains a temporal punishment that is due,[96] and it is for this that we must offer satisfaction through fasting, almsgiving, prayers, and the like (ch. 14). It is not only by falling from faith that the grace of justification is lost.[97] Committing any other mortal sin causes it to be lost, even if faith remains (ch. 15).

Certitude of Being in a State of Grace (Chapters 9, 12–13)

We should believe that it is only "freely, by divine mercy for Christ's sake," that sins are forgiven. But sins are not forgiven on the ground of a boastful confidence that they have been forgiven.[98] Nor is it necessary, for forgiveness and justification, to believe with certainty that one has been forgiven and justified.[99] We should not doubt God's mercy, Christ's merit, or the efficacy of the sacraments, but at the same time, we can be apprehensive about our own spiritual state, since "no one can know, with a certainty of faith which admits of no error, that he has obtained the grace of God" (ch. 9).[100] Just as one cannot be completely sure of one's

95. See can. 29.
96. See can. 30.
97. See cans. 27–28.
98. See can. 14.
99. See can. 13.
100. "This formula denied the certitude of faith in the sense in which the Thomists understood [and denied] it while a certitude stemming from faith as conceived by the Scotists was left an open question" (Jedin, *History of the Council of Trent*, 2:297–98).

present state, so one cannot know for certain whether one is elect,[101] because of the possibility of sin and the uncertainty whether one will then repent. "It is not possible, except by a special revelation, to know whom God has chosen for himself" (ch. 12). We should hope firmly in God's help, but we cannot be sure of the final outcome with absolute certainty,[102] although, unless we neglect God's grace, he will bring to completion the work that he has begun (ch. 13). God does not abandon those who are justified unless he is first abandoned by them (ch. 11).

After Trent

The Tridentine Decree on Justification is one of the most impressive achievements of the council. The leaders of the council had reported to Rome that "the significance of this Council in the theological sphere lies chiefly in the article on justification, in fact this is the most important item the Council has to deal with."[103] But reading it can give one a false impression of the importance of the doctrine within Roman Catholicism. The decree was needed, and the doctrine received the attention that it did, because of the Protestant challenge. For the inner life of the Roman Catholic Church, however, the doctrine was not very important. In 1564 Pope Pius IV promulgated the Creed of the Council of Trent. Justification is mentioned just once in passing: "I embrace and accept each and every article on original sin and justification declared and defined in the most holy Council of Trent."[104] Shortly afterward, in 1566, his successor, Pope Pius V, promulgated a *Catechismus ex Decreto Concilii Tridentini*, the so-called Roman Catechism. This contains only scattered passing references to justification, mostly in the context of teaching on the sacraments.[105] The sacramental system is as central

101. See can. 15.
102. See can. 16.
103. Cited in Jedin, *History of the Council of Trent*, 2:171. Catholic writers often cite Harnack's judgment: "The Decree on justification, although a product of art, is in many respects remarkably well constructed; indeed, it may be doubted whether the Reformation would have developed itself if this Decree had been issued at the Lateran Council at the beginning of the century, and had really passed into the flesh and blood of the Church." But he goes on to point out that the decree was in fact a consequence of the Reformation and so should not be overrated (A. Harnack, *History of Dogma*, 7 vols. [New York: Russell and Russell, 1958], 7:57.) He also proceeds to present a very negative exposition of the decree (60–71). "In spite of all appearance to the contrary, the interest that really governs the whole Decree is the desire to show how there can be an attainment to good works that have weight in the sight of God" (61).
104. Leith, *Creeds of the Churches*, 440.
105. *The Catechism of the Council of Trent*, trans. J. Donovan (Dublin: W. Folds & Son, 1829), 65–66, 90, 111, 138, 141, 149, 152, 181, 184, 346, 505–6. I am indebted to Bruce

to the catechism as the doctrine of justification is peripheral, and the need to offer satisfaction for our sins receives the sustained exposition denied to justification.[106] Justification needed to be treated in response to the Protestant threat, but at the heart of the Christian life in Roman Catholicism is not justification but the sacramental system. The council fathers turned from justification to the sacraments, and the Decree on the Sacraments begins with the observation that all true righteousness begins with the sacraments; having been begun, increases through them; and, if lost, is restored through them.[107]

Conclusion

At Regensburg, Protestant and Roman Catholic theologians reached a temporary agreement on justification. This was based upon the acceptance of both inherent and imputed righteousness and on the recognition that because of the imperfection of our inherent righteousness, Christ's righteousness needs to be imputed to us in order for us to be acceptable to God. The Catholic theologians most responsible for this agreement (Gropper and Contarini) shared the Reformers' conviction about the imperfection of our inherent righteousness and so were willing to embrace the concept of imputed righteousness.[108] These convictions were held no less deeply by Seripando, who had the key role of writing drafts of the Tridentine Decree on Justification. Despite Seripando's passionate advocacy, both points were rejected by the council fathers and excluded from the final version of the decree.

The Tridentine Decree on Justification is a vitally important document, but we must not fall into the mistake of simply equating it with the Catholic doctrine. Trent is what the Roman Catholic Church chose to say at that time in response to what it then understood the Reformers to be saying. To understand what the Roman Catholic Church today is saying to what it now understands Protestants to teach, we need to listen to contemporary Roman Catholic theology. Probably the most objectionable statement in the Tridentine decree is that "nothing more is needed for the justified to be considered, by the works which they have done in God, to have fully satisfied God's law (according to the state of this life)

Winter, in an unpublished paper, for the idea of contrasting the catechism with the decrees. R. Preus, *Justification and Rome* (St. Louis: Concordia Academic Press, 1997), 121, makes the same point but wrongly claims that the term "justify" is used only three times.

106. *Catechism of the Council of Trent*, 285–94.

107. Leith, *Creeds of the Churches*, 425.

108. I am grateful to Smith, "Calvin's Doctrine of Justification," for first drawing my attention to this point.

and to have truly merited eternal life" (ch. 16). The highly important *Catechism of the Catholic Church* (1994) summarizes the teaching of Trent on justification but also adds a quotation from Thérèse of Lisieux on the imperfection of our righteousness, which effectively neutralizes that objectionable statement.[109]

Excursus

The Regensburg Agreement (1541), Article 5

The Justification of Man

1) No Christian should doubt that after the fall of our first parent all men are, as the apostle says, born children of wrath [Eph. 2:3] and enemies of God [Rom. 5:10] and thereby are in death and slavery to sin [Rom. 6:16–20].[110]

2) Likewise no Christian should question that nobody can be reconciled with God, or set free from slavery to sin, except by Christ, the one mediator between God and men [1 Tim. 2:5], by whose grace, as the apostle said to the Romans, we are not only reconciled to God [5:10] and set free from slavery to sin [6:18, 22] but also made sharers in the divine nature [2 Pet. 1:4] and children of God [Rom. 8:14–16].

3) (1) Likewise it is quite clear that adults do not obtain these blessings of Christ except by the prevenient movement of the Holy Spirit, by which their mind and will are moved to hate sin. (2) For, as Saint Augustine says, it is impossible to begin a new life if we do not repent of the former one. (3) Likewise, in the last chapter of Luke [24:47], Christ commands that repentance and forgiveness of sin should be preached in his name. (4) Also, John the Baptist, sent to prepare the way of the Lord, preached repentance, saying [Matt. 3:2], "Repent, for the kingdom of heaven is drawing near." (5) Next, man's mind is moved toward God by the Holy Spirit through Christ, and this movement is through faith. Through this [faith] man's mind believes with certainty all that God has transmitted, and also with full certainty and without doubt assents to the promises made to us by God, who, as stated in the psalm [145:13], is

---

109. *Catechism of the Catholic Church* (London: Geoffrey Chapman, 1994), §2011.

110. The translation of art. 5 is my own, based on a text reconstructed from the versions given by Bucer, Eck, Gropper, and Melanchthon. A very similar translation appeared in Lane, *Justification by Faith in Catholic-Protestant Dialogue*, 233–37.

faithful in all his words. From there he acquires confidence on account of God's promise, by which he has pledged that he will remit sins freely and that he will adopt as children those who believe in Christ, those, I say, who repent of their former life. (6) By this faith he is lifted up to God by the Holy Spirit, and so he receives the Holy Spirit, remission of sins, imputation of righteousness, and countless other gifts.

4) (1) So it is a reliable and sound doctrine that the sinner is justified by living and efficacious faith, for through it we are pleasing and acceptable to God on account of Christ. (2) And living faith is what we call the movement of the Holy Spirit, by which those who truly repent of their old life are lifted up to God and truly appropriate the mercy promised in Christ, so that they now truly recognize that they have received the remission of sins and reconciliation on account of the merits of Christ, through the free goodness of God, and cry out to God, "Abba Father" [Rom. 8:15; Gal. 4:6]. (3) But this happens to no one unless also at the same time love is infused, which heals the will so that the healed will may begin to fulfill the law, just as Saint Augustine said. (4) So living faith is that which both appropriates mercy in Christ, believing that the righteousness that is in Christ is freely imputed to it, and at the same time receives the promise of the Holy Spirit and love. (5) Therefore the faith that truly justifies is that faith which is effectual through love [Gal. 5:6]. (6) Nevertheless it remains true that it is by this faith that we are justified (i.e., accepted and reconciled to God) inasmuch as it appropriates the mercy and righteousness that is imputed to us on account of Christ and his merit, not on account of the worthiness or perfection of the righteousness imparted to us in Christ.

5) (1) Although the one who is justified receives righteousness and through Christ also has inherent [righteousness], as the apostle says, "you are washed, you are sanctified, you are justified, etc." [1 Cor. 6:11] (which is why the holy fathers made use of [the term] "to be justified" even to mean "to receive inherent righteousness"), nevertheless, the faithful soul depends not on this but only on the righteousness of Christ given to us as a gift, without which there is and can be no righteousness at all. (2) And thus by faith in Christ we are justified or reckoned to be righteous, that is, we are accepted through his merits and not on account of our own worthiness or works. (3) And on account of the righteousness inherent in us, we are said to be righteous because the works that we perform are righteous, according to the saying of John: "whoever does what is right is righteous" [1 John 3:7].

6) Although fear of God, patience, humility, and other virtues ought always to grow in the regenerate because this renewal is imperfect and enormous weakness remains in them, it should nevertheless be taught that those who truly repent may always hold with most certain faith that

they are pleasing to God on account of Christ the mediator. For it is Christ who is the propitiator, the High Priest and the one who prays for us, the one the Father gave to us and with him all good things [Rom. 8:32].

7) Seeing that in our weakness there is no perfect certainty and that there are many weak and fearful consciences, which often struggle against great doubt, nobody should be excluded from the grace of Christ on account of such weakness. Such people should be earnestly encouraged boldly to set the promises of Christ against these doubts and by diligent intercession to pray that their faith may be increased, according to the saying "Lord increase our faith" [Luke 17:5].

8) (1) Likewise every Christian should learn that this grace and this regeneration have not been given to us so that we might remain idle in that stage of our renewal which we at first obtained but so that we may grow in everything into him who is the head [Eph. 4:15]. (2) Therefore the people must be taught to devote effort to this growth, which indeed happens through good works, both internal and external, which are commanded and commended by God. To these works God has, in many passages from the Gospels, clearly and manifestly promised on account of Christ a reward—good things in this life, as much for the body as for the soul (as much as seems right to divine providence), and after this life in heaven. (3) Therefore, although the inheritance of eternal life is due the regenerate on account of the promise, as soon as they are reborn in Christ, nevertheless God also renders a reward to good works, not according to the substance of the works, or because they come from us, but to the extent that they are performed in faith and proceed from the Holy Spirit, who dwells in us, free choice concurring as a partial agent.

9) The joy of those who have performed more and better works will be greater and more abundant on account of the increase of faith and love, in which they have grown through exercises of that kind.

10) (1) Now those who say that we are justified by faith alone should at the same time teach the doctrine of repentance, of the fear of God, of the judgment of God, and of good works so that all the chief points of the preaching may remain firm, as Christ said, "preaching repentance and the remission of sins in my name" [Luke 24:47]. (2) And that is to prevent this way of speaking [i.e., *sola fide*] from being understood other than has been previously mentioned.

7

Justification and the *ordo salutis*

A. T. B. McGowan

Introduction

The title I was given for this contribution was "Justification in the *ordo salutis*." I have taken the liberty of changing this slightly to "Justification and the *ordo salutis*." In the course of my preparation, it became clear that the question I needed to answer was not simply "Where does justification fit into the *ordo salutis*?" but "Is the construction of an *ordo salutis* an appropriate way to deal with the doctrine of justification?" This perhaps requires a word of explanation.

As one who stands within the Reformed theological tradition and has an interest in the history of this tradition, I have been fascinated to observe a changing approach to this subject. For most of its history, Reformed theologians have generally sought to understand and explain the application of redemption by means of an *ordo salutis* method, namely, by demonstrating the relationship between the various doctrines in terms of the order in which they impact on the human condition. So, for example, some have argued that the *ordo salutis* begins with effectual calling, which leads to regeneration, which in turn produces faith, which leads to justification, and so on. It might almost be said that these various doctrines were conceived of in terms of a domino effect, such that, the process having begun, one follows from the other automatically.

In more recent Reformed theology, however, theologians have chosen to approach the application of redemption by focusing on union with Christ instead of following an *ordo salutis* method. Paradoxically, this union-with-Christ method has been adopted by two schools of thought within Reformed theology that, in most other respects, are normally opposed to one another, namely, neoorthodoxy, on the one hand, and the theologians associated with Westminster Theological Seminary in Philadelphia, on the other hand. Not surprisingly, there is a marked contrast in the way in which these two schools use the union-with-Christ method, leading to quite different conclusions.

In order to open up the discussion, this chapter is divided into four sections: first, a brief general introduction to the concept of the *ordo salutis*; second, an identification of some of the important theological issues raised in the endeavor to discern the place of justification within the *ordo salutis* in Reformed theology; third, a discussion of the union-with-Christ methods as developed within neoorthodox theology and by scholars associated with Westminster Theological Seminary; and fourth, an attempt to draw some conclusions and suggest possible ways forward for Reformed theology.

The *ordo salutis*

Louis Berkhof defines the *ordo salutis* in this way: "The *ordo salutis* describes the process by which the work of salvation, wrought in Christ, is subjectively realized in the hearts and lives of sinners. It aims at describing in their logical order, and also in their interrelations, the various movements of the Holy Spirit in the application of the work of redemption."[1]

The origins of the term have been traced to two Lutheran scholars, Frank Buddeus and Jakobus Karpov, writing between 1724 and 1739.[2] As Sinclair Ferguson notes, however, the concept "has an older pedigree, stretching back into pre-Reformation theology's attempts to relate the various experiential and sacramental steps to salvation. In this context Luther's personal struggle may be viewed as a search for a truly evangelical *ordo salutis*."[3]

The difficulty experienced in developing an *ordo salutis* is that the biblical evidence for the creation of an *ordo salutis* does not lie on the surface of the text but has to be deduced and inferred from various

1. L. Berkhof, *Systematic Theology* (Grand Rapids: Eerdmans, 1996), 415–16.
2. S. B. Ferguson, "Ordo salutis," in *New Dictionary of Theology*, ed. S. B. Ferguson and D. F. Wright (Downers Grove, IL: InterVarsity, 1988), 480–81.
3. Ibid.

places.[4] This problem, however, did not deter many of those within the Reformed tradition from developing an *ordo salutis*, drawing their structure from Romans 8:28–30 and elsewhere.

Within Reformed theology, the development of an *ordo salutis* included three main considerations. First, it was recognized that God takes the initiative in salvation and that he does so through his Word and by his Spirit. Second, the *ordo salutis* was developed in such a way as to give proper expression to the Calvinistic theology and its understanding of the application of salvation. Third, it was clearly understood that the *ordo salutis* must account for the two problems that fallen human beings face, namely, their broken relationship to God and their polluted, sinful condition. Thus in the *ordo salutis* the various doctrines were divided into two groups: those which described the change in the sinner's relationship to God and those which described the renovation and renewal of the human condition.

The construction of an *ordo salutis* in order to describe the work of the Holy Spirit in the application of redemption was essentially a Reformation and post-Reformation development. As Berkhof writes:

> The doctrine of the order of salvation is a fruit of the Reformation. Hardly any semblance of it is found in the works of the Scholastics. In pre-Reformation theology scant justice is done to soteriology in general. It does not constitute a separate locus, and its constituent parts are discussed under other rubrics, more or less as *disjecta membra*. Even the greatest of the Schoolmen, such as Peter the Lombard and Thomas Aquinas, pass on at once from the discussion of the incarnation to that of the Church and the sacraments.[5]

Berkhof goes on to say that "Calvin was the first to group the various parts of the order of salvation in a systematic way,"[6] while recognizing that this was a very preliminary attempt at such a process. Indeed, we might say that Calvin's *ordo salutis* was very simple, consisting of faith, justification, and sanctification.[7] As Ronald Wallace has written, "Calvin defines what we receive from Jesus Christ by faith as a 'double grace,' or a twofold benefit, the whole of which can be summed up for the purpose of theological discussion under two headings: Justification and

---

4. As Gerrit C. Berkouwer, *Faith and Justification*, trans. Lewis P. Smedes (Grand Rapids: Eerdmans, 1954), 31–32, has demonstrated.

5. Berkhof, *Systematic Theology*, 417.

6. Ibid.

7. See John Calvin, *Institutes of the Christian Religion*, ed. J. T. McNeill, 2 vols. (Philadelphia: Westminster, 1977), III.xi–xviii.

Sanctification."[8] Geoffrey Bromiley argues that the way in which Calvin dealt with the relationship between justification and sanctification was itself highly significant:

> Perhaps Calvin's most important contribution to the understanding of justification is his reuniting of two things which for purposes of clarity had in a sense been divided, namely, justification and sanctification. Now obviously neither Luther nor Cranmer nor others meant to keep the two apart. Their anxiety to relate faith to works bears ample testimony to this. On the other hand, the Reformers in general can hardly be said to have presented a comprehensive view of Christian salvation and the Christian life in a way which brings out the full relationship of justification and sanctification. This was to be the great achievement of Calvin.[9]

Berkouwer puts it slightly differently, arguing that in discussions about the *ordo salutis*, the emphasis should be on salvation in Christ, and this he sees in Calvin: "Though one does not find an *ordo salutis* in Calvin, in the sense of its later development, there is nonetheless an order, perhaps better called an orderliness, which is determined by salvation in Christ. Salvation in Christ—this is the center from which the lines are drawn to every point of the *way of salvation*. The lines themselves may be called faith."[10]

Those who followed Calvin, however, developed the *ordo salutis* considerably. This was particularly true of Theodore Beza on the Continent and William Perkins in England, both of whom developed charts (*tabulae*) in which the various doctrines were located in a logical (although not necessarily chronological) order. Perkins's "golden chain" was particularly decisive for Puritan theology. The *ordo salutis* developed by Perkins involved, first, effectual calling, which produced faith; second, justification, involving the remission of sin and the imputation of righteousness; third, sanctification, which involved mortification, vivification, and repentance; and, finally, glorification and life eternal.[11]

It is important to point out, however, that the *ordo salutis* as developed by Beza and Perkins was not driven and controlled by a predestinarian or deterministic worldview as some have argued.[12] Richard Muller, in a

---

8. R. S. Wallace, *Calvin's Doctrine of the Christian Life* (Edinburgh: Oliver & Boyd, 1959), 23.

9. G. W. Bromiley, *Historical Theology: An Introduction* (Grand Rapids: Eerdmans, 1978), 237.

10. Berkouwer, *Faith and Justification*, 29.

11. See W. Perkins, "A Golden Chaine," in *The Work of William Perkins*, ed. I. Breward (London: Sutton Courteney, 1970), vol. 3 and accompanying diagram.

12. J. B. Torrance, "Strengths and Weaknesses of the Westminster Theology," in *The Westminster Confession in the Church Today*, ed. A. I. C. Heron (Edinburgh: Saint Andrew, 1982), 40–53.

profound and scholarly analysis of the relationship between Christology and predestination in early Reformed theology, states,

> It would be a mistake to say that there were no deterministic tendencies in Beza's thought, but these tendencies existed in tension with a christo-centric piety and a very real sense of the danger of determinism. Beza did not produce a predestinarian or necessitarian system nor did he ineluctably draw Reformed theology toward formulation of a causal metaphysic. Nor did he develop one *locus* to the neglect, exclusion, or deemphasis of others. Beza's role in the development of Reformed system may better be described as a generally successful attempt to clarify and to render more precise the doctrinal definitions he had inherited from Calvin and the other Reformers of the first era of theological codification.[13]

Rather than predestination, the key to the *ordo salutis* in early Reformed theology was effectual calling. This was defined as that work of God the Holy Spirit whereby the outward call of the gospel was combined with the effectual call of the Spirit. In the first half of the seventeenth century, theologians tended to define the term "effectual calling" in such a way as to include regeneration. This is reflected in the "Westminster Confession of Faith," which has a chapter on effectual calling[14] but no chapter on regeneration. In the later seventeenth century, for example, in John Owen, a clearer distinction was made between effectual calling and regeneration, with much more stress being placed on the latter.[15] The general shape of the *ordo salutis* was thus clarified. It was argued that effectual calling produces regeneration. Faith, as the first fruit of regeneration, came next; the *ordo salutis* then divided into two streams. On the one hand, faith led to justification and adoption, thus dealing with the sinner's relationship to God; on the other hand, faith led to repentance and sanctification, thus dealing with the sinner's inner condition.

Internal debates occasioned some of the discussions about the *ordo salutis* in seventeenth-century Reformed theology. For example, Jacobus Arminius and the Remonstrants wanted to put faith before regeneration in order to emphasize the human decision, as over against the Reformed view that regeneration must precede faith in order to emphasize *sola gratia*. It is in this context that Berkouwer refers to Arminianism as "this particular over-estimation of faith as a spiritual achievement."[16]

13. R. A. Muller, *Christ and the Decree: Christology and Predestination in Reformed Theology from Calvin to Perkins* (Durham, NC: Labyrinth, 1986), 96.

14. See "Westminster Confession of Faith," ch. 10.

15. John Owen, *The Works*, ed. W. H. Goold, 16 vols. (London: Banner of Truth, 1966), 3:188–366.

16. Berkouwer, *Faith and Justification*, 87.

This is only one example of the many variations among Reformed scholars on the *ordo salutis*. A more recent example concerns the disagreement between the Dutch theologians Abraham Kuyper, Herman Bavinck, and G. C. Berkouwer. Kuyper taught that justification was from eternity, in order to stress the priority of grace. Berkouwer sums up Kuyper's position thus: "If justification is a divine act of grace which no human merit can achieve, then it must also precede faith . . . as eternity 'precedes' time."[17] Kuyper's argument is that justification is from eternity by grace but is "appropriated" in time through faith. Bavinck rejected this theory of eternal justification because, he argued, it is not taught in Scripture and could be used in respect of many other doctrines as well.[18] He did, however, want to affirm with Kuyper that "all the benefits of the covenant of grace are established in eternity."[19] Berkouwer later comments, "This concept of eternal justification reveals how a speculative logic can invade a scriptural proclamation of salvation and torture it beyond recognition. This is the danger of an apparently consistent logical process which at first imperceptibly and then quite finally estranges itself from scriptural reality."[20] He concludes by agreeing with Bavinck in rejecting Kuyper's notion of eternal justification and does so in quite strong terms: "He who allows justification and redemption to ascend out of time into eternity is never again able to avoid the fatal conclusion that everything occurring in time merely formalizes or illustrates what has been molded in eternal quietness. Even the terrible reality of the cross is swallowed in the deep, still waters of eternity."[21] The concept of the *ordo salutis*, then, was developed in post-Reformation theology, although the precise "order" of the doctrines varied considerably from scholar to scholar.

Justification in the *ordo salutis*

We must now turn more specifically to the place that has been given to justification in the *ordo salutis*. In general, we can say that justification has been regarded by most scholars as following upon faith, which in turn is brought about by effectual calling and/or regeneration. There

17. Ibid., 145.

18. For an overview of Bavinck's views on the *ordo salutis*, see R. Gleason, "Did Herman Bavinck Teach an '*ordo salutis*' in His Theology?" http://www.riforma.net/storia/bavinck/Did%20Herman%20Bavinck%20Teach%20an%20Ordo%20Salutis.doc (accessed April 24, 2005).

19. Berkouwer, *Faith and Justification*, 147.

20. Ibid., 150.

21. Ibid., 151.

are, however, at least three significant issues on which Reformed theologians have been divided in relation to justification, namely, imputation, the nature of saving faith, and the place given to repentance.

Imputation

Justification was defined in forensic terms as the remission of sin and the imputation of righteousness, all of which in later Reformed theology was set in the context of a federal structure including a covenant of redemption, a covenant of works, and a covenant of grace. Just as the sin of Adam was imputed to all those whom he represented in the covenant of works, on the basis that he was their federal head, so the righteousness of Christ is imputed to all those whom he represents as federal head in the covenant of grace.

This matter of imputation is vital to any proper understanding of the Reformed view of justification. Indeed, the very nature of the imputation became a significant issue. This is demonstrated by the way in which the confessional documents present the doctrine of justification. More specifically, it is highlighted by the way in which the "Savoy Declaration" differs from the "Westminster Confession of Faith" on the issue of imputation. The "Savoy Declaration" is, on most matters, almost identical to the "Westminster Confession," on which it was based. On justification, however, there is an interesting difference.

Note first of all this section from the "Westminster Confession" statement on justification:

> Those whom God effectually calleth, he also freely justifieth: not by infusing righteousness into them, but by pardoning their sins, and by accounting and accepting their persons as righteous; not for any thing wrought in them, or done by them, but for Christ's sake alone; not by imputing faith itself, the act of believing, or any other evangelical obedience to them, as their righteousness; but by imputing *the obedience and satisfaction of Christ unto them*, they receiving and resting on him and his righteousness by faith; which faith they have not of themselves, it is the gift of God.[22]

When we come to the statement on justification in the "Savoy Declaration," however, one part has been changed and expanded. As Alan Clifford puts it, "Through alterations proposed by John Owen, the teaching on imputation became even more explicit."[23]

22. From "Westminster Confession," ch. 11, sec. 1 (emphasis mine).
23. A. C. Clifford, *Calvinus* (Norwich, UK: Charenton Reformed, 1996), 83.

Those whom God effectually calleth, he also freely justifieth; not by infusing righteousness into them, but by pardoning their sins, and by accounting and accepting their persons as righteous; not for anything wrought in them, or done by them, but for Christ's sake alone; nor by imputing faith itself, the act of believing, or any other evangelical obedience to them, as their righteousness; but by imputing *Christ's active obedience to the whole law, and passive obedience in his death for their whole and sole righteousness*, they receiving and resting on him and his righteousness by faith; which faith they have not of themselves, it is the gift of God.[24]

This was not an alteration that all Reformed scholars accepted. William Cunningham, for example, in discussing this issue, pointed out that it was not to be found in the writings of Calvin:

It is to be traced rather to the more minute and subtle speculations, to which the doctrine of justification was afterwards subjected; and though the distinction is quite in accordance with the analogy of faith, and may be of use in aiding the formation of distinct and definite conceptions,—it is not of any great practical importance and need not be much pressed or insisted on, if men heartily and intelligently ascribe their forgiveness and acceptance wholly to what Christ has done and suffered in their room and stead. There is no ground in anything Calvin has written for asserting, that he would have denied or rejected this distinction, if it had been presented to him. But it was perhaps more in accordance with the cautious and reverential spirit in which he usually conducted his investigations into divine things, to abstain from any minute and definite statements regarding it.[25]

No matter which position is taken on the issue of the imputation of the active and passive obedience of Christ, however, one thing is clear: imputation is at the very heart and center of the Reformed understanding of justification.

Faith

Another issue that Reformed theologians have debated in their thinking about justification is the nature of saving faith and the location of faith in the *ordo salutis*. In general, Reformed theologians have taught that faith is the formal or instrumental cause of justification and is not in itself meritorious. That is to say, faith is not something that sinners bring to God from out of themselves, in exchange for which God justifies

24. From "Westminster Confession," ch. 11, sec. 1 (emphasis mine).
25. W. Cunningham, *The Reformers and the Theology of the Reformation* (Edinburgh: Banner of Truth, 1967), 404.

them. Rather, faith is a free gift of God, by the instrumentality of which justification is obtained.

Some Reformed theologians have also been concerned lest the significance of faith be lost by regarding it simply as another step in the *ordo salutis*. Berkouwer, for example, expresses the concern in this way:

> If the *ordo salutis* were really intended to be a straight line drawn through a sequence of causal factors it would be open to the same objections that we have against the Roman Catholic concept of the function of faith as a preparatory phase preceding justification or infused grace. Reformation theology has always protested that faith thus loses its central and total character and becomes a mere step on the way of salvation. In contrast to this devaluation of faith, the Reformation confessed *sola fide*, meaning thereby to emphasize the universal significance of faith. In this way faith possesses no unique functional value; it rests wholly in God's grace. Theological study of the *way of salvation*, or *ordo salutis*, must, then, always revolve about the correlation between faith and justification. It must simply cut away everything which blocks its perspective of this *sola fide*. Heresy always invades the *ordo salutis* at this point, and this is why it is so necessary to realize that the entire *way of salvation* is only meant to illuminate *sola fide* and *sola gratia*. For only thus can it be confessed that *Christ is the way*.[26]

He underlines this point and concludes by stressing that "it is perpetually necessary for the Church to reflect on the *ordo salutis*, or, as we think better to say on the *way of salvation*. The purpose of her reflection is not to refine and praise the logical systematization. It is to cut off every way in which Christ is not confessed exclusively as *the Way*."[27]

We can now take the argument a step further and say that the righteousness of Christ is imputed through the instrumentality of faith, a faith that is not itself meritorious and that exists only because of God's grace.

Repentance

In formulating its understanding of the place of justification in the *ordo salutis*, Reformed theology has often been divided over the place of repentance. There were some Scottish theologians, for example, who argued that repentance was a condition of salvation and therefore must come before justification in the *ordo salutis*.[28]

26. Berkouwer, *Faith and Justification*, 32–33.
27. Ibid., 36.
28. Principal James Hadow of St. Mary's College of the University of St. Andrews took this view during the "Marrow Controversy" in the early 1800s. See the discussion

There have been Reformed theologians who wanted to put repentance before justification in the *ordo salutis* but who would certainly not regard justification as conditional upon repentance. Robert Reymond, for example, argues on scriptural grounds that repentance comes before justification.[29] His *ordo* is this: effectual calling, regeneration, repentance unto life, faith in Jesus Christ, justification, definitive sanctification, adoption (and the Spirit's sealing), progressive sanctification, perseverance in holiness, and glorification.[30] Despite repentance coming before justification (and even faith), he is careful to insist that faith is the sole instrument of justification and that repentance is "not to be rested in as if it were itself a satisfaction for sin or the cause of pardon, for repentance *per se* is and can be neither."[31]

On the whole, however, Reformed theologians have viewed repentance as following upon justification as a result rather than going before it as a cause. Irrespective of the view taken on the place of repentance in the *ordo salutis*, however, Reformed theologians are at least in agreement that neither justification nor the faith that is its instrumental cause are occasioned by repentance, which must, rather, be regarded as a non-meritorious but necessary accompaniment to faith.

Union with Christ

As we now turn to consider the two schools of thought that, in their teaching concerning the application of redemption, have followed the union-with-Christ method as over against an *ordo salutis* method, it must not be imagined that the Reformed theologians of earlier centuries ignored this vital doctrine. We noted earlier the emphasis on effectual calling in early-seventeenth-century theology. We should also note that it was characteristic of these theologians to see effectual calling as that which unites believers to Christ. Heinrich Heppe writes, "At the root of the whole doctrine of the appropriation of salvation lies the doctrine of *insitio* or *insitio in Christum*, through which we live in him and he in us."[32] Heppe goes on to quote Witsius: "The goal to which we are called is Christ and communion with himself. . . . The result of this communion

---

in A. T. B. McGowan, *The Federal Theology of Thomas Boston* (Carlisle, UK: Paternoster, 1997), 168–84.

29. R. L. Reymond, *A New Systematic Theology of the Christian Faith*, 2nd ed. (Nashville: Thomas Nelson, 1998), 706.

30. Ibid., 711.

31. Ibid., 722.

32. H. Heppe, *Reformed Dogmatics* (London: Harper Collins, 1950), 511. I am grateful to my colleague Nick Needham for directing me to this section of Heppe.

is communion in all the benefits of Christ, in grace as well as in glory, to both of which alike we are called."[33]

Similarly, Owen among the English Puritans and Thomas Boston among the Scottish covenant theologians are good examples of scholars who gave due emphasis to union with Christ. Owen followed in the general line of those we have noted above. "For Owen, then, such order as there is in the *ordo salutis* would seem to be: Effectual Calling; Regeneration; Faith; Repentance; Justification; Adoption; and Sanctification."[34] Yet Owen could speak about union with Christ as "the sole fountain of our blessedness."[35] His understanding was that this union took place by the indwelling of the Holy Spirit through effectual calling.[36] This was a very significant element in his overall understanding of the *ordo salutis*. Ferguson sums up Owen's position in this way: "Thus divine election, and the outworking of it through the *ordo salutis* find their meeting place in *union with Christ*. This union, and all aspects of the plan of salvation are, for Owen, the application and fruit of the covenant of grace. To become a Christian is therefore to be taken into covenant with God in Christ, by the Holy Spirit."[37]

Boston was an orthodox covenant theologian who developed the *ordo salutis* in line with Calvinist theology and understood the place of justification accordingly. He argued that effectual calling leads to regeneration, which in turn produces faith, by which we are justified. Nevertheless, he placed such emphasis upon union with Christ as to be able to say,

> It is the leading, comprehensive, fundamental privilege of believers, 1 Cor. iii.23. 'Ye are Christ's.' All their other privileges are derived from and grafted upon this, their justification, adoption, sanctification, and glorification. All these grow on this root; and where that is wanting, none of these can be. All acceptable obedience comes from the soul's union with Christ, John xv.4. Hence faith is the principal grace, as uniting us to Christ.[38]

Clearly, Boston saw no incompatibility between emphasizing an *ordo salutis* and at the same time recognizing that union with Christ is vital for salvation. For example, in another place Boston insists, "Union with Christ is the only way to sanctification."[39] He was also very clear in his

---

33. Ibid.

34. S. B. Ferguson, *John Owen on the Christian Life* (Edinburgh: Banner of Truth, 1987), 35.

35. Owen, *Works*, 11:336.

36. Ibid., 11:337–41.

37. Ferguson, *John Owen on the Christian Life*, 36.

38. Thomas Boston, *The Complete Works*, ed. S. McMillan, 12 vols. (London: William Tegg, 1853), 1:549.

39. Ibid., 2:9.

specifications as to the nature of this union with Christ. It was not an external union, such as might exist, for example, between a ruler and his subjects. Rather, it was an internal and spiritual union. He does not regard the benefits that flow from union with Christ as being like benefits that might be passed on to us externally but, rather, as benefits that flow because of the nature of the union. In seeking to explain this union and the benefits that accrue from it, he uses an illustration. The benefits we receive by union with Christ are not like those of the beggar who is thrown some money by a rich man but, rather, like those of a poor, debt-ridden widow who, by marrying the rich man, has her situation transformed.[40]

This view is shared by Berkhof, who writes, "Since the believer is 'a new creature' (2 Cor. 5:17), or is 'justified' (Acts 13:39) only in Christ, union with Him logically precedes both regeneration and justification by faith, while yet, chronologically, the moment when we are united with Christ is also the moment of our regeneration and justification."[41]

We must recognize, however, that although these scholars gave a place (sometimes a significant place) to union with Christ, they did so without any intended critique of the *ordo salutis* method. Those we are now to consider place emphasis upon union with Christ with the clear theological intention of raising questions about the validity of the *ordo salutis* method.

Union with Christ in Neoorthodoxy

On the basis of his christological approach to theology, Karl Barth views the application of redemption from the perspective of Christ rather than from the perspective of the individual human being. He does not regard justification, adoption, sanctification, and so on as a series of separate but connected events or processes in the life of the believer. Instead he emphasizes that all of these blessings come to human beings as a direct result of their being united to Christ.[42] Barth was particularly concerned that the relation between justification and sanctification should be properly understood.[43]

For Barth, questions such as whether regeneration precedes effectual calling, or whether justification has a logical priority over regeneration, are largely irrelevant. For him, all of these are embodied in Christ, and

40. Ibid., 1:545. I am grateful to my colleague Noel Due for pointing me to an almost identical passage in his beloved Luther: Martin Luther, *Three Treatises* (Philadelphia: Fortress, 1966), 286–87.
41. Berkhof, *Systematic Theology*, 450.
42. *CD* IV/3.2:520–54.
43. *CD* IV/2:499–511.

we come to share in all of them as we are united with Christ. In this context, it is interesting to note the recently published lectures of Barth on the "Reformed Confessions," lectures that date from the very earliest days of his academic career.[44] In them Barth touches upon the *ordo salutis* in the "Westminster Confession of Faith." His objection is not the same as that of later Barthians, who have argued that the "Westminster Confession" puts predestination at the head of the *ordo* and works out everything logically from there.[45] Rather, Barth's objection is that, by placing such a heavy emphasis upon the application of redemption and upon the means by which the individual believer finds peace and assurance, it seeks "to make Reformed theology into anthropology."[46] He asks, "Why could the successors of John Knox celebrate the Pyrrhic victory of Puritanism in the Westminster Confession so that they gave up their Scots Confession and exchanged the idea of the 'holy city' for the deficient idea of the 'order of salvation,' the theology of the assurance of salvation?"[47]

T. F. Torrance followed the main tenets of Barth's theology in this matter of union with Christ, as in other areas, although preferring to call himself an Athanasian rather than a Barthian! As Duncan Rankin has demonstrated, however, there is a significant difference between Torrance and Barth in their developed positions.[48] Torrance built his theology around two separate notions of union with Christ: first, an incarnational (or carnal) union, which is with all humanity by the very act of incarnation, and, second, a spiritual union that is only between Christ and believers. It is not at all clear how one moves from the first union to the second or indeed (given that Torrance is not a universalist) how unbelievers fall out of the first union. The key point for our discussion, however, is that the union itself is presented in such a way as to obviate the need for a forensic explanation of the atonement.

The position is outlined with considerable clarity by Trevor Hart, who argues that both traditional Protestant theology and traditional Catholic theology have made the mistake of understanding salvation as the application of "benefits."[49] In contrast to this, he argues, we must see salvation in terms of our union with Christ, who has already, in the

44. Karl Barth, *The Theology of the Reformed Confessions* (Louisville: Westminster John Knox, 2002).
45. See Torrance, "Strengths and Weaknesses of the Westminster Theology."
46. Ibid., 151.
47. Ibid., 151–52.
48. See W. D. Rankin, "Carnal Union with Christ in the Theology of T. F. Torrance" (Ph.D. thesis, University of Edinburgh, 1997).
49. Trevor Hart, "Humankind in Christ and Christ in Humankind: Salvation as Participation in Our Substitute in the Theology of John Calvin," *Scottish Journal of Theology* 42 (1989): 67–84.

incarnation, taken up sinful human flesh, united it with the divine, and purified it from all sin. When we are united to Christ, we share in that reconciled and purified humanity.[50]

In Barth, Torrance, and Hart, then, justification is not conceived of in forensic terms, involving the imputation of the righteousness of Christ and the nonimputation of sin, but, rather, in terms of the participation in, and the sharing of, Christ's righteousness.

Union with Christ in Westminster Calvinism

We now turn to the second group of theologians who have focused attention on union with Christ rather than on the traditional *ordo salutis* method. We must keep in mind the trenchant criticism that McCormack applied to the Barthian scholars who did likewise. We must ask whether, in taking this position, these Westminster Seminary theologians have somehow managed to maintain forensic justification including the nonimputation of sin and the imputation of the righteousness of Christ.

From the influence of Gerhardus Vos and John Murray, there gradually developed within Westminster Theological Seminary (WTS) an approach to the application of redemption that seeks to draw together strands of the two positions considered so far. There is indeed an emphasis upon the union-with-Christ method, but there is also a commitment to forensic justification including the imputation of Christ's righteousness.

To understand how this position holds together, we must consider an important work by Richard Gaffin. Originally a doctoral dissertation submitted to WTS under the title "Resurrection and Redemption: A Study in Pauline Soteriology," in 1969, it was published in 1978 as *The Centrality of the Resurrection*.[51] Gaffin argues that the key element in understanding Paul's soteriology is the resurrection of Christ and that a redemptive-historical outlook is "decidedly dominant and determinative."[52] He argues that it is not possible to understand either the accomplishment or the application of redemption without focusing on the union between Christ and believers in resurrection. The resurrection of believers is entirely dependent upon Christ's resurrection, both historically (already realized) and eschatologically (we will be raised).[53]

---

50. These themes are also explored in several of the essays contained in Trevor Hart and Daniel Thimmell, eds., *Christ in Our Place: The Humanity of God in Christ for the Reconciliation of the World* (Carlisle, UK: Paternoster, 1989).

51. Richard Gaffin, *The Centrality of the Resurrection: A Study in Paul's Soteriology* (Grand Rapids: Baker, 1978).

52. Ibid., 135.

53. Ibid., 60.

On the basis of this study, Gaffin argues that the traditional *ordo salutis* ought to be revisited. In particular he raises three problems with the traditional *ordo salutis*. First, he notes the failure to take seriously the eschatological perspective of the Pauline doctrine: "The traditional *ordo salutis* lacks the exclusively eschatological air which pervades the entire Pauline soteriology."[54] Second, he points out that the various elements in the *ordo salutis* are traditionally regarded as separate acts, which he regards as a serious mistake: "Nothing distinguishes the traditional *ordo salutis* more than its insistence that the justification, adoption and sanctification which occur at the inception of the application of redemption are separate acts. If our interpretation is correct, Paul views them not as distinct acts but as distinct aspects of a single act."[55] Gaffin emphasizes this point by showing the difficulty the traditional method has in dealing with the relationship between the various doctrines in the *ordo salutis* and the doctrine of union with Christ. That is to say, if union with Christ comes before these various acts, then why are they necessary? If, on the other hand, union with Christ follows these other acts, does that not devalue its meaning and significance?

Gaffin's third issue in relation to the traditional *ordo salutis* concerns the prominent place given to regeneration and whether this is compatible with Paul's soteriology. His concern is whether a "distinct enlivening act (causally or temporally) prior to the initial act of faith" might actually constitute a "distortion of Paul's viewpoint."[56] He does not elaborate on this point, however, saying that it "brings us to the limits of this study,"[57] although he clearly believes it to be an important question for further work.

Gaffin's view has been very influential at WTS, and others have followed his line of reasoning, including Sinclair Ferguson, who writes, "Union with Christ must therefore be the dominant motif in any formulation of the application of redemption and the dominant feature of any 'order' of salvation."[58]

There is, however, a marked difference between the understanding of union with Christ as developed by Gaffin, Ferguson, and others and as developed by the neoorthodox theologians. As we saw in the previous section, particularly in Torrance and Hart, neoorthodoxy views union with Christ as an alternative to a forensic understanding of atonement with its key component of imputation. In Gaffin, Ferguson, and the WTS theologians, the forensic element is retained. The imputation of

54. Ibid., 137.
55. Ibid., 140.
56. Ibid., 142.
57. Ibid.
58. Ferguson, "Ordo salutis," 480–81.

the righteousness of Christ to believers remains a key element in their theology; it is simply that the means by which this imputation is effected is located in the prior doctrine of union with Christ.

This position has not gone unchallenged, related as it is to the development of John Murray's modified covenant theology, in which he argued against a legal "covenant of works" in favor of a gracious "Adamic administration." Meredith Kline and others, particularly Mark Karlberg, have argued that this failure to pursue a clear law/grace antithesis is a departure from Reformed theology and endangers the doctrine of justification, which they believe to be dependent upon this antithesis.[59] We do not have time to discuss this argument here, but it is interesting to note that Karlberg goes so far as to say that Murray, Norman Shepherd,[60] Gaffin, and Ferguson have moved toward a "Barthian" theology!

Summary and Conclusions

We have seen, then, that Reformed theology has characteristically dealt with the application of redemption in terms of an *ordo salutis*. Within this *ordo salutis*, justification has normally been placed after faith and before sanctification. Faith itself is seen as a gift of God, which is granted in effectual calling/regeneration. This is to ensure the priority of grace and to avoid any notion that justification could be earned or achieved by sinful human beings.

This schema, however, entails several difficulties. First, there is the difficulty of establishing the order in which the various doctrines are to be placed (based on very little direct scriptural evidence) and whether the sequence is logical or chronological. Second, there is the danger of viewing the various doctrines as mere steps in a sequence, which, having once begun, will continue until complete. Third and most significant, there is the problem of ascertaining the precise relationship between the steps in the *ordo salutis* and the act of God whereby he unites believers to Christ.

In order to avoid these difficulties, particularly the third, some modern Reformed theologians have largely abandoned the use of an *ordo salutis* method and opted instead to view the various doctrines in the *ordo salutis* not as a series of connected acts and processes but, rather, as aspects of union with Christ. We considered briefly two schools of thought within Reformed theology that have taken this approach, and

59. Mark W. Karlberg, *The Changing of the Guard: Westminster Theological Seminary in Philadelphia* (Unicoi, TN: Trinity Foundation, 2001).

60. The particular focus of Karlberg's argument is Norman Shepherd, *The Call of Grace* (Phillipsburg, NJ: P & R, 2000).

we have noted the differences between them. In particular, we noted the crucial difference, namely, that the neoorthodox understanding of union with Christ obviated the need for a clear forensic doctrine of the imputation of the righteousness of Christ. The WTS theologians, on the other hand, maintained both the doctrine of union with Christ, as the key to understanding the application of salvation, and a clear forensic doctrine of imputation.

In my view, we have a great deal to learn from Gaffin, Ferguson, and others in this regard. It is not necessary to abandon totally the concept of the *ordo salutis*. It may well be important to retain the concept in order to clarify the nature of the various doctrines and to guard against mistakes in the relationship posited between them.[61] Two things, however, are certainly clear: first, the doctrine of justification by faith cannot be properly and fully understood unless it is seen in the context of union with Christ; second, any understanding of justification that fails to maintain a forensic notion of the imputation of the righteousness of Christ cannot claim to be Reformed.

61. My colleague Noel Due has pointed out to me that this is precisely the method adopted in the "Heidelberg Catechism," where the various doctrines encompassed by the *ordo salutis* are set in the context of union with Christ. See qq. 32, 36, 55, 56, 59–61.

PART 3

The Protestant Doctrine of Justification

*Continuities and Discontinuities in Current
Challenges to the Traditional View*

8

Justitia aliena

Karl Barth in Conversation with the Evangelical Doctrine of Imputed Righteousness

Bruce L. McCormack

Introduction

Where does Karl Barth stand in the welter of conflicting views surrounding the doctrine of justification today? Does his doctrine of justification stand firmly in the stream of reflection upon that theme flowing from the Reformation—even while correcting the traditional Protestant account in important ways? Or do his corrections finally amount to a *break* with the Protestant tradition? Is Barth's doctrine more compatible, in the final analysis, with the contemporary accounts of justification emerging from within the so-called New Perspective in Pauline studies than it is with the doctrines of Luther and Calvin?

For some time I have been convinced of the need for a lengthy, well-considered treatment of Barth's relation to the New Perspective. Certainly, such a task would be a demanding one—all the more so given that we are not speaking of a single position when we speak of the New Perspective but of, rather, a variety of positions. Needless to say, I am not going to attempt anything quite so grand here.

But the question of where Barth stands in relation to the controversies of our day can be addressed in a preliminary way in relation to the claims of a single writer. And, really, it needs to be in light of the recent publication of Douglas Harink's *Paul among the Postliberals*.[1] Harink's book, it should be noted, is not about Karl Barth in the first instance. It asks what follows for systematic theology and ethics if, as Harink thinks, the Reformers were fundamentally in error in their understanding of Paul's theology and the representatives of the New Perspective are fundamentally right. But his first substantive chapter is devoted to the theme of justification, and in that context Karl Barth does indeed play a central role. Harink's claim is that Barth's doctrine of justification anticipated in all its essential features Harink's own version of Paul's teaching on this subject. Having reflected at some length on Harink's claim in the light of a fresh reading of the relevant materials in Barth, my conclusion is that it depends for its success on something of a caricature.

Though Harink does succeed in lifting up interesting parallels between Barth and some current versions of the doctrine of justification, his characterization of Barth's teaching on the subject is ultimately misleading as a consequence of three tendencies. The first tendency is to make the second edition of Barth's commentary on Romans to be the decisive source for elaborating Barth's doctrine. Scant attention is given to the *Church Dogmatics*. The second is a tendency to polemicize against the Reformation—with the result that Harink often presents his readers with either-or decisions that, for his part, Barth would have refused to make. To name but the most significant example: the sharp contrast that Harink sets up between, on the one hand, justification understood as an "objective" apocalyptic event in which God vindicates both the people of God and himself through the upholding of his covenant with Israel and, on the other hand, justification understood as a "subjective" event having to do with the standing of the individual before God invites the reader to make a decision for the former and against the latter. Barth's doctrine of justification has the virtue of showing precisely why this is a false alternative. And this observation leads to the third tendency. Harink tends to suppress anything in Barth's teaching that collides with the picture he draws. At the points where he does (rather grudgingly) acknowledge such elements, he quickly dismisses them on the grounds of inconsistency:

> In *Church Dogmatics*, as in *Römerbrief*, Barth continues . . . to work with the faith/works dichotomy (typically abstracted from its contingent context

1. Douglas Harink, *Paul among the Postliberals: Pauline Theology beyond Christendom and Modernity* (Grand Rapids: Brazos, 2003).

in the Pauline writings) as a way of protecting the priority of God's action. And in truly Protestant fashion, Barth seems to have far more to say and speculate about the character of "faith" than Paul was ever interested in doing. This, to my mind, runs not only against the grain of Paul's logic, but also against Barth's own best insights into the character of faith itself as a "work" and as obedience.[2]

In truth, however, Barth's appropriation of the Reformation doctrine is much too comprehensive and far too complete to allow for the judgment that it constitutes an inconsistency on his part.

My thesis, in what follows, is that—contra Harink—a relationship of shared interest exists between Karl Barth and today's defenders of classical Protestant teaching on justification. Granted, his doctrine is not precisely theirs. But the two are compatible on the most fundamental level. Again, this is not to deny the parallels that Harink is able to establish between Barth's teaching in *Romans* especially and some of the exegetical conclusions now emerging under the banner of the New Perspective on Paul. But these parallels touch only upon Barth's corrections of the Reformation doctrine; they do not offset in any way the still deeper-lying continuity that joins him to the Reformation. My argument will unfold in the following way. It begins with a discussion of John Calvin's doctrine of justification in the conviction that it was he, more than anyone else, who contributed to the final form of what most of us once learned to understand as the Protestant and "evangelical" view. The second section turns to Harink, outlining his objections to the classical Protestant doctrine, his alternative to it, and his use of Barth. The third section (which will constitute the bulk of the essay) turns to Barth, showing why he must finally be seen as an ally of the traditional Protestant and evangelical view in the context of today's debates.

The Traditional Evangelical Doctrine of Justification

The Protestant doctrine of justification did not emerge overnight, as it were, with Luther's theological "conversion." The doctrine that would eventually be enshrined in all the major Protestant confessions was the product of a fairly lengthy process of elaboration whose high point came with the Osiandrian controversy of 1551. It was only in the light of this controversy that the full ramifications of the emerging Protestant conception were seen—above all, by John Calvin—and the doctrine given

2. Ibid., 54, n. 53.

its more finished form.[3] For this reason, Calvin will be our guide to the traditional doctrine.

Calvin's doctrine of justification is easily stated and unproblematic in itself. Problems have arisen in recent years regarding the proper interpretation of it only because issues touching upon its relation to other elements in his soteriology (e.g., union with Christ, regeneration, and sanctification) have so driven the discussion that the doctrine itself threatens to disappear from view.

For Calvin, justification is a *forensic* or legal concept. That is to say, it is a term that finds its home in the setting of a court trial. Its fundamental significance is that of vindication, a declaration of innocence with respect to a charge, an acquittal. And so Calvin says, "'to justify' means nothing else than to acquit of guilt him who was accused, as if his innocence were confirmed."[4] The "as if" of this statement is necessitated by the fact that the accused, in this case, is the sinner, who in himself or herself is anything but innocent of the charge. God is the just Judge, who must judge rightly if God is to remain faithful to himself. What, then, happens?

> Justified by faith is he who, excluded from the righteousness of works, grasps the righteousness of Christ through faith, and clothed in it, appears in God's sight not as a sinner but as a righteousness man. Therefore, we explain justification simply as the acceptance with which God receives us into his favor as righteous men. And we say that it consists in the remission of sins and the imputation of Christ's righteousness.[5]

Justification has two principal parts—a negative nonimputation of guilt and, corresponding to it, a positive imputation of Christ's righteousness. Closer investigation shows that these two parts stand in an ordered relation to each other. It is the positive imputation of Christ's righteousness that grounds—and even necessitates, once the decision has been made by God to do it—the remission of sins. So the just Judge

---

3. For a sketch of this development in greater detail, see Bruce L. McCormack, "What's at Stake in Current Debates over Justification? The Crisis of Protestantism in the West," in *Justification: What's at Stake in the Current Debates*, ed. Mark Husbands and Daniel J. Treier (Downers Grove, IL: InterVarsity, 2004), 96–103. A word should be said here about the relation of the present essay to the one cited here. In the earlier essay, I was not engaged in an exposition of Barth's doctrine as is the case here. Rather, I was asking myself what an *evangelical* doctrine might look like which—without abandoning the framework of assumptions within which it was first elaborated historically—sought to listen carefully to Karl Barth. Here I am no longer working strictly within that framework but seeking to engage Barth more directly within his own framework of assumptions so that the compatibility between the two might emerge more clearly.

4. John Calvin, *Institutes* III.xi.3.

5. Ibid., III.xi.2.

acts justly in that he forgives those whom he "clothes" with Christ's righteousness. Clothed with Christ's righteousness, covered by him, they are already in him what they are only gradually being made in themselves: the "new humanity." And on this basis, they are declared innocent even though as yet, in themselves, they are nothing of the sort. So much by way of definition.

That this quickly became the standard Protestant view may be ascertained by even the briefest perusal of the confessional documents written in the immediate aftermath of Calvin's careful work on the subject. Within the Reformed realm, the idea of the imputed righteousness—or, alternatively, the imputed obedience[6]—of Christ plays a prominent role in defining justification in the "French Confession" of 1559 (art. 18), the "Scots Confession" of 1560 (ch. 15), the "Belgic Confession" of 1561 (art. 23), the "Second Helvetic Confession" of 1566 (ch. 15), the "Heidelberg Catechism" of 1563 (q. 60),[7] and the "Westminster Confession of Faith" of 1647 (ch. 13).[8] On the Lutheran side, it plays a significant role in the "Formula of Concord" of 1577.[9] And although John Wesley had some doubts about the idea of a positive imputation of Christ's righteousness—wondering whether the lack of an explicit use of the language in the New Testament did not serve to call the idea itself into question and worrying about whether the idea of imputation could be used as a "cloak that covers our own continuing unrighteousness"[10]—he did finally affirm it as sound teaching.[11]

One final word on Calvin's doctrine of justification will be of utmost importance when we come to an evaluation of Barth: the theological concern that comes to expression in Calvin's insistence upon a positive imputation of Christ's righteousness is that the ground or basis for our justification is to be found in the "alien" righteousness of Christ and in

6. In Calvin's hands at least, the two phrases—"imputed righteousness" and "imputed obedience"—function as virtual synonyms. The link between the two is provided by his conviction, made clear in his debate with Osiander, that what is made ours by divine imputation is the "acquired righteousness" of Christ—i.e., that righteousness which is Christ's by virtue of his obedience unto death—as opposed to the "essential righteousness" which is proper to Christ's deity as such and which he, as the eternal Son, brings with him into the incarnate state. See ibid., III.xi.5.

7. See Arthur C. Cochrane, *Reformed Confessions of the 16th Century* (Philadelphia: Westminster, 1966), 150, 174, 204, 256, and 315.

8. Philip Schaff, ed., *The Creeds of Christendom*, 3 vols. (Grand Rapids: Baker, 1990), 3:626.

9. *Epitome* 3.2, in *The Book of Concord: The Confessions of the Evangelical Lutheran Church*, ed. and trans. Theodore G. Tappert (Philadelphia: Fortress, 1959), 473.

10. Kenneth J. Collins, *The Scripture Way of Salvation: The Heart of John Wesley's Theology* (Nashville: Abingdon, 1997), 93.

11. From John Wesley's sermon "The Lord Our Righteousness" (1765), in *The Works* (Grand Rapids: Baker, 1996), 5:237.

that alone. And the pastoral concern that comes to expression in it is that if we find the ground for our justification in something God is doing in us—we do not have to go to the extreme of finding it in something we do (so-called works righteousness) but *even if only* in something God is doing in us—then we will have effectively undermined Christian assurance. For God's work "in us" is never complete in this life. It knows of periods of growth and flourishing, but it also knows of periods of extreme aridity. If we were to look to ourselves for our assurance, all would be lost. As Calvin puts it in the "French Confession," we must "rest simply in the obedience of Christ which is imputed to us." For "we could not find rest elsewhere, but should always be troubled. . . . We are never at peace with God till we resolve to be loved in Jesus Christ, for of ourselves we are worthy of hatred."[12] When we turn to Barth, the question we will need to be asking ourselves is this: Can Barth do justice to both of these concerns—the theological and the pastoral—even if he does not employ the concept of a positive imputation of Christ's righteousness in precisely the same way and within the same framework of assumptions? But before undertaking this task, we will summarize briefly the charge that Harink has brought against the traditional Protestant doctrine of justification, his alternative to it, and his reading of Barth's doctrine.

Harink's Critique of the Traditional Protestant Conception and His Alternative

According to Douglas Harink, the Protestant and evangelical notion that an individual must have faith in Jesus Christ in order to be saved rests upon a foundation that was first laid in Luther's mistaken translation of the phrase *pistis Christou Iēsou* in Galatians 2:16.[13] The genitives found in this passage are rightly understood as subjective rather than objective genitives—meaning that it is not our faith *in* Christ but, rather, the faith *of* Christ, *his* faithfulness to God on behalf of God's people, that justifies. Where this mistranslation held sway, justification was wrongly conceived of as "an inner and individual matter."[14] Moreover, the doctrine built upon this foundation assumed a degree of centrality for Protestant theology that it did not possess for the apostle Paul.[15] Paul is able to tell the story of his conversion, for example, without any reference to the dialectic of law and gospel, the contrast of faith and works, or even his

12. Cochrane, *Reformed Confessions of the 16th Century*, 150.
13. Harink, *Paul among the Postliberals*, 26–27.
14. Ibid., 25.
15. Ibid.

own personal faith in Jesus Christ.[16] Nor does Paul's earliest articulation of his gospel (1 Thessalonians) display any worries over "works righteousness," thus demonstrating that he did not have an automatic reflex toward discussion of the relation of faith and works and could indeed give an account of the gospel without it.[17] In truth, Harink says, "Paul attacks only 'works of law' or 'works' when Gentile believers . . . wished to take Torah observance upon themselves (to come 'under Torah') as a necessary completion of their justification or when anyone else . . . wished to require Torah observance of Gentile believers as a necessary completion of their justification."[18] And since this issue did not arise for Paul in every one of the churches he founded, justification (as one way, among others, of speaking of God's action in Christ) was not a theme that was central to all of his epistles.

For Harink, justification or, as he prefers, "rectification" is an objective act of God. It is

> the definitive, apocalyptic act of the one God of Israel in Jesus Christ, whereby this God, through the death and resurrection of the Faithful One, conquers the powers which hold the nations in bondage and reconciles the world to Himself in order that he might create in Christ a new people, indeed, finally, a whole new world, in which loyalty, obedience and faithfulness to the one God of Israel is made possible among the nations in the power of the Holy Spirit. In this way, God demonstrates His own justice, that is, His faithfulness to the promise which he made to Abraham to bless not only Israel but also the nations and so too the whole creation.[19]

"Justification" is not an answer to the monk's question "How do I [as an individual] lay hold of a gracious God?" In truth, it is not really about the individual's relationship to God at all. Justification is, rather, a question of how the God of Israel sets right the relation of Israel (and of Gentile Christians) to the nations; it is a question of how God vindicates himself through the vindication of the people of God, thereby dethroning the false gods of the surrounding nations. "Participation" in all of this is understood as taking place through baptism. In baptism, we are "united" to Christ in his death and resurrection—a concept that Harink construes in terms of being brought into conformity to the pattern of obedience found in Jesus' faithfulness.[20] Through our faithful living in

16. Ibid., 30–32.
17. Ibid., 32–38.
18. Ibid., 39.
19. Ibid., 44.
20. Ibid., 42.

all of its dimensions, we demonstrate ourselves to be the people of the one true God.

It is understandable that Harink should have begun, in the appeal to Barth that immediately follows this sketch of Paul's doctrine of rectification, with the justly famous second edition of Barth's commentary on Romans. Harink is, after all, interested in the relationship between Paul and Barth. And it is here that he finds the richest source of parallels. The "overriding theme of Barth's entire commentary," he says, is the destruction of all idolatry through the "irruptive, disruptive even destructive apocalypse of Jesus Christ," which brings about the "eradication of all human pretensions of having God in hand and the world under control."[21] The doctrine of justification is interpreted, in turn, through the lens provided by this central concern.[22]

> By connecting the gospel of justification with the criticism of idolatry, Barth anticipates one of our key findings about Paul's message to the nations: justification, that is the rectification of the nations, is in the first place about the first commandment, the exclusive priority of the one God of Israel, not only for Israel but for the nations of the world. Barth emphasizes, with Paul, that God's revelation in Jesus Christ is *God's apocalyptic triumph* over all the enslaving powers and gods of this world, a triumph that in turn delivers idolaters (for Barth, that means all of humankind) from the imprisonment to these other, finally immanent and impotent, powers and gods. Precisely so, it is also a demonstration of God's faithfulness.[23]

Harink does find a certain "abstractness" in Barth's handling of his apocalyptic theme.[24] Barth's translation of *pistis Christou Iēsou* in Romans 3:22 as "through his [God's] faithfulness in Jesus Christ" lacks something of the concreteness of Christ's faithfulness, in his view. But he notes that Barth takes up the theme of Christ's faithfulness in Romans 5:18–19, especially where he "speaks of Christ as 'the new subject, the EGO of the coming world. This EGO receives and bears and reveals the divine *justification* and election. . . .' Noteworthy here is Barth's claim that Christ is the one toward whom God's justification is directed in the first place. . . . Sinful humanity is justified only because God first

---

21. Ibid., 47.

22. Ibid., 50: "In Barth as in Paul the language and meaning of justification and faith is consistently subsumed within this unreserved apocalyptic horizon. Barth sees that justification is simply another way of saying that in the cross and resurrection God puts to death the whole cosmos and raises it again from the dead. Justification is about God's deed of new creation."

23. Ibid., 47–48.

24. Ibid.

justifies Jesus."[25] If Barth's treatment of justification in *Romans* suffers from a weakness, it lies in the fact that Barth was so preoccupied with overcoming the psychologizing of pietists and liberals that he failed to show "how the shape of Jesus' faithful obedience might provide a visible, normative pattern for the concrete shape of the Christian life"[26]—but this, Harink thinks, is a problem that is remedied in the *Church Dogmatics*.

As he turns to the *Church Dogmatics*, Harink is confident that the most important decisions regarding the themes of justification and faith have already been made in *Romans*. Here, too, he says, "justification is wholly God's work, directed first towards Jesus Christ 'who lives as the author and recipient and revealer of the justification of man' (*Church Dogmatics* IV/1.629); in and through Jesus Christ humanity itself is wholly justified. Therefore, justification cannot be 'completed' or 'made effective' through human faith." Indeed, faith is now understood as a human "work"; "so how can it be thought to contribute to our justification?"[27] Barth moves beyond the position articulated in *Romans* in one respect only. He now is able to give greater room to the theme of the *imitatio Christi*—not as something that contributes to our justification but as that which brings us into conformity to the Christ who achieves it on our behalf.

Harink's account of Barth's doctrine of justification in its historical evolution fascinates not so much for what it says as for what it leaves unsaid. This is not the place to enter fully into his exposition of *Romans*; our focus must rather be directed to the *Church Dogmatics*. Suffice it to say that Harink's presentation of the thoroughly eschatological character of that commentary and its preoccupation with idolatry is right on the mark. His formulation of the central theme of the whole is largely sound, though elements emerge here and there in the commentary itself that are not easily reconciled with this formulation—inconsistencies around the edges, as it were. The most important of these jarring elements is the appearance of the language of acquittal in the midst of the apocalyptic horizon that Barth paints in such vivid colors in Romans 3:21–22a.[28] It is when we turn to Harink's handling of the *Church Dogmatics* that the problems begin to mount up.

Harink is absolutely right to ascribe to Barth the view that justification is complete in Jesus Christ. The individual's faith in Christ does not

---

25. Ibid., 51, citing Barth, *The Epistle to the Romans*, trans. Edwin C. Hoskyns (Oxford: Oxford University Press, 1933), 181.

26. Harink, *Paul among the Postliberals*, 52.

27. Ibid., 53.

28. Harink does seem to be aware of such inconsistencies, and the element of "acquittal" appears in a passage that he himself cites—suggesting that he could not have been unaware of it. See ibid., 46. Cf. Barth, *Epistle to the Romans*, 92.

add anything to it or even make it effective. But this in no way makes faith *in* Jesus Christ superfluous or unnecessary, in Barth's view. Nor does it mean that faith in Jesus Christ has no rightful place within the bounds of the Christian doctrine of justification. What Harink misses, as he turns from *Romans* to the *Church Dogmatics*, is the shift that takes place in the overarching frame of reference within which justification is treated. In contrast to the approach taken in *Romans*, Barth's treatment of the doctrine of justification in the *Church Dogmatics*—like his treatment of the atoning work of Christ—takes place within a *forensic* framework.[29] This is why Barth's treatment of justification in the *Church Dogmatics* fairly bristles—as we shall see—with language drawn from the courtroom.

Even more important, the "trial" that is in view here is not concerned directly but, at most, indirectly with the charge brought by the surrounding nations against Israel (and Gentile Christians)—namely, that their God is not the true God. The priorities that governed Barth's exposition in *Romans* have here been reversed. God's act of self-vindication in Jesus Christ takes the form of a judicial verdict that is directed not to the nations in the first instance but to the "man of sin" who has broken the covenant.[30] In Jesus Christ, God vindicates himself through the condemnation and destruction of this "man" and the wholly just acceptance of the new and obedient "man" in his place.

But the doctrine of justification is not complete when it has touched only upon what has taken place for us in Christ. It must also concern itself with the faith of the individual, which recognizes and accepts as true and valid the justifying sentence of God in both its negative and positive significance (as condemnation and as acquittal). "How do I lay hold of a gracious God?" is not the only question to be asked in Christian soteriology, Barth says, but it is an inescapable one.[31] And why is

---

29. Although the atonement is not a theme to which Harink gives sustained attention, it is probably significant that the few remarks he makes about it have a decidedly Abelardian tilt. Harink could almost get away with this where *Romans* is concerned, but the *Church Dogmatics* is a completely different matter. Barth first came under the influence of Anselm after his move to Göttingen in 1921 (and therefore after the completion of the second edition of *Romans*), and from that point on, his thinking about the twin themes of atonement and justification was carried out within a judicial or forensic frame of reference. It should be noted that Barth was quite explicit about this in the *Church Dogmatics*. See *CD* IV/1:274. For a discussion of Barth's appropriation of the traditional Protestant/evangelical penal-substitution theory of the atonement, see Bruce L. McCormack, "The Ontological Presuppositions of Barth's Doctrine of the Atonement," in *The Glory of the Atonement: Biblical, Theological, and Practical Perspectives*, ed. Charles E. Hill and Frank A. James (Downers Grove, IL: InterVarsity, 2004), 346–66.

30. *CD* IV/1:94.

31. *CD* IV/1:108.

the faith of the individual not superfluous or unnecessary? Because it is the form that the human response to the work of God in Christ must take insofar as this work consists in a justifying sentence[32]—just as that response must take the form of love insofar as this work consists in the divine direction given to human life in this world (sanctification)[33] and the form of hope insofar as this work consists in the calling to be a witness to the divine promise of eternal life (vocation).[34] And because there is no such thing as a genuine obedience apart from the faith *in* Jesus Christ from which it takes its rise. To play off faith against obedience, as Harink is inclined to do, as though the former is only and always a "work" in the negative sense of that term while the latter stands alone as the only proper response to a justification that is complete and effective in Christ, is to miss Karl Barth's doctrine. In the final analysis, the kinds of change that would have to be effected in Barth's doctrine of reconciliation as a result of Harink's reading of it would not be merely cosmetic. Indeed, it would ultimately have to be revised in its entirety.

A close examination of Barth's doctrine of justification will now demonstrate the truth of these assertions.

Karl Barth's Doctrine of Justification

Traditional evangelicals will likely find it a bewildering experience coming to Barth's treatment of the Christian life for the first time. It is as if they were traveling over a familiar stretch of road. All of the landmarks long known to them are there. But somehow the landmarks do not appear in the right places. Nothing is quite where it is supposed to be. And the longer they seek to solve the riddle created by this sensation, the landmarks themselves seem to undergo slight changes in their appearance, making these evangelicals wonder whether they were right to think they were traveling over familiar ground in the first place. For traditional evangelicals seeking to come to grips with Barth, what produces this bewilderment and confusion is what appears to them to be a loss of "realized eschatology" in Barth's treatment of the Christian life. They will want to ask: Is there no justification of individuals in the here and now of their lives, no divine declaration pronounced on them in a moment in their own history? And is there no experience corresponding to this divine declaration with respect to these individuals, no realiza-

32. *CD* IV/1:93–99.
33. *CD* IV/1:99–107.
34. *CD* IV/1:108–22.

tion of righteousness in their lives, no "impartation" of righteousness to them individually, as ones who stand before God?

Let me concede here at the outset that there is good reason for this experience of bewilderment. It is not the case that the traditional evangelicals' sense of Barth's doctrine is altogether wrong—far from it, though the conclusions they are likely to draw on the basis of it will be premature and ultimately wrong. For it is not as though there is no "realized eschatology" whatsoever in Barth's treatment of the Christian life—though his tendency to describe it in sharply paradoxical statements and by means of dramatic images makes it difficult for the evangelical to recognize it. What is ultimately at stake in the differences between the traditional evangelical doctrine of justification and Barth's doctrine of justification, however, is a difference on the level of the theological ontology that is entailed in each. Most evangelicals (and this includes those who would consider themselves "progressive") will not think the problems through this far; indeed, most specialists in Barth's theology never think the problems through this far. But it is, in fact, on the level of theological ontology that the real divergence takes place.

The question is this: does the existence of a substantial difference on the level of theological ontology render impossible the existence of a tremendous amount of shared theological and pastoral concern between traditional evangelicals and Barth on this head of doctrine? My own answer is no. Barth's doctrine, while not "evangelical" in the widely accepted Anglo-American meaning of the term today, is most certainly Protestant—not Orthodox, not Catholic, but *Protestant*. It is even *radically* Protestant. But precisely in its radicality, it never loses contact with the concerns (theological and pastoral) which motivated Calvin, especially, in the formulations of his doctrine.

Some Formal Definitions and Relations

For Karl Barth, the word "justification" is a term that is rightly employed to describe the *whole* of the reconciling activity of the triune God (including both "objective" and "subjective" soteriology). Employed in this way, the only comparable terms in his theology are "sanctification" and "vocation."[35] These terms, too, describe the whole of the reconciling activity of God. So, when we turn to a consideration of "sanctification,"

---

35. In his *Church Dogmatics*, Barth treats these three "aspects" of the doctrine of reconciliation in three distinct movements of thought that are to be found in §61 (justification), §66 (sanctification), and §71 (vocation). I will not be discussing "vocation" here but will confine my attention to the relation of the two terms that, since the Reformation, have been most under discussion in Protestant circles—"justification" and "sanctification."

for example, we are not dealing "with a second divine action to be placed alongside of justification, preceding or following it temporally. The action of God in His reconciliation of the world with Himself in Jesus Christ is a single action."[36] Justification and sanctification are "two different aspects of the one saving event."[37]

Here already an important difference from the traditional evangelical view announces itself. Barth takes 1 Corinthians 1:30 with a degree of seriousness hitherto unseen in the Protestant tradition. That text reads, "He [God] is the source of your life in Christ Jesus, who became for us wisdom from God, and righteousness and sanctification and redemption."[38] "Justification" is something that takes place in Jesus Christ, in his death and resurrection. Only because and insofar as it takes place in him is it effective "for us." Seen in this light, it is important that we should avoid setting up "a dualism between an objective procuring of salvation there and then and a subjective appropriation of salvation here and now."[39] For much of the Protestant tradition, "justification" could be regarded as taking place in Christ only in an improper sense. Actual justification, it was thought, occurs in the historical existence of the believer; what takes place in Christ provides only the basis for a further act of God in the present that is to be distinguished from it.[40] For Barth, this way of thinking fails to understand that *what Jesus Christ accomplishes is not merely the possibility of reconciliation but the reality of it.* Expressed even more concretely: justification is not first made effective when the Holy Spirit awakens faith in us; rather, the Spirit awakens faith in us so that we might live from and toward the reality of a justification that is already effective for us even before we come to know of it.[41] The traditional "dualism," Barth added, also overlooks "the simultaneity of

36. *KD* IV/2:567–68; *CD* IV/2:501. (As all the texts quoted from Barth's *Church Dogmatics* appear here in my own translations, I will cite them first from the German edition and then provide the corresponding place they can be found in the English translation—which will sometimes, though not always, make it clear why a fresh translation was desirable.)

37. *KD* IV/2:569; *CD* IV/2:503. Hans Küng's way of speaking of this is misleading: "Barth regards the all-encompassing event, which includes justification too, as reconciliation—the central work of God, standing between creation and consummation. Justification is only *one* aspect, if a vital one, of reconciliation." To put it this way is to take the word "aspect" (which Barth does indeed use) in a quantitative sense, as though justification were a *part* of the work of reconciliation. But this is precisely what Barth seeks to avoid. See Küng, *Justification: The Doctrine of Karl Barth and a Catholic Reflection* (Philadelphia: Westminster, 1981), 24.

38. All scriptural citations are from the New Revised Standard Version.

39. *KD* IV/2:569; *CD* IV/2:502–3.

40. John Murray, *Redemption Accomplished and Applied* (Grand Rapids: Eerdmans, 1955), 84–85.

41. A great deal hangs on this "from and toward." Its significance will be explained in the following section, "The Material Content of Barth's Doctrine of Justification."

the one work of salvation, whose Subject is the one God through the one Christ through the one Spirit—'being more closely (!) bound together than in a mathematical point.'"[42] In back of this reminder stands Barth's commitment to an understanding of the Trinity that will not allow the axiom *Opera trinitatis ad extra sunt indivisa* to be suppressed or set aside by a doctrine of appropriations. What God does may well be experienced by us as distinct events, but this does not mean that they are distinct in precisely the same way for God as well.

Barth's objection to the elaboration of a dualism between an objective accomplishment of salvation and its subjective appropriation is accompanied by a divergence from another traditional form of Protestant theology. Barth rejects the concept of an *ordo salutis*—or at least he does so to the extent that it is thought of as "a *temporal* succession [of acts] in which the Holy Spirit brings forth His effects . . . here and now in men."[43] Barth would not have disagreed that *some* sequencing in the *opera trinitatis ad extra* is necessary. For him, as for the tradition, divine acts that take place in eternity (election and glorification) come "before" and "after" those which take place in time. His scruples against the concept of an *ordo salutis* are directed strictly toward those elements believed traditionally to take place in time, in the life history of the believer. His objection has to do with the attempt to order into a temporal sequence the concepts of calling, regeneration, faith and repentance, justification, adoption, sanctification, and perseverance. And the concern that comes to expression in this objection has to do with the close proximity of this largely seventeenth-century discussion to the "psychologistic pragmatics" of much late-nineteenth- and early-twentieth-century theology: the ease with which what began as a discussion of the works of the Holy Spirit became instead a discussion of a series of awakenings, movements, actions—perhaps even "steps"!—of a religious and moral kind, which were alleged either to take place in the consciousness of the Christian or to be undertaken by the Christian.[44]

But it is not just that the rejection of dualism is *accompanied* by the rejection of the concept of an *ordo salutis*. This is correct as far as it goes, but it does not go far enough. I put it this way initially because this is how a good many of those influenced by Barth's critique of the concept of an *ordo salutis* have thought about it. And in thinking about it in this way, they have failed to see that Barth's rejection of dualism, his insistence on the unitary character of the reconciling work of the triune God as Jesus Christ and as Holy Spirit has *as its necessary consequence*

42. *KD* IV/2:569; *CD* IV/2:503.
43. *KD* IV/2:568; *CD* IV/2:502.
44. Ibid.

his critique of the concept of an *ordo salutis*. The latter follows the former as night follows day. And because this is so, it is not the case that Barth's objections to an *ordo salutis* can be adequately addressed simply by insisting that the distinctions are (largely) logical rather than chronological.[45] His insistence on the unitary character of the work of God in Christ and in the Holy Spirit means that the work of Christ *is* effective as such, that the work of the Spirit does not complete it or give to it an efficacy it does not otherwise have.[46] The work of Christ and the work of the Spirit belong to a *single* movement of God toward the creature, a movement that entails both the accomplishment of the work of Christ and the awakening of individuals to this accomplishment.

This does not mean that it will not still be necessary to order the "forensic" concepts (justification and adoption) to the "new humanity" concepts (regeneration, sanctification, and glorification). But such an ordering will no longer be seen as the ordering of *distinct acts* of God but as the ordering of two descriptions of a single divine activity. The concerns expressed in the traditional *ordo salutis* discussion, however, do not simply disappear in this view; rather, they are taken up into a new frame of reference. Barth does, in fact, devote considerable energy to thinking through the relation of justification to sanctification as two aspects of a single unified work.

Barth's thinking in this connection runs thus: if it is true that justification and sanctification take place in Jesus Christ in the first instance, then the locus for determining the relation between them has shifted

45. It is not at all uncommon to find Barth scholars who are happy to follow him in his rejection of an *ordo salutis* but who will then complain that they find in him an underdeveloped pneumatology. What such scholars fail to realize is that you cannot have Barth's critique of the traditional concept of an *ordo salutis* in the absence of his rejection of a dualism in the work of Christ and the Holy Spirit, for the latter is the ground of the former. When Barth says of the work of Christ that in it "our wrong has really and definitively become a thing of the past" or that "it is no longer there because it has been extinguished," such claims lead quite directly to the "underdevelopment" of which so many complain. See *KD* IV/2:617–18; *CD* IV/2:553. The issue here is this: Do we really believe that Christ accomplishes the *reality* of reconciliation? Or do we believe that what he accomplishes is merely the *possibility* of it? If we are willing to say the former, we should be a little more hesitant to join the throng of those complaining of an underdeveloped pneumatology in Barth.

46. Hans Küng's remark in this connection rests upon a misunderstanding of a fundamental nature: "Reconciliation is applied and made real through the work of the Holy Spirit" (*Justification*, 26). Seen in the light of the fundamental nature of the mistake made here, it is very difficult to understand what Barth was thinking when he wrote to Küng that "your readers may rest assured—until such time as they themselves might get to my books—that you have me say what I actually do say and that I mean it in the way you have me say it" (ibid., xxxix). Küng's is an excellent book in many ways, and its significance in ecumenical history cannot be overestimated. But Barth's blanket endorsement of what it attributes to him cannot be sustained by close analysis.

from what takes place in us to what takes place in Christ. Calvin's *simul* in the relation of the two remains, but the reason given for it no longer has anything to do with the pragmatics of addressing Tridentine criticism.[47] Indeed, the fact that justification and sanctification take place simultaneously is now seen to be *necessitated* by the way in which the divine and human elements are united in Christ in the singularity of his person. The unity of the divine and the human in the God-man means this: reconciliation is effected in and through a unitary movement of God toward the human in Jesus Christ, a movement that embraces both the humiliation of God (in which is our justification) and the exaltation of the human (in which is our sanctification). Humiliation and exaltation are not two, perhaps successive, movements but a single movement—and necessarily so, since it is in and through the life, death, and resurrection of the one God-human in his divine-human unity that both take place. And so, justification and sanctification *must* be, in the very nature of the case, worked out simultaneously. It could not have been otherwise.

But if the two are simultaneous, does one still have a certain priority over the other? Once we have been careful to eliminate any suggestion of a temporal priority, Barth does not hesitate to make justification be the *prius* and sanctification the *posterius*. Justification is to be regarded as "the first moment and aspect of the one event of salvation, the one that grounds the second and to that extent is superior to it"; sanctification is to be regarded as "the second moment and aspect of the one event of salvation, the one that is made possible by the first and to that extent is inferior to it."[48] Barth says this even while acknowledging that what is second in execution may well prove to be first in intention where God's priorities are concerned. It could well be that sanctification is the true goal of the covenant of grace. So, why then say that justification is the *prius*? Here again Barth's answer is christological. It is in virtue of the divine self-humiliation (i.e., the incarnation of the Logos) that there also takes place the exaltation of the human. And in complete correspondence to this christological state of affairs, it is in virtue of

the forgiveness of his sins and his establishment as God's child—both completed in God's gracious judgment and sentence—that man is called, made willing and ready for discipleship, conversion, the doing of good works, the bearing of his cross. It is in virtue of the fact that he stands before God as one justified by Him that he is sanctified by Him. Clearly,

47. On the relation of justification and regeneration/sanctification in Calvin's theology, the classical treatment is found in Wilhelm Niesel, *The Theology of Calvin* (Grand Rapids: Baker, 1980), ch. 9. For the importance of Catholic polemic for Calvin's *ordo docendi*, see pp. 130–31.

48. *KD* IV/1:574; *CD* IV/1:507.

if one asks after the *structure* of this entire event, justification must be accorded the priority over sanctification.[49]

It should be noted that Barth is able to accord justification a priority over sanctification—much of the Reformed tradition wavered on this point—only because he has removed justification from the "in us" sequence of the traditional *ordo salutis*. What he has achieved by this move is that "justification" is now set free to be descriptive of the whole of God's reconciling work and not just one aspect of it. Where this move is not made, vacillation will always occur over how to relate justification to regeneration/sanctification.

But how, finally, does the fact that Barth regards justification as having a certain priority over sanctification relate to the question (much discussed today) of the "centrality" of the doctrine of justification? Douglas Harink would have us believe that the doctrine of justification had a minimal importance for Barth's theology of reconciliation as a whole—on the grounds that it takes up little space in the *Church Dogmatics* relative to the whole.[50] Here, as is often the case, the importance of a theme will not be decided by a simple quantitative analysis. We have already seen that Barth makes justification the ground of sanctification. So the question of centrality will not be as easily disposed of as Harink thinks.

Now, admittedly, Barth does say, "The *articulus stantis et cadentis ecclesiae* is not the doctrine of justification as such but rather its ground and its summit: the confession to Jesus Christ, 'in whom are hidden all the treasures of wisdom and knowledge' (Col. 2:3): the knowledge of *His* being, *His* activity for us, to us, and with us."[51] But notice: Barth does not deny that justification is in every conceivable sense "the doctrine by which the church stands or falls." He only says that it is not this *as such*. That is to say, this status does not belong to the doctrine of justification in isolation but only insofar as it is understood in combination with sanctification and vocation and only insofar as all three are subordinated to the being and activity of Christ in its entirety, which all three serve to confess. When justification no less than sanctification and vocation is subordinated to the being and activity of Christ in this way, then its rightful place as the *prius*, the foundation of sanctification and vocation, can be readily acknowledged. In this precise sense, justification is of central importance for Karl Barth.

The stage has now been set for showing in greater detail why Barth's doctrine is compatible with the traditional evangelical doctrine.

49. *KD* IV/1:574; *CD* IV/1:507–8.
50. Harink, *Paul among the Postliberals*, 46, n. 44.
51. *KD* IV/1:588; *CD* IV/1:527.

The Material Content of Barth's Doctrine of Justification

Justification for Barth, as for the traditional evangelical view, consists most fundamentally in acquittal. But it will not come as a surprise, in light of the foregoing, if I now add that, for Barth, it is also much more than that. Barth defines justification materially as the act of divine judgment that restores the covenant of grace that God made with the human race in eternity-past. It is an act of judgment that consists in the *sentence*[52] by means of which, first, the right of the covenanting God is upheld and maintained in the face of human sin and, second, the right of God's human covenant partner—a right that had belonged to that partner as a consequence of the covenant of grace but that had been forfeited through sin—is restored or returned. This is the definition in brief; now for an explanation of its meaning.

Barth's Christocentric Doctrine of Justification

Perhaps the best place to begin is with the recognition that the meaning of the right of God of which Barth speaks cannot be ascertained from a vantage point outside the history in which God establishes and, in the face of opposition, upholds the covenant of grace. The right of God will always be wrongly construed where it is based in some conception of natural law or general moral principles. "The exposition of the doctrine of justification has always suffered from the fact that the attempt was made to define God's right in the activity that is here to be clarified by means of a hypothesis that has been audaciously maintained on the basis of one's own maxims, on the basis of an allegedly recognizable natural or moral law."[53] God's right is a right that God has given to himself in

---

52. *KD* IV/1:576; *CD* IV/1:516. The word *Gericht*, which I have decided to translate here (with Geoffrey Bromiley) as "sentence," is to be distinguished from the word *Urteil* ("judgment" in a more generic sense) by the fact that *Gericht* is a word that has its home in the halls of justice. And so it can also be used to refer to the *Recht sprechende Behörde* (the magistrates as holders of an office). It is closely connected with *Gerichtsbarkeit* ("culpability before the law"), *Rechtsprechung* ("the sentence pronounced on one accused of a crime and bound over to a court"), etc. On these points, see *Wahrig Deutsches Wörterbuch*, 6th, newly rev. ed. (Gütersloh: Bertelsmann Lexikon, 1997), 545. As Barth uses the term *Gericht*, it is a virtual synonym of *Rechtsprechung*, as the title given to the section that deals with the meaning of justification makes amply clear: "Des Menschen Freispruch." See *KD* IV/1:634; *CD* IV/1:568. Curiously, Bromiley opts to translate *Freispruch* as "pardon," but this constitutes a significant weakening of the term's significance and of the linguistic connection in which Barth's use of that word stands to *Gericht*. *Freispruch* is a legal term whose meaning, once again according to *Wahrig* (p. 503), is "gerichtliche Feststellung der Unschuld des Angeklagtens" ("a legal determination of the *innocence* of the accused"—emphasis mine).

53. *KD* IV/1:590–91; *CD* IV/1:529. Cf. also the small-print section, *KD* IV/1:576; *CD* IV/1:516–17.

establishing the covenant of grace. How, then, could it in any way be known and understood apart from a knowledge of the history of God's covenantal relationship with the human race?

A similar insight can be found in the very best defenses of the traditional evangelical position. Against the traditional view, many through the centuries have claimed that an imputation of the innocence of Jesus Christ to the sinner who stands before the bar of God's justice would call into question every concept of justice known to human beings. For every human judge has a sworn obligation to uphold a law that requires him or her to mete out justice to the accused on the basis of "proof beyond a reasonable doubt" of the latter's guilt or innocence, and on that basis alone. For a judge to pronounce a verdict of guilty, only then to transfer the sentence due another, would not only be arbitrary; it would be a violation of the law, which would make the judge who did such a thing to be most "unjust." But as D. A. Carson has recently argued, the judge in this case is under obligation to uphold and enforce a law of someone else's creation (a legislature, perhaps); the law that God must uphold and defend, on the other hand, is a "law" of God's own creation, a "law" that God has given with his eternal covenant of grace, a "law" that not only establishes God's "right" but also opens up the way in which this "right" may be upheld in the case of violations of it.[54] What Carson has said here, in effect, is that every attempt to assess the "legality" of the trial described in Romans 3:19–26 on the basis of an appeal to the situation that pertains in even the best human courtrooms is bound to mislead. Such analogy as exists between them is simply too inexact. Barth would only add to this observation that the source of the error lies ultimately in the attempt to make a judgment on the basis of general principles rooted in natural reason. If there are analogies between the criminal proceeding spoken of in Romans 3 and human versions of the same, the analogy must run from Romans 3 to the human court of law and not the other way around. To think analogically in the other direction will necessarily result in a damaging distortion of the contingent reality that is God's covenantal relationship with the human race, and thereby a loss of its uniqueness.

But now this emphasis upon the contingent character of God's right as established in the covenant gives rise to another question that must be dealt with before proceeding to Barth's account of *how* God justifies. By finding in a contingent divine decision the basis for the right of God that is upheld in justification, has Barth not gone a long way toward making the divine justice in justification to be an arbitrary act on God's part?

---

54. D. A. Carson, "Atonement in Rom. 3:21–26," in *Glory of the Atonement*, Hill and James, 132–33.

Evangelical theologians have typically been very concerned to insist that what God does in justification is not only *not* done arbitrarily; what God does is right in the more important sense that God is being faithful in this act to his own justice and therefore to his very being as just. What God does is right because what God is seen to be doing here manifests perfectly what God is as the one who is always just in himself.

Barth would certainly agree that there is a valid concern in this, one that he, too, would want to uphold. He would only add that the reason we are in a position to be certain that what God does is in accordance with God's true being as just is not that what God does is thought simply to manifest God's being as just but that what God does *constitutes* God's being. The difference between Barth's view and the traditional evangelical view at this point is ontological—and because ontological, then also epistemological. The traditional view holds that God's being is something complete in itself, apart from and prior to whatever God does. But to put it this way raises the question whether we can ever really know the being of God that lies in back of God's activities. If we cannot, then we may want to believe that God's activities perfectly manifest God's true being; we may hope this is true, but we would never be in a position to really know it. If, on the other hand, God is self-caused being in the sense that God gives being to himself in the eternal act of entering into the covenant of grace with human beings, then there is no being of God above and prior to the covenant. The true being of God is his being in the covenant of grace. And therefore, when God does what is necessary to restore the covenant, we can know with certainty that he is doing that which is faithful to God's being as just. We can *know*—and not only hope—that God is faithful not only to his promises but also to himself.[55] As suggested earlier, the truly decisive departure between Barth's doctrine of justification and the traditional evangelical view occurs in the realm of theological ontology—that is to say, in the realm of reflection in which a decision is made as to the right ordering of God's eternal act to God's eternal being. There will be more to say about this in the next section, "Participation and 'Imputation.'"

What we have established through this discussion of God's right is that the ontological ground of Barth's doctrine of justification is to be found in the covenant of grace and not in a being of God abstracted from this covenant. It is the being of the *living God* with which Barth is concerned, the being of God in his covenant.

---

55. *KD* IV/1:592; *CD* IV/1:530–31: "It is precisely the God who, in the justification of sinful humanity and, therefore, as the gracious God is present and active, who is just and is in the right. He is just in Himself—not as subordinated to an alien law, but as the One who is Himself the origin, ground and revealer of every true law. That is the *backbone* of the event of justification."

What we must understand next is what necessarily takes place when the God who is faithful to himself, the God whose right is absolutely superior to the wrong of humanity, encounters this wrong. The "wrong of man," as Barth puts it, "cannot remain his own private business." In the very nature of the case, it is a wrong that occurs within the human's relationship to God; it is directed *essentially* toward God's right and therefore toward God himself. The "wrong of man" contradicts God's right; it places itself in opposition to it. God would not be God, the living God of the covenant, if God were content merely to be in the right over against this wrong, if God simply acquiesced in its existence. God would not be God if he did not *exercise* his right through the judgment of this wrong, through the negation, the overcoming, indeed the destruction not only of this wrong but of "man as the doer of it." God would not be God if he failed to do any of this, because, in failing to do it, God would be cooperating in this opposition to his right and would thereby enter into contradiction with himself. God's right, after all, is what God is; God cannot allow it to be contradicted without contradicting himself.[56]

But this means, then, that the situation of sinful humanity could not be more dire. The judgment of God must, if God is to be God, result in the destruction of both sin *and the sinner*. Therefore the crisis into which "the man of sin" has placed himself through his rejection of God's right could not be more absolute. The inbreaking of the divine judgment is the inbreaking of a catastrophe. The very existence of the "man of sin" has now become an impossibility, and if, in spite of this, he continues to exist for a time, he does so only as one whose very being is characterized by a "sickness unto death."[57]

And yet the real human in time is not only the "man of sin." He is this but he is also much more. That the real human in time continues to exist as the "man of sin," that God sustains him in his existence for a time, is a function of the fact that he is also—at the same time—the elect of God, chosen before the foundations of the world to be God's partner in a kingdom of peace. God would not be God on this side as well if God were not to keep the promise bestowed upon the human race in its election, if the "No" of God's destructive wrath were not succeeded by God's "Yes" of acceptance and mercy, if the wrong of the fallen human were not positively replaced by a "new right" of the reconciled human, if the fallen human were not set aside and replaced by the righteous

56. *KD* IV/1:597; *CD* IV/1:535.

57. *KD* IV/1:602; *CD* IV/1:539. The frequent use of language made famous in Barth's second commentary on *Romans*—the language of "crisis," "catastrophe," and the Kierkegaardian phrase "sickness unto death"—is a visible demonstration of the fact that Barth's depiction of the situation of the sinner here in the *Church Dogmatics* has lost nothing of the seriousness that it possessed in his early theology.

human.[58] But how can this be? How can God fulfill the promise made to the sinful man in the covenant if, in order to be God, he must destroy this man? That God must act righteously on both sides—first on the side of upholding God's own right through the execution of a sentence upon the "man of sin," and then also on the side of restoring to the covenant partner a grace-given right that the latter had forfeited—is also clear. The very Godness of God is at stake in the question of how God can act righteously on both sides. But how can God do this? How can God maintain himself in the right against the wrong of the human even as God gives right to a human who is in the wrong? This is the special problem of the doctrine of justification.

This problem is seen in its real depth and breadth, however, only where it is also seen that God would, once again, not be God if the dividing of the "old" sinful human on the left hand and the "new" human on the right were to result in a dualism, a tearing apart of the one human who is both the "man of sin" and the elect of God, so that there were now two distinct groups of people, toward each of which God would now be acting righteously *on one side only*. In truth, however, the division that is described by the "man of sin" on the left hand and the elect of God on the right hand is a division that cuts through the existence of every individual human at its very root.[59] For Barth, "the only alternative"—and he means this "only" with strict seriousness—is to "understand the divine work of dividing the human on the left and the right as the initiation of a history in which the human on the left is the *Whence* and the human on the right the *Whither* of the *one* human, he himself the former as the one he was and still is, he himself once again the latter as the one who will be and to that extent already is."[60]

So, justification involves a history, a movement from unrighteousness to righteousness.

The justification of man by God is an *event* between God and man, not a static relation between the being of the One and the being of the other but rather the being of God and the being of man in a definite *movement* that cannot, as such, be reproduced in two pictures that could be laid alongside each other and contemplated together. It takes place as a *history* of God with man. And that which is twofold but also one in it is the righteousness and grace of the one *God above*, judging and acquitting, killing and making alive, and, in correspondence to this divine activity, the dark Whence and the bright Whither of the one *man below*, his transition and stepping forth out of that yesterday into this tomorrow, his coming from his wrong,

58. *KD* IV/1:605; *CD* IV/1:542.
59. *KD* IV/1:603; *CD* IV/1:541.
60. *KD* IV/1:606; *CD* IV/1:543.

which is finished and annihilated, and therefore from his own death and his going toward his new right and thereby his new life.[61]

For those with ears to hear, Barth's solution to the problem of justification has already been announced. The history described in the passage just cited is the history of Jesus Christ, the God-human, the Judge judged in our place. The human who lives in correspondence to the divine activity of judging and acquitting, of killing and making alive, is the man Jesus. And Jesus' transition, his stepping forth from the dark Whence of the "man of sin" and into the bright Whither of new right and new life is the transition from his death on the cross to his resurrection from the dead. Thus it is *in him*, in the event of the cross, that the "man of sin" is condemned and destroyed. And it is *in him*, in the event of the resurrection, that we are pronounced innocent and given a new right and a new life.[62] *He* was "handed over to death for our trespasses and was raised for our justification" (Rom. 4:25). In him? For Barth, we cannot put this too strongly. It is not in ourselves that we see and experience the destruction of the "man of sin." It is not in ourselves that we see and experience righteousness. The transition from the one to the other occurs in a "today" that is not our own. "The today of *our* true and real transition from wrong to right, from death to life and therefore the today of judgment that falls upon us through God's righteousness and grace, is to us indeed a strange today."[63]

As mentioned earlier, Barth's doctrine of justification was Protestant and radically so. We now see the reason. If justification is to be found always and in every moment in Jesus, in a today that is always alien to us but is real in him, then justification must always be for us—not just in the initiating moment of our Christian lives but in every subsequent moment—a *justitia aliena* (an "alien righteousness") because it is the

---

61. *KD* IV/1:608; *CD* IV/1:545. Here again the echoes of the early Barth are quite pronounced. The statement that the dark Whence of the human and his bright Whither cannot be described in two pictures that would be laid alongside each other, to be contemplated together, recalls Barth's claim, made in his lecture at Tambach in 1919, that the knowledge of God entails the humanly impossible attempt to "draw the bird in flight." Such an attempt may succeed in capturing the bird, but in the nature of the case, it will only be the bird frozen in a moment of time. The movement, the flight itself, will be lost. See Karl Barth, "Der Christ in der Gesellschaft," in *Das Wort Gottes und die Theologie* (Munich: Chr. Kaiser, 1925), 40; English translation, "The Place of the Christian in Society," in *The Word of God and the Word of Man* (Gloucester, MA: Peter Smith, 1978), 282–83.

62. The verdict of innocence pronounced in the resurrection is, of course, a verdict pronounced on Jesus himself. But because we are already "in him" by virtue of our election, it is pronounced on us as well—at the same time. See *KD* IV/1:620; *CD* IV/1:556: "His innocence, the innocence in which he bore and bore away our sin, the innocence which was manifested in the resurrection, was and is our innocence."

63. *KD* IV/1:611; *CD* IV/1:548.

justitia Christi.[64] It is precisely this emphasis that, as Hans Küng has rightly observed, will immediately call forth from the great majority of Catholic critics the battery of terms by means of which Catholics through the ages have always sought to vanquish the Protestant doctrine of justification: terms such as "imputation and extrinsicism, juridicism and forensicism."[65] And yet it is in terms echoing traditional Catholic polemic that evangelicals, too, are likely to react to the radicality of Barth's christocentric treatment of justification. They, too, will worry about whether Barth does not make justification be something that takes place in a transcendent realm, over our heads, so to speak. They, too, will worry about whether Barth's doctrine amounts to anything more than a "nominalistic 'as if.'"[66] They, too, will wonder whether Barth does not make God guilty of a "legal fiction."

Of course, the source of evangelical worries will be different from that of their Catholic counterparts. Evangelicals will, after all, want to continue to insist upon a clear, conceptual distinction between justification and sanctification—something their Catholic counterparts will be less concerned to do. But in spite of this difference, evangelicals will likely hold that what Barth has done is reduce the divine work of justification without remainder to the divine work of atonement. Surely, they will say, this is Christocentrism gone mad! In the words of Hans Küng, "How do we know that what Christ has done really applies to us?"[67] Are we ever really affected by it? Karl Barth most certainly has answers to these questions, answers that we must now consider. But we should not fail to notice that the mere fact that such questions can be raised at all offers strong testimony to the fact that Barth's doctrine is not only Protestant but radically so.

Participation and "Imputation"

This discussion has already said in a variety of ways that, for Barth, justification is not a matter of our subjective experience. But Barth does not stop there. For he also insists that Jesus' "history is as such our history and even our *most proper* history (in a way that is incomparably more direct and more intimate than anything we think ourselves to know as our history)."[68] Now, if this equation cannot be ventured on the basis of subjective experience, on what basis can it be made? Barth's answer

---

64. *KD* IV/1:613; *CD* IV/1:549.

65. Küng, *Justification*, 33.

66. The phrase is employed by Barth himself to describe a position he has every intention of overcoming in a way more definitive than heretofore. How he accomplishes this will become completely clear only in the next section. See *KD* IV/1:577; *CD* IV/1:517.

67. Küng, *Justification*, 39.

68. *KD* IV/1:612; *CD* IV/1:548.

takes us deep into his theological ontology. We noted earlier that the truly decisive point of division between Barth and evangelicals takes place in the realm of theological ontology. We must now take a brief look at Barth's ontology in an effort to understand why it is that Christ's history is *as such* our history, why it is that "participation" in Christ is not something that has first to be realized by means of an independent work of the Holy Spirit but is already real even as the God-man carries out his work.

The place to begin is, once again, the covenant of grace. What happens in the covenant of grace and the divine election that comes to expression in it is that God chooses to be God in a covenant with sinful man. It must be emphasized that the covenant is with *sinful man*. Not the "neutral" human who lives in a paradisaical situation but the sinful human is the object of God's electing grace. But because this is so, God had to address the problem of sin and the sinner already in the covenant itself. This God did by choosing reprobation for himself and mercy for us. In Jesus Christ, God chose to be the God who would suffer and die in reprobation. And in Jesus Christ, God determined that we sinners would be the beneficiaries of a restored covenantal relation. The crucial point here is that this act, this eternal decision, is basic to Barth's theological ontology. It is an eternal decision in which both the being of God *and the being of the human* are constituted by way of anticipation, by looking forward to the appearance in time of the one God-human in whom both the humiliation of God and the exaltation of the human take place.

Two immediate consequences of this move deserve mention. First, as was suggested above, the fact that God has eternally chosen to be God as the reprobate human means that no question can remain as to God's right in taking the place of those who stand convicted and condemned before the bar of the divine judgment. That this is an altogether lawful act is guaranteed by the fact that when God does this in time, God is only acting in a way that is faithful to his true being as constituted in the covenant of grace. No injustice can be conceived here. Second, the fact that God has eternally chosen that our true, "essential" being would consist in the exalted humanity of Jesus Christ means that no question can remain as to God's right in pronouncing us innocent. What we truly are is not that which we, in our fallenness, have made ourselves to be; what we truly are is what we are determined by God to be in Jesus Christ. That this is an altogether lawful act is guaranteed by the fact that when God pronounces a verdict of acquittal in the resurrection of Jesus Christ, He is telling the truth about the true being of us all. Again, no injustice can be conceived here.

The problem of participation in Christ is thus to be resolved in the doctrine of election. What is decisive for participation is the eternal divine *determination*. In God's electing grace, we are "in Christ" long before the appearance of Jesus in time. This does not mean, parenthetically, that history has been rendered insignificant. History could not have any greater significance if even the being of God is constituted eternally, in and for itself, by that which God will undergo as human in time. But we do learn from this why the Holy Spirit need do nothing further to make us participants in Christ. This we already are by virtue of the divine election. What, then, is the purpose of the Holy Spirit's work? The purpose of the Spirit's work is to awaken us to the truth about who and what we are, to the truth that in Jesus Christ we are justified sinners, so that we may then live in a way that corresponds to what we are in Christ.

Barth does not make use of the language of a positive imputation of Christ's righteousness. The fact that he does not should not, by this point in our exposition of his doctrine, come as a surprise. "Imputation"—understood as a *distinct* act of God the Father in the power of the Holy Spirit, an act in which the work of Christ is made to be efficacious for the individual to whom it is "applied"—has been set aside. The reason is that it so compartmentalizes the work of Christ and the work of the Holy Spirit as to make the former ineffectual in itself apart from the latter. But Barth's spare use of the language of imputation (and usually only in the negative sense of the nonimputation of sin) does not at all mean that he has simply dismissed from further consideration the content that the notion of a positive imputation of Christ's righteousness once communicated. What it does mean is that Barth has taken up this content and employed it in his own way.

What I want to suggest in concluding this section is, first of all, that the work that was done by the concept of "imputation" in the older Protestant theology is done in Barth's theology by the doctrine of election—and, specifically, by that covenant of grace by means of which the content of the doctrine of election is filled out. It is still the divine verdict of acquittal that stands at the heart of justification. But the divine "imputation" has been relocated, so to speak; it has been made basic to the gracious election of God, so that when the divine verdict is pronounced in time, it is the manifestation of a decision already made in eternity. And second, this conceptual labor is carried out within a framework that is even more thoroughly and consistently forensic than the framework within which the older Protestant doctrine of justification was thought out. In Barth's hands, "forensicism" is not simply a tool for thinking through the atoning work of Christ and justification; it is the frame of reference that is basic to the whole of his soteriology. As such, it also makes possible the elaboration of a theological ontology consistent with the twin doctrines of atonement and justification. What has happened in Barth is that forensicism has been made basic to his ontology and his concept of "participation." After all, what could be more consistent with forensic thinking than to make "being" a function of decision and act? And the reason all of this is important is that when the concept of "participation in Christ" is introduced, its meaning will not contradict the ontology implied by the forensic treatment of atonement and justification.

What is manifestly clear is that the theological and pastoral concerns that originally came to expression in the language of a positive imputation in Calvin's theology, for example, have not been lost to view. To the contrary, the language of imputation wanted to say that the basis for our justification is to be found, always and at every moment, in the "alien righteousness" of Christ and not in ourselves. And this concern has been met fully and completely. It is for this reason, above all, that Barth's doctrine of justification is a natural ally of the older Protestant conception.

The Being and Existence of the Justified Sinner

The Christian life, for Barth, is a life that is lived "in transition," a life poised on a knife's edge between past and future. *The* transition (the movement from past to future that has actually arrived at its goal) has already taken place in the movement of Jesus from his death to his resurrection. *In him*, Jesus, the death of the "man of sin" has taken place, and yet this is not something that we can find in any event of our own lives; it is not something we can perceive as a determination of our own existence.[69] However true it may be that "in Christ" I am no longer the "man of sin," yet in myself I find that I am. Indeed, wherever I look at myself in my "physico-psychical existence," I find no evidence of that death.[70] I am still the "old man." The struggle described by Paul in Romans 7:14–25 is a description of me.[71] The "law of sin" is at work in me, making me captive to sin (v. 23). Granted, I could know nothing of this if I did not already know that what Paul says in Romans 8:1 is true: "There is therefore now no condemnation for those who are in Christ Jesus." And yet, in and for myself, I am still the "old man."

By the same token, the exaltation of the human has already taken place in Jesus Christ—but once again, this is not something that we can find in any event of our lives. "That we will live as those who are righteous is not an immanent determination of our existence."[72] In Jesus Christ

---

69. *KD* IV/1:616; *CD* IV/1:552.

70. *KD* IV/1:656; *CD* IV/1:589.

71. Barth's exegesis of Rom. 7 and 8 belongs to some of the most compelling exegesis to be found in his writings. See *KD* IV/1:648–59; *CD* IV/1:581–91.

72. *KD* IV/1:619; *CD* IV/1:554.

my future has been secured. I will be the exalted, the righteous human, but I am not yet that person.

And so the Christian life is a life "in transition." As such, it mirrors imperfectly *the* transition that has already taken place in Christ, imperfectly because, in and for ourselves, the past ("the old man") is not yet past and the future ("the new man") has not yet arrived. In and for ourselves, the transition in question takes place in those moments in which we hear the word of acquittal spoken to us in revelation—and this is a point of great significance.

It is not at all the case that justification takes place over my head, in a transcendent sphere or in a remote past with which I stand in no real connection. There is indeed a justification of the individual by faith. In that the Holy Spirit awakens me to faith, I am able to see nothing but negation as I look toward my past, and nothing but affirmation and promise as I look ahead to my future. In that I live by faith, I am no longer the man I was, and I am already the man I will be. And yet, given that this is not a description of my existence as such but of my true being, given that faith here is quite clearly "the conviction of things not seen" (Heb. 11:1), God's justification of me as an individual takes place at a "mathematical point"[73] without before or after on the level of my lived existence. It is never a completed action in my life's history. I cannot look back on a date in my past and say, "On that date I was justified."[74] God's justification of me is something that is new each morning; it is something that breaks in upon me in spite of my continuing unwillingness to live as one who is justified. Justification is an ever-to-be-repeated event in which I am caught up in the "breaking-out of the acquitted man."[75] At no point is justification my secure possession or a predicate of my existence in this world. Justification is a completed action in Jesus Christ alone; in my history it is something that can only take place (present tense) in each new moment. So long as I remain the "old man" on the level of my lived existence, justification must take place in all my present moments.

Clearly, Barth has stretched the relationship of our true being in Jesus Christ and our lived existence to the breaking point. That he has done so has much to do with his worries over the psychologizing of Christian faith. But the battle against psychologism is only a symptom of something lying deeper. Ultimately, Barth's point is that of a radical Protestant. His point is that the word of divine acquittal that is heard by individuals and

---

73. *KD* IV/1:657; *CD* IV/1:589.

74. Barth says of Paul that he, too, never understood the beginning of his justification as a past event only but as a beginning that is renewed in each new moment. "Every morning and every evening his situation, too, is the situation of departure in the midst of sin" (*KD* IV/1:651; *CD* IV/1:583).

75. *KD* IV/1:642; *CD* IV/1:576.

understood to be valid and effective for them does not find its ground in them. The ground of our justification is always, at every moment of our earthly existence, to be found in Jesus Christ. *Justitia aliena*—first, last, and always, the doctrine of justification is about alien righteousness.

It was noted earlier that evangelicals would probably be inclined to find too little realized eschatology in Barth. And now we see why. Clearly, Barth holds that the future is already present—for faith. But since faith, in his view, does not possess its object, the element of realization here will likely seem too little for most evangelicals. Be that as it may, the one thing Barth's view does not do is render faith *in* Jesus Christ superfluous where justification is concerned. Faith may not be the cause of our justification, but there is no justification of the individual without it.

Justification by Faith Alone

The "essence" of the faith that justifies, Barth once wrote, does not lie in the fact that it is *fiducia* ("trust"), though it is also this.[76] The essence of faith lies in the fact that it is God's gift. On the other hand, the fact that genuine faith is a gift of God takes nothing away from the fact that it is a human act, a human "work," if you will. It is precisely in its character as both gift and human work that it has a role to play in justification.

> Even as grounded in the work and gift of God, the work of faith is still a human work. And its part in the justification of man is that it alone is the human work . . . that is adapted, that corresponds, on the human side, to his divine justification. Not because of its intrinsic value. Not because of its particular virtue or any particular power of its own. But because God accepts it as the human work that corresponds to His work. Because, according to the phrase adapted from Gen. 15:6 (Gal. 3:6; Rom. 4:3f.), it is "reckoned" (ἐλογίσθη) to man by God as δικαιοσύνη, as a righteous human work, that is, as a work that corresponds to His righteousness. God recognizes not that by this action man fulfils a condition or attains something that makes him worthy of the divine acquittal but that in this action of man, and this action alone, His acquittal actually comes fully into its own. God recognizes that in this way, and only in this way, but in this way seriously and fully, His work and Word will be accepted, "realized" by man, that in this action of man to which He awakens and calls him, His own action has its counterpart and analogy.[77]

Everything that Barth says against the contrast of faith and works—as though faith were not also a human work—is said within the horizon of

76. Karl Barth, "Reformierte Lehre, ihr Wesen und ihre Aufgabe," in *Das Wort Gottes und die Theologie*, 207; English translation, "The Doctrinal Task of the Reformed Churches," in *The Word of God and the Word of Man*, 263.

77. *KD* IV/1:686; *CD* IV/1:615.

this positive appreciation of the role of faith in justification. And so, when he says, for example, "There is always something wrong and misleading when the faith of a man is referred to as his way of salvation in contrast to his way in wicked works. . . . Faith is not an alternative to these other ways,"[78] he is not turning away in the least from his earlier assertion that it is in this human action alone that God's acquittal "comes fully into its own." He is, moreover, simply reiterating a point that was already well understood in the Reformed Reformation especially, namely, that although faith alone is finally suited to receive and acknowledge what God has done, it can in no way bring into play what God has done and make it effective. But this much it does do. And because it does this much, it has an important part in Barth's doctrine of justification.

Conclusion

Much in Harink's exposition of Barth is important and valuable. He understands that justification, for Barth, is something that is complete and effective in Jesus Christ; the awakening to faith adds nothing to this completed action, nor does it give to it an efficacy that it does not have in itself. Harink also knows that Barth refuses to contrast faith and works as ways to God. But missing in his exposition is the forensic context within which these claims are given their meaning and significance. Nowhere do we find in his treatment any discussion of the forensic categories of "guilt," the divine "sentence," "penalty," "verdict," "condemnation" and "acquittal," or faith as the divinely accepted form of correspondence to that "acquittal."

In the final analysis, Karl Barth's doctrine has to be seen as standing in broad agreement with the older Protestant conception. Certainly, he has shifted the locus of interest from pneumatology to Christology. But he did not simply eliminate the importance of the individual's awakening to faith by the Spirit. Barth's doctrine constitutes an extension and radicalization of the Reformation doctrine; it does not constitute a break with it.

78. *KD* IV/1:687; *CD* IV/1:616.

9

The Lutheran-Catholic Declaration on Justification

Henri A. Blocher

On October 31, 1999, in the city of Augsburg, Germany, high officials of the Lutheran World Federation and the Roman Catholic Church solemnly affirmed, through a "Joint Declaration on the Doctrine of Justification," that whatever differences remain between their theologies of this article no longer warrant ecclesial division. The choice of place and date was a powerful symbol: Augsburg, which gave its name to the first Lutheran Confession of Faith, and October 31, the anniversary of Luther's bold initiative, the posting of the 95 Theses. After several years, the dust of media excitement has fallen and the heat of enthusiasm, or of *rabies theologorum*, has cooled down; it is now possible to make use of earlier reactions and to venture a global assessment of the "limited consensus" that was reached.

The Augsburg event was the fruit and culmination of a long process (as paragraph 6 of the "Joint Declaration" recalls). A possible starting point would be the work of the Roman Catholic theologian W. H. van de Pol of Nijmegen, as early as 1948.[1] The breakthrough of Hans Küng's

---

1. In W. H. van de Pol, *Het christelijk dilemma: Katholieke Kerk-Reformatie* (Roermond en Maaseik, Neth.: J. J. Romen, 1948), according to Gerrit C. Berkouwer, *Faith and Justification*,

famous dissertation followed in 1957. The "Malta Report," which was penned by a group of Roman Catholic and Lutheran theologians in the autumn of 1971 (published in 1972), as the swan song of the Second Vatican Council era, boosted ecumenical hopes by its confidence in a feasible agreement. The work of the Joint Commission then started (1972). It benefited from parallel endeavors, most important among them the Lutheran–Roman Catholic dialogue in the United States, which produced what remains the most enlightening documentary source, rich with precious information that draws the reader into the theologians' common work.[2] There exists a fair probability that the thinking behind Augsburg 1999 was of the kind more openly displayed in the American documents.

The unique weight of the "Joint Declaration" attaches to the official involvement of the churches. It was not only the child of some scholars' brains, of some more or less representative scholars; the chairman and general secretary of the Lutheran World Federation signed it, and so did the chairman of the Pontifical Council for Promoting Christian Unity, Edward Cardinal Cassidy, with effective support from the Congregation for the Doctrine of the Faith (headed by Cardinal Ratzinger) and with the pope's personal blessing. The process was neither smooth nor easy. A significant number of Lutheran churches, both within and without the federation, rejected the statement. The chairman of the large Missouri Synod, A. L. Barry, denounced "a betrayal of the Gospel of Jesus Christ."[3] More than 150 theological teachers, among them Ingo Dalferth and Gerhard Ebeling, appended their signatures to a protest. In addition to shorter expressions of his stance, the prestigious Tübingen systematician Eberhard Jüngel has authored a powerful synthesis of his views on justification that contains sharp comments on the "scandal" and "macabre" attitudes, which the "Joint Declaration" reflects, among Lutheran participants in dialogue.[4] Behind the scenes in the Vatican,

---

trans. Lewis B. Smedes (Grand Rapids: Eerdmans, 1954) 39; Klaas Runia, "Justification and Roman Catholicism," in *Right with God: Justification in the Bible and in the World*, ed. D. A. Carson (Carlisle, UK: Paternoster; Grand Rapids: Baker, 1992) 199, who quotes from W. H. van de Pol, *Karakteristiek van het reformatorische Christendom* (Roermond en Maaseik, Neth.: J. J. Romen & Zonen, 1952). Both write the name "van der Pol"; but all other sources (Congar, Subilia, etc.) offer "van de Pol."

2. H. George Anderson, T. Austin Murphy, and Joseph A. Burgess, eds., *Justification by Faith*, Lutherans and Catholics in Dialogue 7 (Minneapolis: Augsburg, 1985). Runia, "Justification and Roman Catholicism," 210–12, frankly exposes that ARCIC II (the work of the Anglican–Roman Catholic International Commission) does not bear the comparison.

3. From a press release of October 15, 1999, quoted by Raoul Dederen, "The Joint Declaration on the Doctrine of Justification: One Year Later," *Ministry* 72, no. 11 (2000): 13.

4. Eberhard Jüngel, *Das Evangelium von der Rechtfertigung des Gottlosen als Zentrum des christlichen Glaubens: Eine theologische Studie in ökumenischer Absicht* (Tübingen:

fierce arm wrestling was taking place: the Vatican's "Official Response" of June 25, 1998, dismayed the more ecumenically minded and seemed to wreck hopes of a joint signing (the Lutheran World Federation Council had just voted on the text one week before). Finally the progressive party got the upper hand—with a propitiatory "Annex" added, in line with the body of the "Joint Declaration."

Measuring Convergences

One cannot and should not repress the naive questions that immediately arise: Did they truly agree? If they did, how were they able to?

The title was carefully worded: "Joint Declaration" (*Gemeinsame Erklärung*) and not a "Common Confession of Faith." The signatories disclaim having reached agreement on the whole doctrine of justification (§5); they have reached "a consensus on basic truths" (*Konsens in Grundwahrheiten*, §§5, 13, 14, 43), with divergences still unresolved on some points that belong to the doctrine and some that are connected with it (§43). This cautious openness, however, should not become a pretext for belittling what was achieved in the eyes of those who took part: they rejoice in "a shared understanding of justification" (§14) that had not been dreamt of since the year 1560.

Was it indeed achieved? A few remarks may be helpful on the procedure that was followed. To escape paralysis in the fetters of old anathemas, a subtle balance was maintained between contextual, that is, historical, relativity and permanent validity in doctrinal statements (§7: not disowning the past but welcoming new insights). Beyond dispelling misunderstandings and caricatures, the legitimate diversity of languages and "conceptualities" was stressed as a key factor to explain differences: not to explain them away but to press the venom out of them, to render them inoffensive (§40). The target, rather than agreement per se, is the affirmation that differences "are no longer the occasion of doctrinal condemnations" (§§5, 41 with the "protective" addition in 42: "Nothing is thereby taken

---

Mohr [Siebeck], 1998). Referring to Lutheran efforts to show, "durch einen unglaublichen Eiertanz," that the "Formula of Concord" did not rule out works as a means of preserving and confirming the gift of righteousness, Jüngel writes, "Ich erwähne diese Peinlichkeit, weil sie symptomatisch ist für die Verteidigung tridentinischer Positionen durch lutherische Theologen im Interesse der Ökumene," and asserts that the statement that the "Formula" does not bear upon the corresponding Catholic doctrine "gehört zu den Skandalen, für die die *Gemeinsame Erklärung* einmal als theologie-geschichtliches Beispiel gelten wird" (176–77, n. 136); and again, 200, n. 215: "Es gehört indessen zu den makabren Seiten des Streites um die *Gemeinsame Erklärung*, daß deren lutherischen Apologeten—Bischöfe, Oberkirchenräte, aber auch Theologieprofessoren—den Vorgang damit gerechtfertigt haben."

away from the seriousness of the condemnations," i.e., they still count as warnings). Nowhere are the criteria spelled out. Participants appear to have relied on their own feeling as to what was acceptable and what was not. As a contribution to the American dialogue, George Lindbeck had shrewdly pondered the difficulty of *proving* contradiction and highlighted the distinction between agreement and compatibility.[5]

Did the framers yield to the facility of ambiguous phrases? Such has been the plague of many an ecumenical document! As far as I can see, the answer is "no." The Augsburg declaration is almost a model of univocal talk, with one minor exception.[6] If one accepts in principle interconfessional dialogue, one is not likely to do much better. It is comforting to observe able thinkers truly concerned with theology, with finding a gracious God and not only a gracious neighbor, with the gospel and not only its sociopolitical implications.

Have, then, Roman Catholics changed? Undoubtedly, in Augsburg they subscribed to propositions that Protestants through the centuries thought they would never accept. In the "Joint Declaration" they firmly said, "Justification thus means that Christ himself is our righteousness, in which we share through the Holy Spirit in accord with the will of the Father. Together we confess: By grace alone, in faith in Christ's saving work and not because of merits on our part, we are accepted by God" (§15). They added, "Our new life is solely due to the forgiving and renewing mercy that God imparts as a gift and we receive in faith, and never can merit in any way [*in welcher Form*]" (§17). They explained that the beneficiary's "personal consent" is "itself an effect of grace, not . . . an action arising from innate human abilities [*aus eigenen Kräfte*]" (§20). And most precisely: "Whatever in the justified precedes or follows the free gift of faith is neither the basis of justification nor merits it" (§25).

Cardinal Cassidy answered journalists that these statements are in agreement with the decrees of Trent. Could he say otherwise? When the documents of Trent and Augsburg are placed side by side, a naive reader may feel asked to stretch hermeneutical goodwill beyond capacity. Does not canon 9 (appended to the Tridentine Decree on Justification) pronounce anathema on whosoever will say that the godless is justified by faith alone, that is, with nothing else being required by way

5. George Lindbeck, "A Question of Compatibility: A Lutheran Reflects on Trent," in *Justification by Faith*, Anderson, Murphy, and Burgess, 230–31.

6. The last sentence of §24, "They [Catholics] do not thereby deny that God's gift of grace in justification remains independent of human cooperation," can be understood as meaning either that justification itself is the gift, independent of cooperation, or that the gift is God's contribution toward a synergistic justification. Even in the former case, a distinction between initial justification and justification fully confirmed might produce some haziness.

of cooperation?[7] Does not canon 24 similarly condemn the affirmation that good works are only the fruit and signs of justification received, not the cause of its increase?[8] Canon 32 affirms (by expressly putting anathema on the contrary thesis) that good works truly merit the increase of grace, life eternal, and even the increase of glory.[9] Is this "basically" the Reformers' understanding?[10] One is tempted to follow Barth when he asks Hans Küng, with typical Barthian humor, about Küng's reading of Trent: "Don't you agree that I should perhaps be permitted to plead mitigating circumstances for the considerable difficulty I had trying to discover in that text what you have found to be true Catholic teaching? How do you explain the fact that all this could remain hidden for so long and from so many, both outside and inside the Church?"[11]

One should beware, however, of reflex reactions. Catholics have a grand hermeneutical tradition of paradoxical subtlety. One remembers the maxim *Extra ecclesiam nulla salus*, whose interpretation was reversed (by 180 degrees), in the course of history, from an exclusive to an all-inclusive understanding. In his debate with Bossuet, we are told, Pasteur Claude thus summarized the bishop's position: "Jesus Christ said 'Drink ye all of it,' but the church knows he meant, 'Don't drink ye all,'" and Bossuet did not indeed deny the fact. And it must be granted, in all fairness, that evangelicals do not escape similar straits. A number of them consider that Paul's "I do not permit a woman to teach," if properly understood, does not rule out a woman becoming a pastor today (in the present writer's estimate, there are weighty considerations in favor

7. "Si qui dixerit, sola fide iustificari, ita ut intelligat, nihil aliud requiri, quo ad iustificationis gratiam consequendam cooperatur . . . A[nathema] S[it]."

8. "Si qui dixerit, iustitiam acceptam non conservari atque etiam non augeri coram Deo per bona opera, sed opera ipsa fructus solummodo et signa esse iustificationis adeptae, non etiam ipsius augendae causam: A. S."

9. "Si quis dixerit, hominis iustificati bona opera ita esse dona Dei, ut non sint etiam bona ipsius iustificati merita, aut ipsum iustificatum bonis operibus, quae ab eo per Dei gratiam et Iesu Christi meritum (cuius vivum membrum est) fiunt, non vere mereri augmentum gratiae, vitam aeternam et ipsius vitae aeternae (si tamen in gratia decesserit) consecutionem, atque etiam gloriae augmentum: A. S."

10. Canon 11 seems to aim at the Reformers as it condemns the view that justifying grace is only God's favor ("esse tantum favorem Dei"), and likewise canon 12 when it condemns the view that "justifying faith is nothing else than trust in the divine mercy that remits sins for Christ's sake, or that by this trust alone we are justified" ("Si qui dixerit, fidem iustificantem nihil aliud esse quam fiduciam divinae misericordiae peccata remittentis propter Christum, vel eam fiduciam solam esse, qua iustificamur: A. S."). Runia, "Justification and Roman Catholicism," 198–200, seriously doubts that Trent and the Reformers could be shown to have said essentially the same thing.

11. Karl Barth, introduction, in Küng, *Justification: The Doctrine of Karl Barth and a Catholic Reflection* (Philadelphia: Westminster, 1981), as quoted by Runia, "Justification and Roman Catholicism," 200.

of this stance). Could it be, then, that the subtle, paradoxical interpretation of Trent by recent Roman Catholic theologians falls within the parameters of ecclesial and theological responsibility—in other words, that one could accept it as an option?

The "Joint Declaration" refers to modern studies (§13). It is clear that Catholic participants in the Joint Commission have imbibed recent Catholic theology. In the book produced by the American dialogue, Avery (now Cardinal) Dulles's chapter sheds much light on this influence, for it shows how potent Karl Rahner's has been.[12] The Rahnerian motif, itself in harmony with modern sensitivities (with modern resentment at the thought of a divine Judge), that "grace is not rare," grace is to be interpreted as the self-communication of God, explains the main emphasis in the "Joint Declaration": all by grace. "By grace alone" (a nearly universal grace for the modern) *is* a Catholic conviction. Since there were convinced Augustinians among the council fathers at Trent, they likely secured the *possibility*, at least, of an Augustinian reading of the Tridentine paragraphs and canons.[13] The other emphasis in the "Joint Declaration" also helps one to see its text with Catholic eyes: the emphasis on Christ our righteousness. The christocentric cast allows Catholics to say, "Thus justifying grace never becomes a human possession to which one could appeal over against God" (§27); they can maintain *inherent* righteousness (with Trent and tradition) and yet deny "possession" if this righteousness is Christ himself indwelling believers. If it is Christ, it remains in some way "extrinsic," and the language of the Reformers may be adopted. This point is connected with the revision, in twentieth-century Catholic theology, of the notion of *gratia creata*: no longer a "thing" in us but a participative relationship with God in Christ.[14] If one adds the flexibility of the notion of merit since the Middle Ages, the puzzle of Roman Catholic theologians and officials signing Lutheran-sounding statements begins to take lighter colors.

12. Avery Dulles, "Justification in Contemporary Catholic Theology," in Anderson, Murphy, and Burgess, *Justification by Faith*, 256–77.

13. Jüngel, *Das Evangelium*, 157ff., forcefully brings out the (deliberate) ambiguity of the redaction of the council decrees; he states (159) that when one scrutinizes it, this document shows itself full of compromises and cleverly unclear, "als durchsetzt von Kompromissen, als in vielerlei Hinsicht zweideutig und als 'vor lauter Klugheit unklar,'" the last phrase being borrowed from F. Loofs.

14. See Lindbeck, "A Question of Compatibility," 238 (referring to Maurice de la Taille, Émile Mersch, Karl Rahner, and Edward Schillebeeckx), and Dulles, "Justification in Contemporary Catholic Theology," 258–59 (following Karl Rahner, who argues his case on the basis of the beatific vision, a fine illustration of Rahnerian subtlety). Lindbeck suggests that "when Aristotelian categories are given a participationist interpretation, they can no longer be as easily misused as they were in the sixteenth century" and thus *gratia infusa* may be compatible with Reformation doctrine.

And what about Lutherans? They did not renounce the *simul pecca-tor et justus*, nor the qualification of concupiscence as sin, even after baptism. They did not impose the *sola fide*, however, to Jüngel's bitter deploration.[15] What may be even more intriguing is the omission of any significant debate on an issue that would seem to deserve pride of place: the *meaning* of justification. Traditionally, Lutherans and Protestants (at least orthodox Protestants) were wont to stress that to justify is to declare, to pronounce, right with God and *not* to make righteous (by transforming effectively human nature, *habitus*, behavior). Justification is a matter of imputation. Such ways of speaking are strangely muffled in the "Joint Declaration." Roger S. Evans complains, "The words 'im-pute' (with one exception in parag. 22), 'declare,' and 'by faith alone' are missing."[16] Though not perfectly accurate,[17] this observation calls for vigilant reading. Indeed, positive evidence matches the negative one: while Catholics consistently define justification as "the forgiveness of sins and being made righteous by justifying grace" (§27), Lutherans express no disapproval—they simply avoid using it themselves in the body of the document. It is found, however, in the head for section 4.2, and in "Annex" 2A, they "confess together" with Catholics that justification is "being made righteous." This may signal a significant departure from the former confessional position and may have a part in the preference, throughout the "Joint Declaration," for the language of "forgiveness of sins" combined with the "gift of life" rather than for more explicitly forensic terms.

Historical precedent does provide excuses for such a departure if one feels excuses are needed. Melanchthon, who was responsible for the strong emphasis on the forensic sense of "justification" (since about 1530), of which his philological studies and his exegesis of the Epistle to the Romans had convinced him,[18] was ready to yield to Roman and imperial pressures on this issue, and even the "Formula of Concord" is not as clear-cut as one would expect.[19] Luther himself did not achieve

15. Jüngel, *Das Evangelium*, 200, n. 215.

16. Roger S. Evans, "Justification in Lutheranism and Catholicism: From Conflict to Conversation," *Ministry* 72, no. 11 (2000): 25.

17. The verb "to impute" is found not only in §22 (God no longer imputes to them their sin) but also in the biblical §10 ("reckon" in the English version, but it is the same *anrechnen* in the original); §23 speaks of the "declaration" of forgiveness (*Zuspruch*), and §12 uses *Gerechtsprechung* in German, "pronouncing righteous," in its quotation of Rom. 5:18.

18. Otto Ritschl, *Dogmengeschichte des Protestantismus*, vol. II/1, *Orthodoxie und Synkretismus in der altprotestantischen Theologie* (Leipzig: J. C. Hinrichs, 1912), 226–73, on Melanchthon's evolution, esp. 247–53.

19. John F. Johnson, "Justification according to the Apology of the Augsburg Confession and the Formula of Concord," in *Justification by Faith*, Anderson, Murphy, and Burgess, 193–94.

transparency. Although the kinship of his thought with the doctrine of *theōsis* (as claimed by the Finnish school of Luther studies)[20] can be discerned only in the younger Luther at most and although present-day preferences generally tend to exaggerate the place of effective renewal in his notion of justification—whereas it was first and centrally imputation—he did, to the end of his life, hold several themes in tension: acquittal and the gift of the new life.[21] Signatories of the "Joint Declaration" may plead, to some extent, that they go back to Luther.

In any case, these theologians were not seventeenth-century orthodox divines! The Lutheran World Federation Lutheranism is Lutheranism revised in the light of modern certainties or preferences. The 1963 assembly of that Federation in Helsinki revealed a high degree of uncertainty about the message of justification today, and, from many, a vocal dissatisfaction with the older confessional stance, including the distinction between imputed and imparted righteousness.[22] Participants in the American dialogue emphasized that the New Testament offers us diverse "images" and "pictures," among which justification is just one in many.[23] They expressed their adherence to the historical-critical method.[24] One perceives a faint echo of such statements in the "Joint Declaration" (§§8–9). In fact, the Lutheran input into the work of the Joint Commission (that led to Augsburg) sounds much more conservative than the average Helsinki paper and even the dominant tone in the U.S. dialogue.[25]

Some of the most brilliant Lutheran theologians of the last decades have advocated a *dialectical* version of Luther's thought and message: antithetical statements are both valid at the same time, *simul peccator et justus*, when we move from what is true in ourselves (under judgment) and true of us "in Christ" (under grace), and back again (for dialectics must not freeze, with thought resting in one static truth).[26] Now, it may be

20. Cf. William T. Cavanaugh, "A Joint Declaration? Justification as Theosis in Aquinas and Luther," *Heythrop Journal* 41, no. 3 (2000): 165–280.

21. O. Ritschl, *Orthodoxie und Synkretismus*, 147–48. Henri A. Blocher, "Justification of the Ungodly (*sola fide*): Theological Reflections," in *Justification and Variegated Nomism*, ed. D. A. Carson, Peter T. O'Brien, and Mark A. Seifrid, 2 vols. (Grand Rapids: Baker, 2001–2004), 491–93, gives a little more development to this point.

22. As the U.S. Lutheran–Roman Catholic "Common Statement" (in, *Justification by Faith*, Anderson, Murphy, and Burgess, 45–46) recalls, §§84–87.

23. Ibid., §§90, 91, 99, 122, 128, 132, 158.

24. Ibid., §122.

25. The evangelical (*evangelikale* and pietist) wing in the Lutheran church, especially the German church, had little say, if any, in the process. Such a keen theologian as Eberhard Hahn, from the Albrecht-Bengelhaus in Tübingen, had sharply criticized Helsinki.

26. Robert W. Bertram, "Recent Lutheran Theologians on Justification by Faith: A Sampling," in *Justification by Faith*, Anderson, Murphy, and Burgess, 241–55; Gerhard O.

argued that dialectics and forensic logic are alternative ways of accounting for Christ being our righteousness *extra nos*, for righteousness of faith being *aliena*; it is *aliena* and extrinsic either because it is the reckoning to our credit of the substitute's work and payment on the cross or because the believer's relationship to Christ is *simul* identity and nonidentity, yes and no. A dialectical interpretation (that goes far beyond Luther despite the seeds found in his writings) can lose interest in the forensic accent. Theologians may also harden or soften dialectical antitheses; milder versions become compatible with a Catholic synthesis.

One can thus understand how both groups of theologians, Roman Catholic and Lutheran, were able together to sign the "Joint Declaration"—though sympathetic understanding does not entail joining them as a third party.

Probing Difficulties

What are the most sensitive issues for the framers and signatories of the "Joint Declaration"? And for stricter heirs of the Reformation? They should be identified, described, and evaluated so as to reach a global assessment of the document.

The "Joint Declaration" itself signals some points that remained unresolved but that it dedramatizes. The old *simul peccator et justus* stumbling block (already mentioned) was almost removed. There had been considerable misunderstanding on this issue (strangely, *et poenitens*, which Luther sometimes added, is not mentioned). Lutherans explained that sin, as it remains in baptized believers, is no longer *regnans* but *regnatum* (echoing Rom. 6:14), and this dispelled Catholic suspicions (§29). Catholics recognized that the justified "are continuously exposed to the power of sin still pressing its attacks (cf. Rom. 6:12–14) and are not exempt from a lifelong struggle against the contradiction to God within the selfish desires of the old Adam (cf. Gal. 5:16; Rom. 7:7–10)," so that they "must ask God daily for forgiveness" (§28; cf. "Annex" 2A). This does not seem far off the mark if one considers scriptural language: "While we were still sinners . . ." Whatever difference is left relates to anthropology and styles of thinking—apart from a nagging problem that was curiously put to the side: what about the state of perfection reached by some saints, and especially that of the Immaculate Virgin Mary, according to Roman Catholic traditional discourse?[27]

Forde, "Forensic Justification and Law in Lutheran Theology," ibid., esp. 281–91; Jüngel, *Das Evangelium*, esp. 167, 176, 182.

27. The U.S. "Common Statement," §102, refers to Trent VI, can. 23, which mentions the Blessed Virgin.

Dialogue participants labored hard on the status and role of the doctrine of justification. Is it *the* criterion for everything else or only *a* criterion, as the "Joint Declaration" allows (§18; "Annex" 3)? Other heirs of the Reformation may hesitate to follow traditional Lutherans in their exaltation of this *articulus*: however close to the heart of the gospel, can the doctrine of justification by faith be extracted as a norm above all the rest without express warrant from Scripture? Karl Barth's preference for the confession of Jesus Christ as the supreme criterion may indicate a safer course.[28] Yet Jüngel's passionate and powerful plea, even against his beloved Barth, may generate second thoughts.[29] One may note that emphasis on justification by faith as *the* "Protestant principle," the critical anti-idolatrous principle, lends itself (following Tillichian logic), to promoting a balancing "Catholic principle," as Carl J. Peter cleverly devises.[30]

Agreement to disagree prevailed on concupiscence. The Roman Catholic participants stood by the Tridentine position, which refuses to call sin what remains of original sin after baptism (it is only the "fuel of sin"): that the *fomes peccati*, which is not properly sin, "does not merit the punishment of eternal death" (§30). The extraordinary fact is that Trent's Decree Concerning Original Sin, although it acknowledges that Paul does call it sin (Rom. 6:12–14), boldly claims that it should not be so considered *vere et proprie*.[31] The "Joint Declaration" paragraph grants that it is "objectively in contradiction to God." Motives for denying that it should be considered as sin, in the context of such embarrassing admissions, must be strong indeed! The Catholics' argument is twofold: akin with free-will emphases, "according to Catholic conviction, human sin always involves a personal element and since this element is lacking in this inclination, Catholics do not see this inclination as sin in an authentic sense"; the efficacy of baptism, buttressed by Romans 8:1, is that it takes away sin and whatever is "worthy of condemnation" (still §30). Foundational elements of Roman Catholic theology are involved.

The stakes therefore are not minor. Calvin, as he reviews the decree in *Les actes du concile de Trente, avec le remède contre la poison* (1548), pours devastating irony on it: "If vice is not guilty before God, the sun is dark"; considering that the same inclination was labeled original sin before baptism, with attendant guilt, he mocks, "These horned doctors maintain that the same thing is no longer what it was, though it re-

28. *CD* IV/1:514–28; cf. Runia, "Justification and Roman Catholicism," 213.
29. Jüngel, *Das Evangelium*, 12–42 ("Eine Auseinandersetzung mit Karl Barth," 15–25).
30. Carl J. Peter, "Justification by Faith and the Need of Another Critical Principle," in *Justification by Faith*, Anderson, Murphy, and Burgess, 304–15.
31. Fifth session, June 17, 1546, 5.

mains."[32] He strikes at the root of the doctrine: "These Reverend Fathers allege that God hates nothing in those who are regenerate. I grant them this point: but does it follow that there is nothing hateful?"[33] Freedom from all condemnation (Rom. 8:1) does not imply that there is nothing "worthy of condemnation" (here the breach of logic in §30 is obvious). If one carefully distinguishes between temptation in weakness, as Christ himself underwent, and an inclination contrary to God (the *yetser* of Gen. 6:5 and 8:21), it takes an incredible psychology—with no warrant in the biblical view of humankind—to isolate personal will from it. Even without a conscious deliberation, it is a willful, personal orientation of the heart. Whether there be another, righteous, orientation and a struggle between the two does not cancel the fact: inner inclinations toward evil are sinful. The weakness of the Catholic position here could be a symptom of inadequacies in the notion and grounding of justification.

Apart from a brief mention of the sacrament of penance/reconciliation (§30), the "Joint Declaration" avoids dealing with several controversial issues closely connected with justification. Dialogue in the United States had made bolder advances: on satisfaction that sinners are to offer the church, with the tariffs of penalties and corresponding indulgences (during that period, John Paul II was both issuing indulgences and blessing the Augsburg conclusions), and on purgatory.

Even sympathetic observers, such as André Birmelé (from the Institute for Ecumenical Studies in Strasbourg), point to this omission as *the* problem of the "Joint Declaration." It could hardly be denied that acceptance of justification by faith as understood by the Reformers immediately entailed the rejection of these beliefs and practices, which, for centuries, the overwhelming majority among Roman Catholics, both clergy and laity, have understood in ways incompatible with Reformation faith. The fact awakens horrible doubts as to the genuineness of agreement.

The American dialogue partners suggest a rather radical reinterpretation of penitential satisfactions and purgatory, a view that appears to be widely accepted among present-day theologians (at least in the Western world). We should no longer think of true penalties but only of merciful, though sometimes stern, pedagogical measures to help penitents correct their behavior and appropriate sanctifying grace.[34] Indulgences correspond to organic solidarity within the body of Christ. The pedagogical process and the efficacy of indulgences play a role even in the transition

---

32. John Calvin, *Les actes du concile de Trente, avec le remède contre la poison*, in *Recueil des opuscules, c'est-à-dire des petits traictez, de M. Iean Calvin* (Geneva: Baptiste Pinereul, 1566), 927. My translation from Calvin's French, or Calvin-approved French.

33. Ibid., 926.

34. Dulles, "Justification in Contemporary Catholic Theology," 270–72.

to eternity: hence the place of purgatory and the effect of indulgences even there. Is this enough to soothe Calvin's complaint that purgatory, "a terrible abyss," is "so great a labyrinth that it contains a thousand labyrinths beneath itself"?[35] Catholic theologians are walking or dancing on a tightrope; their very nimbleness witnesses to the extreme difficulty of their task.

On the side of "ecumenical" optimism, there is only one comment that carries dignity: one step at a time (it was urged by Otto Pesch). Theologically, however, one discerns that the underlying issue is that of the status and role of the church. Why do the Rahners, Dulleses, and others so "cleverly" defend improbable theses? They do so in filial deference to her motherly authority. What is at stake in satisfactions is the church's prerogative as dispenser, as mediatrix, of the grace of justification. The sacrament of penance, which Reformers consider a mere invention of men,[36] illustrates the requirement laid upon believers to relate to Christ through the church. Dulles brings this logic to light: the church is an instrumental cause of justification "as prolonging and participating in Christ's symbolic and sacramental mode of causality."[37]

With the word "sacramental," the other burning question surfaces. Lutherans and Catholics in the Joint Commission subscribed to the oft repeated statement that justification occurs in and through baptism (§§11, 16, 25, 27, 28, 30 and "Annex" 2B). The absence of any dissenting voice induces some uneasy feelings.

The traditional understanding of justifying grace in Roman Catholicism, considered to be operative in baptism, was that all *previous* sins were then blotted out and good works were henceforth to ground hope of final justification—with penance as the "second plank" in the case of mortal sins. Though some continuity could be claimed between much patristic teaching and this doctrine,[38] Reformers regarded it as a human scheme that beclouded the gospel.[39] Is the "Joint Declaration" clear

---

35. Calvin, *Recueil des opuscules*, 978.

36. Ibid., 959.

37. Dulles, "Justification in Contemporary Catholic Theology," 261.

38. Robert B. Eno, "Some Patristic Views on the Relationship of Faith and Works in Justification," in *Justification by Faith*, Anderson, Murphy, and Burgess, 111–30.

39. Eno himself, ibid., 130, has caught with perfect lucidity its historical outworking:

If the emphasis on gratuity of salvation and forgiveness of sins without our works is limited to first justification, if justification is identified with the moment of baptism, and if there comes a time when infant baptism is universal, then it is not hard to understand that the word of God's free forgiveness in justification would not impinge very forcefully on the conscience of the average Christian. If this same Christian then is exhorted to live a life of virtue and good works in order to be saved and rewarded in the next life and if in fact he does not live a very good life but is frequently exhorted to repent and threatened with divine judgments if he does not repent and, even if he repent, he is still menaced with

enough to ward off this sort of danger? One wishes it were clearer. As already noted, Catholic signatories maintain the requirement of *sacramental* reconciliation after voluntary sinning (§30) whereas to good works they assign the role of *preserving* righteousness (§38; cf. "Annex" 2D, which claims that Lutherans can agree).

Although Luther's works and Lutheran documents do contain statements on baptism in the same vein, it is unfortunate, even a little misleading, that Lutheran and Catholic understandings should appear to coincide. From reading the "Joint Declaration," one would hardly guess that Luther so strongly proclaimed the preeminence and sole agency of the word, even in baptism; that he stressed that it is operative only through faith (which faith he then attributed to baptized infants), not fearing to border on paradox. Luther's rejection of the *ex opere operato* may rest on misunderstanding, but it is clear that he had no room for the Catholic doctrine of baptismal *character*. Such differences at least deserve some scrutiny.

At any rate, the justifying role baptism receives in the "Joint Declaration" is not acceptable for other Protestants, whether of Reformed or Anabaptist lineage. Despite his subtle diplomatic choice of words—which has sent several modern interpreters on the wrong track—Calvin does not endorse the causative view (Karl Barth was basically right when he wrote that the function of the sacraments for Calvin was cognitive). Many have forgotten his proposition expressly denying that the sacraments confer what they represent.[40] A few times he does use the word "confer,"[41] but the context makes it clear that the sacraments confer as preaching does, as a visible word, so that God fulfills his promise if the promise meets faith in the recipient; more generally the efficacy of sacraments, which Calvin often extols, is that of sealing and confirming, not of causing grace as an instrument. In his *Antidote to Trent*, he protests against the exaltation of baptism as *the* means of justification and underlines that it is but "an accessory or dependence" of the gospel, that to call baptism the instrumental cause of justification is tantamount to calling

---

long and painful purgatorial torments to make up for the penances he cannot do, it is not surprising that a law atmosphere will be generated. People will seek to cut corners, find shortcuts, cheap grace.

40. John Calvin, *Institutes* IV.xiv.17: The sacraments "nous servent de la part de Dieu d'une mesme chose, que les messagers de bonnes nouvelles de par les hommes: c'est asçavoir *non pas pour nous conférer le bien*, mais seulement nous annoncer et desmontrer les choses qui nous sont données par la libéralité de Dieu"; cf. IV.xv.14: "*Non pas* que telles grâces soyent liées ou encloses au Sacrement, ou *qu'en la vertu d'iceluy elles nous soyent conférées*; mais seulement pource que par signe et marque le Seigneur nous testifie sa volonté, c'est asçavoir qu'il nous veut donner toutes ces choses" (italics mine).

41. Cf. Ronald S. Wallace, *Calvin's Doctrine of the Word and Sacrament* (Grand Rapids: Eerdmans, 1957), 163–64; one may add one instance in Calvin, *Les actes du concile*, 987.

the handle of a trowel the instrumental cause of the building.[42] He uses 1 Corinthians 7:14 to deny that baptism makes us children of God, for children of believers are already such before baptism: "Their salvation does not draw its origin from baptism; it is already founded by the Word, and sealed by baptism."[43] As a Reformed Baptist, I could not make this argument mine, but I share Calvin's rejection of a Tridentine position reflected in the "Joint Declaration": Here I stand, I can do no other!

Divergences on sacramental function and causality affect the theology of justification. The *prooemium* of the sixth session of Trent (March 3, 1547) makes the connection: "To complete the salvific doctrine of justification . . . it is appropriate to deal with the most holy sacraments of the church, by which all true righteousness either begins, or grows once it has begun, or is restored if it was lost."[44] If it is true from the Roman Catholic viewpoint, it is also from the Reformation side: baptism is a work, and its addition to faith raises a problem if justification is to remain by faith alone, apart from works. Berkouwer, a shrewd thinker, was aware of this consequence, noting that baptism cannot be thought to bring a grace beyond that of the word: "Nothing is added to the *sola fide*"; "Those who do hold to a second cause—even when acknowledging the *prima causa*—will inevitably begin to place the actual moment of salvation more and more in the second causality which occurs at the moment of baptism."[45]

Interestingly, Tertullian had to wrestle with this difficulty. To the objection of some opponents (critics of baptism) that Abraham was saved by means of bare faith without baptism, he replies that the subsequent prevails over the antecedent, that since the time of Abraham, faith has been enlarged and clothed, in some sense, by baptism.[46] This logic is singularly at odds with Paul's reasoning when writing to Galatians. Luther's own way, not to solve but to ignore the difficulty, was first to ascribe the agency to the word of God "united with water," although he does not account for this alleged union. But is not the word in danger of becoming a kind of energetic fluid, a force that pious imagination fantasizes, with the mere name of "word" left—emptied of its biblical notion? Then Luther, with maximum authority, affirms that baptism is no human

---

42. Calvin, *Les actes du concile*, 943–44.

43. Ibid., 938–39. ("Parquoy leur salut ne prend pas son origine du Baptesme, ains estant desia fondé par la Parolle, est seellé par le Baptesme," 939). He also denies that John 3:5 refers to baptism.

44. "Ad consummatione salutaris de iustificatione doctrinae . . . visum est, de sanctissimis Ecclesiae sacramentis agere, per quae omnis vera iustitia vel incipit, vel coepta augetur, vel amissa reparatur."

45. Gerrit C. Berkouwer, *The Sacraments*, trans. Hugo Bekker (Grand Rapids: Eerdmans, 1969), 86, 115.

46. Tertullian, *Baptism* 13.

work but the work of God.[47] Still, however active God is thought to be in baptism, baptism itself remains something that disciples do as they obey the Lord's command to them.[48] To claim that it is no human work flies in the face of all evidence; it is the violent suppression of an embarrassing fact. Roman Catholic theology achieves greater consistency, as it solves the problem by intimate union or fusion between the church and the Lord: if the priest is an *alter Christus*, if the church is Christ himself prolonged, the *Ur-Sakrament*, the rite participates in the divinization of the church. Such a logic (although some Catholic theologians today try to distance themselves from it) can be detected, for example, in Carl Peter's strategy.[49] But this is the view of the church that the Reformation was supposed to change.

Digging Deeper

Searching beneath expressed theses to unearth motives and discover ramifications may be useful. Some comments, at least, on issues underlying choices in the "Joint Declaration" may stimulate further reflection.

The first question does not look very deep; it bears the stamp of common sense: Why did traditional Protestants strenuously battle for a strictly forensic sense of justification and against any overlapping of justification and sanctification, although they confessed that these always go together—*sola fide nunquam sola*?[50] Why did Catholics stubbornly resist? Why have Lutheran participants in dialogue and many theologians softened the older stance?

To some, biblical philology and exegesis still possess normative value. It is difficult to deny that the hiphil form of *tsdq* and the Greek verb *dikaioō* never mean "to make righteous" (*justum facere*). "To justify" is the antonym of "to condemn," and a few looser or borderline cases do not warrant lodging under that word the thought of actual transformation.[51] But the theological and spiritual motive carries an even greater

47. On this point, Jüngel, *Das Evangelium*, 199, follows Luther: "Was sich hier als *Handlung* vollzieht, ist alles andere als ein menschliches Werk." He criticizes, however, W. Pannenberg's sacramentalistic tendency, which he sees leaning toward the Roman Catholic position (n. 208).

48. Recognized by the Reformed theologian Auguste Lecerf, "Des moyens de la grâce, la Parole, le baptême, la sainte Cène: Notes dogmatiques II," *Revue réformée* 6, no. 22 (1955): 37.

49. Peter, "Justification by Faith," 310–11.

50. Jüngel, *Das Evangelium*, 219 (borrowing from Paul Althaus's title).

51. The only passage in the Old Testament that could lend itself to an interpretation in terms of real renewal is Dan. 12:3, where the *maskilim*, the wise and faithful teachers

weight: the traditional Protestant conviction refers to the absolute character of the divine demand (the sense of which is akin to the fear of God, so typical of Reformed piety). Only *perfect* righteousness escapes God's condemnation: "All who rely on observing the law are under a curse, for it is written: 'Cursed is everyone who does not continue to do *everything* written in the Book of the Law'" (Gal. 3:10 TNIV; cf. 5:3; James 2:10).[52] The eyes of the Thrice Holy One are too pure to tolerate the smallest residue of evil (Hab. 1:13). A few dead flies are enough to spoil the whole bottle of perfume (Eccles. 10:1). Isaiah 64:6 reveals that our works of righteousness, the purest of our deeds, are still so marred by what displeases the Lord that they can only evoke in him the utmost abhorrence. Woe unto us if our acceptance ultimately is based, even in part, on inherent righteousness—that beginning of effective righteousness still mingled with so much unworthiness! We are "undone," lost and condemned. Luther revived Augustine's insight: since the first commandment requires our all, we are breaking the law of God with the slightest omission or imperfection (cf. Matt. 5:48).[53] Calvin develops the same arguments in his refutation of Trent.[54] If justification is purely forensic and Christian assurance is based upon justification alone, then our assurance can be firm and certain because justification is itself complete. If assurance were based on sanctification (as expressed in our works), then it could never be firm and certain.

Assurance is the correlative of the sense of dreadful demand. When one totally despairs of self, there is no room left for restless calculation of merits and demerits, no room for the anxious question whether we shall rise up to the standards or fail; an equally total reversal turns the *terrores conscientiae*[55] into perfect peace—if faith has placed us on the *other* ground. The God who justifies the ungodly no longer considers our works and *habitus* but only the absolutely perfect righteousness of Christ; like a garment, it covers our dishonor, and the shame of our nakedness

---

of Maccabean times, are called the *matsdiqim* of multitudes, "those who turn many to righteousness"; but one can understand "those who will so lead them that they will receive a favourable verdict from God's judgement." (The LXX and even Theodotion are too far from a literal rendering to be of help here.)

52. Italics added. The two other references dispose of the view that Paul was not interested in the "all" of his quotation. *Sanhedrin* 81a tells of R. Gamaliel's tears (ca. 90 CE) when, upon reading Ezekiel 18, he realized that, in order to live, one had to do *all* these things commanded; R. Aqiba comforted him by taking the opposite view (according to Hermann L. Strack and Paul Billerbeck, *Kommentar zum Neuen Testament aus Talmud und Midrasch*, 6 vols. [Munich: C. H. Beck, 1922–1961], IV.1, 22); the question was not alien to Judaism.

53. Lindbeck, "A Question of Compatibility," 234–35.

54. Calvin, *Les actes du concile*, 943, 952, 975 (956).

55. See Jüngel, *Das Evangelium*, 195, for the theme in early Lutheranism.

is no longer seen. Such an assurance was a major spiritual-existential benefit of justification by faith alone, in the eyes of the Reformers, a weighty factor in their motivation. Signatories of the "Joint Declaration" agreed to disagree on the matter of assurance, after reducing the distance between themselves (§§34–36). Catholics acknowledged that one cannot "consider God's promise untrustworthy" (§36)—a Rahnerian sense of grace has cast away the anguish of older-style devotion—while Lutherans admitted that believers "are never secure looking at themselves" (§35).[56] Quite obviously, the *pathos* of the Reformers' proclamation of Christian assurance produced only a very faint echo among the Joint Commission.

Theologians who do not follow the "forensic" line are also moved by strong arguments and motives. As to the biblical meaning of "justify," they may easily point to the state of flux, if not chaos, of academic exegesis today: who dares claim a final word? Theologically, they may question the mental picture of the implacable Judge who is supposed to send to eternal hell helpless creatures, just for dead flies in their bottles. They suggest that this picture represents the false absolutization of human standards, of forensic principles that are used metaphorically or hyperbolically in Scripture to express the experience of grace. It is a projection of a neurotically guilt-ridden conscience or a fantasy produced by superego sadism. The true God of Scripture is instead the compassionate Father, who "knoweth our frame" (Ps. 103:14 KJV); his judgments, in the service of redemptive love, are mellowed with *epieikeia*. God shows greater love and mercy when, instead of putting to our account a righteousness that remains "alien," he gives us the ability to cooperate in justification, and he graciously accepts our works, though imperfect, and rewards them with eternal life as a father does with his fledgling children.

The quest for assurance, the reply goes on, is also born of the neurotically "terrified conscience." The Reformers' solution is not satisfactory. On the one hand, it is embarrassed by the countless New Testament warnings about sins, the commission of which rules out any access to ultimate life; those who do them shall not inherit the kingdom of God. On the other hand, it appears that assurance ever eludes our grasp. Lutheran tradition admits that salvation may be lost. For the strict Reformed, there remains, against the background of the unfathomable decree of predestination, the question of the individual's faith as genuine: I can never rely enough on my works (and feelings and reasonings) to prove the authenticity of my faith.

---

56. In the U.S. dialogue, agreement was reached (§156, point 9): "Of themselves they remain capable of losing justification."

A few remarks may help to assess the strength of each case. Exegetical issues may be settled only by exegesis; this has to be left to other treatments of the theme of justification.[57] Theologically, it would be difficult to adjudicate in the abstract between the two hypotheses: false absolutization of our sense of justice, or adequate perception of the truly absolute claims? The concrete contents of Scripture, however, seem to endorse the logic of absolute demand. Our Lord went further than anyone along this line (e.g., Matt. 5:19–20, 22, 28). Terrified conscience, in view of terrifying judgments announced—the Bible is full of such. If one replies that it is imagery, the picture of the lenient father is no less anthropomorphic and is equally vulnerable to psychoanalytic suspicion. The biblical Father shows his mercy first by providing atonement and offering a pure gift of righteousness, not by closing his eyes on human imperfections. Promises of restoration, promises of grace regularly look beyond and through judgment; justification of the ungodly involves no condoning of any modicum of ungodliness. It is possible because of Christ, the Righteous One who died for the unrighteous, so that God remains absolutely just while he justifies undeserving sinners who simply trust in Jesus (*dikaion kai dikaiounta ton ek pisteōs Iēsou*, Rom. 3:26). The gentle acceptance of our works is a consequence, rather than a cause, of our justification.

Behind the motives of those who leave the Reformers' line, one may scent the subtle agnosticism of much modern theology—about the cognitive import, the ontological "purchase," of the language of Scripture. Metaphorical dimensions too often become a pretext for undermining the seriousness of biblical standards of righteousness, demands of holiness, and representations of God as Judge—with preferences tainted by modern humanistic sensitivity, which is then allowed free play.

God gives a greater grace (James 4:6). Since a simultaneous change wrought within the human person, progressive enabling, fatherly discipline, the gracious acceptance of our imperfect works, and even the matching of them by gracious "rewards" are all maintained in the doctrinal scheme of traditional Protestants, together with perfect acquittal by faith alone, one wonders how any greater grace could be bestowed on humankind. It is grace the greater of which cannot be conceived.

Assurance indeed remains a delicate topic, probably because it cannot be separated from living faith itself. Calvin warns that attempts to penetrate God's counsel are "a true abyss to engulf our souls."[58] Assurance disengaged from faith degenerates into worldly *securitas*: we cannot reach

---

57. Carson, O'Brien, and Seifrid, *Justification and Variegated Nomism*, vol. 2, contains a wealth of painstaking and persuasive exegetical studies of relevant texts.
58. Calvin, *Les actes du concile*, 957.

assurance introspectively but only in the "eccentric" movement of faith, when we look away from ourselves to the mirror of predestination, who was made for us Righteousness, Christ himself. But then we receive and enjoy assurance, being taught and assured by the sure scriptural word that whosoever believes is forever right with God, having peace with him through our Lord Jesus Christ.

The relationship of justification with surrounding beliefs and practices raises the more general problem of the systematic character of doctrine. The critical comments bearing on the "Joint Declaration" that have been offered by the theological research institute of Padua (which publishes the review *Studi di teologia*), with contributions by the able young theologian Leonardo De Chirico, center on Roman Catholicism as a system—and consequently express marked distrust in the face of piecemeal agreements.

There is biblical precedent. Paul argues from bonds of necessity between elements of doctrine, from systematic relationships, when he exclaims, "If justification comes through the law, then [*ara*] Christ died for nothing" (Gal. 2:21 NRSV). At the same time, we cannot claim to master the unity of the whole field of doctrine; we know in part and *en ainigmati* (1 Cor. 13:12). It is possible to agree on essentials and still diverge on secondary matters (Phil. 3:15–16). It would be presumption to rely on inference only; we may draw lines that connect various propositions, but dotted lines only, if independent support, first of all biblical, is not available. Frail we are, frail the proceedings of all theological minds.

On justification and the "Joint Declaration," two organic links may be ascribed paramount importance. With the mention of baptism, the core of ecclesiology (and of sacramental structures and functions) comes into play. The "Joint Declaration" itself points to this organic theological solidarity and confesses that it must be further studied (§43)—the whole field is open for cautious and bold investigation. The foregoing remarks on baptism must here suffice.

The second essential connection binds substitutionary atonement and justification by faith. Reformed theology, in the footsteps of Calvin, brings out the consequence in full light: because Christ bore our sins in our stead, they no longer weigh on our heads—inasmuch we are "in him" as our head. Since Christ paid our legal debt, the ransom of blood, the Judge of all the earth does right when he releases us, free from all condemnation—he has taken responsibility for his people, whom we join by faith. This logic of steel, this logic of gold, stands out in several passages of Scripture. Galatians 3 bases the justification of believers, deliverance from the curse incurred by imperfect obedience to the law, on Christ's being made a curse on our behalf; the formal symmetry of 2 Corinthians 5:21 implies the same reasoning, especially when one sees that Paul is thinking in terms of imputation (v. 19); and Romans 3:23–26 not only establishes the foundation of justification by faith in the atoning sacrifice of Jesus but explains that this is valid even for the forgiveness/justification that Old Testament believers enjoyed although their sins could not be truly atoned for. The link already appears in Isaiah 53: the righteous servant's death is accepted as a proper guilt offering, *asham* (v. 10), and he will lead to justification, *yatsdiq*, the many whose sins he will bear (v. 11). It is disquieting to realize how few, if any, among the Lutheran–Roman Catholic dialogue partners would make this logic theirs.[59]

The last question may raise what, in the eyes of many, was a dead issue: What about the difference between the Lutheran and the Reformed? Is it relevant to our reception (warmer or cooler) of the "Joint Declaration"? Since the wide-ranging "Concorde de Leuenberg" (1973), the two branches of the magisterial Reformation have enjoyed full theological communion—officially, at any rate. Nevertheless, the Reformed were not associated with their Lutheran friends in the dialogue with Roman Catholics. Some regretted this sign or symptom of felt difference, if not indifference. The primary cause was probably the policy that the Vatican chose to follow about thirty years ago, of privileging *bi*lateral dialogues. But this disassociation spurs theological reflection.

The Reformed, it was suggested above, cannot sign the statements on baptism in the "Joint Declaration" if they wish, lucidly, to be faithful to their tradition. They are able to avoid the unclarity in Luther's notion of the word. But do differences go deeper and make convergence with Roman Catholics easier for Lutherans than for Reformed theologians? It has been a striking phenomenon that Roman Catholic scholars have been far more interested in Luther than in Calvin (with the exception of Alexandre Ganoczy). They feel more at ease; they more readily perceive what they can appropriate and how they may respond. Is this meaningful and relevant to reflection on the "Joint Declaration"?

The tools of Herman Dooyeweerd's critical analysis of "ground-motives" may shed some light on the matter. The Augustinian monk Luther, who had been trained as a nominalist theologian, did not break away totally from his past. The ground-motive of his thought remained the nature-grace antinomy[60]—the same as still governs the Catholic worldview. Luther produced a sharply *antithetic* version of nature-grace

---

59. Especially among Roman Catholics (cf. Dulles, "Justification in Contemporary Catholic Theology," 260), whereas three or four generations ago it was still very present in Catholic theology.

60. Herman Dooyeweerd, *A New Critique of Theoretical Thought*; vol. 1, trans. David H. Freeman and William S. Young; vols. 2–4, trans. David H. Freeman and H. De Jongste; 4 vols. (Philadelphia: Presbyterian and Reformed, 1969) 1:512–13, 517; 2:157, 159.

thought, whereas the wonderfully balanced *synthetic* version of Thomas Aquinas prevailed in the Roman Catholic Church. Yet the deep kinship is there, which favors some degree of understanding. Calvin, trained in Renaissance philological and legal studies, was the man of the creation-fall-redemption motive, the other ground-motive (and the biblical one in Dooyeweerd's estimate); hence the strange flavor of his argument for Roman Catholic readers.

This hypothesis receives some corroboration from what might seem, at first, to be a valid objection. The Reformed theologian Karl Barth was the first Protestant thinker (almost since the Reformers) to draw intense and sympathetic attention on the part of Catholic critics.[61] On justification, his account was chosen by Hans Küng when Küng set out to show the essential agreement between Catholic and Protestant doctrines, but precisely because, as Dooyeweerd himself discerned with remarkable penetration, Barth's revolution amounted to a return to the nature-grace ground-motive.[62] Barth's radical reinterpretation of his tradition yields a more intensely antithetical version in the nature-grace key. But some unexpected encounters look less surprising if one digs deeper.

If the last suggestion contributes to historical interpretation, it is also a call for self-examination, finer, more rigorous, reaching deeper, *Deo volente* (Ps. 19:11–14 [12–15 Hebrew]; 139:23–24). Where do *we* stand?

---

61. Starting with Erich Przywara, Hans Urs von Balthasar, and then Henri Bouillard and his major dissertation.

62. Dooyeweerd, *A New Critique*, 1:66.

10

The Doctrine of Justification
in Paul and Beyond

Some Proposals

SIMON GATHERCOLE

Introduction

Writing on justification in Paul and in the New Testament in general is like the life of the theologian in miniature. There is all the joy of expounding the fact that Christ's death means our acquittal before God. The joy that continual reflection on this fact gives is one of the reasons I often feel as if I have the best job in the world. On the other hand, the agony is never far away from the ecstasy. Although all theological exposition requires attention to clarity of expression and careful choice of words, this seems even more pressing than usual with justification. There is a constant sense of the danger of miscommunication, or of "watering down," or exaggeration.

In very brief summary, this contribution is divided into six sections. The first two look at the basis of justification in Paul's discussions of the work of Christ and forgiveness. In the third we come to examine what takes place in the divine act of justification, according to Paul. The fourth section examines Paul's understanding of justification in relation to soteriology more broadly; and the fifth section, in relation to the teaching of the rest of the New Testament on justification. Finally, the sixth section engages in discussion with N. T. Wright's understanding of righteousness and "works of the law."

Justification and the Cross

A frequent criticism of various articulations of justification is that they are unchristological.[1] There is a constant problem of justification being envisaged simply as an act of God *in abstracto*, which has little relation to Christ. We will attempt to confront this problem at the outset by anchoring justification in the atonement. Beginning with the theme of the atonement, then, several passages are important.

Atonement

Galatians 2:21 says, "I do not set aside the grace of God; for if righteousness came through the Law, then Christ died for nothing."[2] The key point to note here is the relation, which underlies the verse, between *the death of Christ* and *righteousness*. Although it is not stated directly, the obvious implication is that Christ's death is what wins righteousness for us. Paul's subsequent reasoning is that since God went to such a length to restore righteousness to us by sending his Son for us, righteousness surely cannot be obtained any other way.

Romans 3 (which we shall examine in more detail later) is the place where we first encounter the connection in Romans. Paul's statement here is as follows: those who have sinned and fallen short of the glory of God "are justified freely by his grace, through the redemption which is in Jesus Christ whom God set forth as the mercy seat to be accessed by faith, in his blood" (Rom. 3:24–25). It is in his death (indicated by "in his blood") that Christ is fully visible as the mercy seat, as the locus of justification and redemption.

Next, Romans 4:25 indicates how, for Paul, this justification is not achieved by the cross in isolation from the resurrection. At the end of

---

1. See the comments in R. B. Hays, *The Faith of Jesus Christ: The Narrative Substructure of Galatians 3:1–4:11*, Biblical Resource Series (1983; repr., Grand Rapids: Eerdmans, 2002), xxix, endorsing Gerhard Ebeling's critique of post-Reformation Lutheran formulations. See the critique of Dunn in P. Stuhlmacher, "Christus Jesus ist hier, der gestorben ist, ja vielmehr, der auch auferweckt ist, der zur Rechten Gottes ist und uns vertritt," in *Auferstehung–Resurrection: The Fourth Durham-Tübingen Research Symposium*, ed. F. Avemarie and H. Lichtenberger (Tübingen: Mohr, 2001), 351–61.

2. All Scripture quotations in this chapter are the author's translation.

Romans 4, Paul is speaking of Christ, "who was delivered over to death for our sins, and was raised to life for our justification." Most commentators rightly avoid a crude reading of this verse that would indicate Christ's *death* as the way sins are dealt with, and then the *resurrection* as the basis for justification. It is clear enough that Paul is telescoping together the cross and the resurrection here, just as he regards "dealing with transgressions" and "justification" as a unity.

The point could hardly be made more clearly than in Romans 5:9: "Therefore, having now been justified by his blood, how much more shall we be saved from wrath through it."[3] Paul is not even arguing here for the death of Christ as the ground of justification; he is assuming it and using it as a basis for his how-much-more argument about assurance in the face of the wrath to come.

Finally, in the light of the strong evidence we have already seen in Romans, the statements in the Adam-Christ contrast in Romans 5 make best sense as contrasting the effects of Adam's sin with Jesus' death on the cross: "So then, just as the one transgression led to condemnation for all, so also the one act of righteousness led to the righteousness of life for all. For just as through the transgression of the one man many were made sinners, so also through the obedience of the one man many were made righteous" (vv. 18–19). In verse 18 Adam's single transgression at the fall leads to condemnation, but Christ's single act of righteousness brings justification for all. In verse 19 Adam disobeyed and so many were made sinners, whereas Christ's obedience to death on the cross made many righteous.

This makes our justification, should we be in doubt of it, as sure and certain as the fact that Jesus died. Since this is a fact that cannot really be disputed, Paul exhorts us to draw the conclusion that we really do have right standing before God. Our justification is anchored repeatedly, for Paul, in the cross and resurrection of Christ.

Other Christological Aspects of Justification

If the primary basis for justification is the death of Christ in the *past*, the way in which Paul describes justification as tied up with the *present* action of Christ is also significant. As Peter Stuhlmacher has noted, Romans 8:34 is an important statement of Christ's role in justification when one considers the parallelism with 8:33: "Who will make an accusation against the elect of God? God is the justifier! Who can condemn them? Christ Jesus has died—what is more, has risen from the dead, and is at

3. Or "through him."

the right hand of God, and is interceding for us!"[4] From passages already noted above, we are familiar with the first two components (Christ's death and resurrection) as instrumental in justification. Christ's heavenly session, however, in which he intercedes on our behalf, also seems still to be a part of Paul's discussion of justification. Christ's present work as our heavenly protector is seen as a kind of extension of the justifying work of his death and resurrection. This should not be pressed, however, since the reference is very brief.

For a clearer example of righteousness as deriving from the present relation to Christ, we can turn to Philippians 3. After Paul's catalog of privileges and achievements according to the flesh, he recounts famously that whatever they once were to him, he now considers them loss. He *has* written them off as a loss, and *continues to do so*, "so that I may gain Christ, and be found in him, not having my righteousness by the Law, but having it through faith in Christ, that righteousness from God by faith, so that I might know him and the power of his resurrection and fellowship in his sufferings, being conformed to his death so that I may somehow attain to the resurrection of the dead" (Phil. 3:8–11).

Here the righteousness by faith is regarded as deriving from that present relationship of faith in Christ, and being "found in him." Being "in Christ" means participating in the sphere of righteousness that he has opened up and that he defines. To be in Christ, then, means to be righteous.

The Reformed tradition's most common way of explicating the christological character of justification (not least by way of Phil. 3), however, has recently aroused considerable controversy. This is the doctrine of the imputation of *Christ's* righteousness (as opposed to an imputed righteousness understood in some other way). A statement by Robert Gundry on the (non)imputation of Christ's righteousness in particular has sparked a response by John Piper,[5] and Gundry and Don Carson have also entered the same debate from different stances.[6] It is not my purpose here to enter this debate. But it should be said that there is clearly a great deal of diversity of opinion on the matter. This is, of course, not sufficient in itself to let discretion take the better part of

4. See Stuhlmacher, "Christus Jesus ist hier."

5. R. H. Gundry, "Why I Didn't Endorse 'The Gospel of Jesus Christ: An Evangelical Celebration' . . . Even Though I Wasn't Asked To," *Books and Culture* 7, no. 1 (2001): 6–9. See further the forceful critique in J. Piper, *Counted Righteous in Christ: Should We Abandon the Imputation of Christ's Righteousness?* (Wheaton, IL: Crossway, 2002).

6. See R. H. Gundry, "The Nonimputation of Christ's Righteousness," in *Justification—What's at Stake in the Current Debates*, ed. M. A. Husbands and D. J. Treier (Downers Grove, IL: InterVarsity, 2004) 17–45; and D. A. Carson, "The Vindication of Imputation: On Fields of Discourse and, of Course, Semantic Fields," ibid., 46–48.

valor. But in this case, the diversity seems to arise out of the complexity of the New Testament evidence, not because one side is particularly hidebound to tradition and the other wallowing in the desire for novelty or for a doctrine that is more amenable to culture. I would not myself deny this traditional understanding of imputation. Still, because of the complexity of the issue, I would propose that the requirement that it is specifically Christ's righteousness that is imputed to believers should not feature on evangelical statements of faith. To make such a finely balanced point an article of faith seems a dangerous strategy. Nonetheless, it is very clear that justification is still christological through and through. Both the cross and the present action of Christ are the vital grounds of justification.

Forgiveness and Justification

We have seen the unbreakable connection between the death of Christ and justification in the passages above. What we have not seen is how the two ideas are connected, which requires a closer look at Romans 3:21–26. At the beginning of this section, we come across "the righteousness of God," which is revealed for all who believe (vv. 21–22) and is demonstrated in God being both "just and the justifier" (vv. 25–26). Probably God's own righteousness is meant in this context rather than a righteousness given by God. As Romans 10:3 implies, this "righteousness of God" is much more likely to be an *action*, rather than an *attribute*, of God.[7] Even if the "righteousness of God" here in 3:21 is not the imputed righteousness that avails before God, the action of God is clearly that of his reckoning of righteousness to the ungodly.

This is to get ahead of ourselves, however. Staying with Romans 3:21–26, the passage seems to be combining at least two elements. First is the Old Testament tradition of God's righteousness as his saving deliverance, as in the numerous references in Isaiah 40–55 or the similar statement in Psalm 98:2: "The Lord has made his salvation known, he has revealed his righteousness to the nations." Second is Paul's more immediate interest, in 3:21–26, in God demonstrating his justice in the punishment of sin at the cross. God's righteousness has come into question in that God has passed over sin. Paul's term *anochē* ("forbearance") refers to God's merciful withholding of his judgment for a season, so that sin does not immediately receive the penalty it merits. Now, however, sin has received its penalty in Christ (although this is seen more clearly in

---

7. S. J. Gathercole, *Where Is Boasting? Early Jewish Soteriology and Paul's Response in Romans 1–5* (Grand Rapids: Eerdmans, 2002), 224.

Romans 8:3 than in Romans 3:25). God's forgiveness of sin can now be seen, then, to be not simply indulgence on God's part but part and parcel of his righteousness. It is this forgiveness that is a vital aspect of God's reckoning righteousness to the ungodly.

The beginning of Romans 8 is also important for understanding the considerable overlap between justification and forgiveness. It has numerous similarities with Romans 3:21–26 in that it also talks of how God's verdict of condemnation is broken as sin is punished in the flesh of Jesus. The condemnation by God has been nullified for those in Christ Jesus because he has provided a sin offering, which in Leviticus 16 brings about both atonement and cleansing from sins. A further neglected passage in this discussion is 2 Corinthians 5, where Paul happily talks of reconciliation and righteousness in the same context as "not counting people's sins against them" (vv. 17–21).

This overlap can be further supported by Paul's near equation of justification and forgiveness, as is clear in the conjunction of Romans 4:1–5 with 4:6–8. Here Abraham and David form parallel cases, even though Abraham is apparently justified whereas David is "only" forgiven. But Paul makes it clear in his discussion of David that justification and forgiveness are almost coextensive. Verses 6–8 read as follows: "Similarly, David also speaks of the blessedness of the man to whom God *reckons righteousness* apart from works: 'Blessed are they whose *wrongs are forgiven* and whose *sins are covered*. Blessed is the man *whose sin the Lord does not reckon*'" (italics added). Despite numerous attempts by a wide variety of very different interpreters to avoid the fact, Paul seems here to be defining the *reckoning of righteousness* as *forgiveness of wrongs, covering sins*, and *not reckoning sin*.

The reason for the difficulty that interpreters have with this idea stems, it seems, from understanding forgiveness in too minimalistic terms. It is sometimes regarded merely as wiping the slate clean, which leaves us at zero—where we have no record of sin against us but no positive righteousness either. Paul, however, combines forgiveness with blessedness and justification (Rom. 4:6–8) and also with reconciliation and justification (2 Cor. 5:18–21). Forgiveness appears, then, not merely as a clearing of the account; it has (and here there is a thoroughly Pauline mixing of metaphors) relational contours as well. Justification is not forgiveness in the sense of the forgiveness of a debt in abstraction from a relationship (e.g., a waiver of a debt to a bank). Rather, it is forgiveness of a personal wrong (disobedience and offense against God's glory), such that forgiveness of the personal wrong means restoration of the relationship. And restoration of the relationship is tantamount to talking of divine acceptance, since the initiative needs to come from the divine side. There has perhaps been too much separation of images such as justification, forgiveness, and reconciliation when such a separation does not really seem to work with Paul; for him, one image often suggests another (Rom. 3:24–26; 5:8–9; 2 Cor. 5:17–21). A nice parallel from Qumran suggests that a sharp distinction between forgiveness and justification would probably not have made much sense to Paul's Jewish contemporaries either:

> As for me, if I stumble, the mercies of God shall be my eternal salvation.
> If I stagger because of the sin of the flesh, my justification shall be by the righteousness of God which endures for ever.
> When my distress is unleashed, he will deliver my soul from the pit and will direct my steps to the way.
> He will draw me near by his grace, and by his mercy will he bring my justification.
> He will judge me in the righteousness of his truth and in the greatness of his goodness he will pardon all my sins.
> Through his righteousness he will cleanse me of the uncleanness of man and of the sins of the children of men,
> that I may confess to God his righteousness, and his majesty to the Most High. (1QS 11:13–15)[8]

Returning to Paul, we can sum up his view as follows. The atonement is the basis for forgiveness in that Christ's death means that God's loving refusal to punish our sin is not indulgence on God's part but, rather, is a function of God's righteousness. What follows from this is that such forgiveness goes hand in hand with justification. This pattern has perhaps not always been clear because of Paul's frequent omission of the category of forgiveness and because of his concern merely to talk of the death of Christ and the justification that results from it.

Justification: The Question of Status, Moral Transformation, and Ontology

We come, then, to the question of what takes place in the divine act of justification. Charles Cranfield expounds the traditional alternatives with his customary clarity:

> We must notice first the centuries-old dispute as to whether *dikaioun* ["to justify"] and . . . its cognates refer simply to status, or to status and also ethical character. Or to put it otherwise, as to whether justification is simply the acquittal of the sinner, or both that and also a making righteous

8. G. Vermes, *The Dead Sea Scrolls in English*, 4th ed. (London: Penguin, 1995), 88.

in an ethical sense, moral regeneration. Roman Catholic scholars have generally maintained that justification includes moral renewal, though they have stated and defended this position in various ways: Protestants have generally taken the opposite view.[9]

Given these alternatives, there seems little doubt that we should prefer the view that justification is a divine declaration of status, a declaration that does not include any infusion of moral righteousness; the latter view is especially to be rejected if the moral righteousness is supposed to be prior to, and a basis for, God's justifying act. God's declarative word is, rather, the justification of the ungodly.

On the other hand, what happens when this takes place? The traditional Protestant view, as far as I understand it, is that in the act of justification, the believer does not actually become righteous but, rather, receives the status of an alien righteousness, the righteousness of God that is alien from first to last. Here, however, there is a potential danger if divine speech or divine reckoning is understood in a way that is not really true to the identity of God.

The principal trouble is if one supposes that God can declare something to be the case (namely, that the sinner is righteous) but that in reality the opposite state of affairs persists: in God's eyes, the believer is *justus* ("righteous"), but his or her real being is fundamentally as *peccator* ("sinner"). We should more properly consider that God's "speech-acts" are what *determine* reality; they do not merely create an alternative, Platonic reality.[10] If God declares a sinner to be righteous, then he or she really *is* righteous. Reality at the forensic level (*justus*) is no less real than the reality made up of human actions (*peccator*).

This is not simply the imposition of a foreign philosophical or linguistic understanding of God's words—it comes from Romans 4. Here God's act of justification (in this case, the justification of Abraham) is described as a reckoning of righteousness and as the justification of the ungodly. Significantly, however, the reference to God justifying the ungodly comes in a series of descriptions of God in the chapter. God is "the one who justifies the ungodly" (v. 5), "the one who makes the dead live and who calls nonbeings into being" (v. 17), and "the one who raised Jesus our Lord from the dead" (v. 24).

Here justification is a typical act of God in that it has the character of a creation from nothing or, more appropriately perhaps, in Karl Barth's phrase, *creatio e contrario*, creation from its opposite. God's word de-

9. C. E. B. Cranfield, *A Critical and Exegetical Commentary on the Epistle to the Romans*, 2 vols. (Edinburgh: T&T Clark, 1975–1979), 1:95.

10. What I have in mind here is the view, sometimes articulated, that although we are *really* sinners, yet, when God looks at us, God sees Jesus.

termines the being and identity of the person who is the object of God's justification, and so this person is really righteous.

> The vital thing is that this judgment has creative power because it is God's Word. As the creative Word of God, it effectively pronounces sinners righteous. This is the Word, as Paul says in the oft-quoted phrase of Romans 4:17, which calls into existence the things which do not exist. It works according to the rule given in Psalm 33:9: "For he spoke, and it came to be; he commanded, and it stood firm." This is also the rule to be applied if we are to understand the forensic judgment of God as he pronounces sinners righteous. The forensic act *is* the effective act of making the ungodly righteous. It *is*![11]

In the light of the explanation of justification as a declaration with creative power, it is proper to see it as constituting a true definition of the being of the believer. The believer has not had an infusion of moral righteousness but is determined by God—in the cross—to be righteous. The righteousness here should not be understood either as an infused moral power or as covenant membership (as we will see in discussion with Wright below). According to Paul, when we are reckoned righteous, it is not that we have done what God requires, such that he is recognizing the status quo. Rather, even as we are ungodly, he declares us righteous. By God's creative word, then, we stand as embodying everything that God requires. In our identity and being we have been determined righteous by God.

This finds further support in Romans 5:19: "For just as through the transgression of the one man many were made sinners, so also through the obedience of the one man many were made righteous." Here Paul describes righteousness as forensic, but not forensic in a nonontological sense. In Romans 5:18 Paul contrasts the "justification of life" (*dikaiōsis zoēs*) with "condemnation" (*katakrima*). So, here the sense is clearly forensic. When the argument progresses, however, the contrast is in Romans 5:19 between the many who are "appointed" (*katastathēsontai*) sinners and those who are appointed righteous. This term, "appointed," has been the subject of a good deal of discussion. The usual meaning of *kathistēmi* is "appoint," as in appointing a person to a position or task.[12] Does Paul in Romans 5 see righteousness as a status of being to which one is appointed? "This is powerful evidence that righteousness in Paul,

---

11. Eberhard Jüngel, *Justification: The Heart of the Christian Faith* (Edinburgh: T&T Clark, 2001), 210–11.

12. In James 3:6 and 4:4, the passive means something close to "is." The latter reference is probably the closest parallel, as it talks of *kathistēmi* with a half-noun/adjective: "whoever wants to be a friend of the world *kathistatai* ['thereby becomes'] an enemy of God."

although forensic, cannot be confined in every instance to forensic categories."[13] On the one hand, then, it is not simply a *reckoned* righteousness that is not real; the verb does not really allow for that interpretation. On the other hand, it is not a righteousness of behavior that is in view here; rather, it is a matter of status. The verb *kathistēmi* has a stronger sense than *logizō* ("I reckon"), although, when seen within a theological understanding of divine reckoning, the senses converge. So, through the obedience of the one man, "many are appointed as righteous."

An obvious question that arises from this should not be avoided. Are believers, now declared righteous, not sinners? Indeed they are, though Paul might not use this term. He might well not use the term because it sounds like a description of one's identity, of one's being, and this fundamental identity is one that God has now eliminated. Nevertheless, we know both from Scripture and experience that we continue to sin. Paul wrote letters to his churches because of it and presumed that the individual continued to struggle with sin after conversion, despite some recent attempts to prove otherwise.[14] To cite just one proof text: "For the flesh desires what is contrary to the Spirit, while the Spirit desires what is contrary to the flesh, for these are opposed to each other, so that you do not do what you want" (Gal. 5:17).[15] But is it not illogical to say that one whose fundamental, God-determined being is "righteous" still continues to sin? Yes; Paul would, I am sure, say that it is completely illogical for those who believe in Christ to continue to sin.

This is not, however, the key point at issue here. What I should like to open up for discussion is the understanding of the "justification of the ungodly." In this connection, Tom Wright's definition of justification as being "reckoned to be in covenant with God" seems too minimal.[16] To cite a longer definition:

> Justification, to offer a fuller statement, is the recognition and declaration by God that those who are thus called and believing are in fact his people, the single family promised to Abraham, that as the new covenant

13. T. R. Schreiner, *Romans*, Baker Exegetical Commentary (Grand Rapids: Baker, 1998), 288, who also notes P. Stuhlmacher, *Gerechtigkeit Gottes bei Paulus* (Göttingen: Vandenhoeck & Ruprecht, 1966), 223–24.

14. See, e.g., T. Engberg-Pedersen, *Paul and the Stoics* (Edinburgh: T&T Clark, 2000), 167.

15. I follow here the interpretation of J. L. Martyn, *Galatians*, Anchor Bible (New York: Doubleday, 1997), 495, as well as my own position outlined in S. J. Gathercole, "A Law unto Themselves: The Gentiles in Romans 2:14–15 Revisited," *Journal for the Study of the New Testament* 85 (2002): 27–49, at 45.

16. N. T. Wright, "The Letter to the Romans: Introduction, Commentary, and Reflections," in *The New Interpreter's Bible*, 13 vols. (Nashville: Abingdon, 1994–2004), 10:393–770, at 490.

people their sins are forgiven, and that since they have already died and been raised with the Messiah they are assured of final bodily resurrection at the last.[17]

This may not sound like a minimalistic definition of justification. We have seen above, however, that God's act of justification is not one of *recognition* but is, rather, closer to *creation*. It is God's *determination* of our new identity rather than a recognition of it. The latter does not seem to sit well with the portrayal of divine action in general and justification in particular in Romans 4. The category of "alien" righteousness is vital in capturing the truth that our righteousness comes only from God and not from ourselves. But it should not be misinterpreted to mean that we are thereby not really righteous.

Justification and Salvation

At least two problems attend the relationship between justification and soteriology more broadly conceived. The first concerns the *ordo salutis*, most controversially in terms of the relationship between justification and sanctification but also in terms of the relation of justification to *regeneration*. The problem in essence is that if faith is a gift of God that is an instrumental cause of justification, then this implies that God *equips* believers for justification rather than justifies the ungodly. (This problem is exacerbated further if one adopts a maximalist definition of faith along the lines implied by Romans 4:18–21, where faith is essentially synonymous with *worship*, as Abraham is depicted as "giving glory to God" [Rom. 4:20; cf. Rom. 1:21–23].) Similarly, regeneration by the Spirit has traditionally been regarded as necessary for faith; so, in what sense are the "ungodly" still ungodly if they have been regenerated?

The other problem surrounds the temporal aspect of justification. One standard line is to take justification by faith in Paul to refer to the "beginning of salvation" or the "initial acceptance before God."[18] The problem with this, however, lies in the fact that in Galatians Paul is insistent that Gentile converts persevere in justification by faith (Gal. 3:1–5). He uses the doctrine precisely to correct a false understanding

17. N. T. Wright, "The Letter to the Galatians: Exegesis and Theology," in *Between Two Horizons: Spanning New Testament Studies and Systematic Theology*, ed. J. B. Green and M. Turner (Grand Rapids: Eerdmans, 2000), 235.

18. Phrases used respectively by J. D. G. Dunn, *The Theology of Paul the Apostle* (Edinburgh: T&T Clark, 1998), 317. (where it is the title of ch. 5, in which justification is discussed); and D. J. Moo, *The Letter of James*, Pillar New Testament Commentary (Grand Rapids: Eerdmans, 2000), 141.

of how the Christian life should be lived. Again, returning to Romans 4:6–8, the blessing of justification by faith is the blessing of forgiveness that David experienced in the midst of his fellowship with God when he fell into sin.

There is, however, a more promising line of attack. In this model, justification can be seen as referring to the totality of salvation, as regarded from a certain point of view. By way of illustrative analogy, Rudolf Bultmann's famous treatment of anthropology may be helpful. In *Theology of the New Testament*, Bultmann tackles the various anthropological concepts, "*soma*," "*psyche, pneuma* and *zoe*," "mind and conscience," and "heart."[19] Some treatments of these terms have attempted to divide up the totality of the human person scientifically by assigning locations and substances to each of these components, albeit occasionally acknowledging that there is overlap between some concepts at points. Bultmann distanced himself sharply from this strategy. In discussion specifically of Paul's use of *pneuma* ("spirit"), Bultmann writes, "He [Paul] does not mean some higher principle within him or some special intellectual or spiritual faculty"; rather, *pneuma* refers to *the person as a whole*, regarded from a particular standpoint.[20] "Man does not consist of two parts, much less of three; nor are *psyche* and *pneuma* special faculties or principles (within the *soma*) of a mental life higher than his animal life. Rather, man is a living unity."[21]

The accuracy of Bultmann's exegesis of Paul here is not the point. The question is whether justification can really be thought of as, quantitatively, a "part" of salvation—whether as a stage in the *ordo salutis*—or as itself a process, which has a beginning, a middle, and an end. Instead, the approach outlined by Bruce McCormack in his essay in this volume seems rather more fruitful, although it is by no means the case that one needs to follow all of Barth on the point. The suggestion here is that salvation should be viewed as a unity, with justification referring to the whole while highlighting a certain aspect. In this model, one does not need to decide on an order of faith, regeneration, and justification. Such an order would be very difficult to prise out of the relevant passages in Paul, and therefore an account that enables them to be viewed as a simultaneous product of divine action has a certain explanatory power.

We have cleared the ground, then, to regard Paul's use of "justify" and "reckon righteous" language as referring to the totality of salvation. What aspects of soteriology does the doctrine of justification bring to the fore, then? The first is clearly that of salvation as consisting in acceptance,

19. R. Bultmann, *Theology of the New Testament* (1952; repr., London: SCM, 1965), 191–227.
20. Ibid., 206.
21. Ibid., 209.

forgiveness, and acquittal; these arise directly out of the sense of the term "justify" as used by Paul. As we have noted already above, there is a constant oscillation between forensic and relational categories in Pauline discussions of justification. Second, the term "justify" must be regarded in terms of how Paul glosses it—as taking place when "faith is reckoned as righteousness" (Rom. 4; Gal. 3). Here the *extra* of salvation is highlighted: that salvation does not arise from within ourselves but simply on the basis of divine action in Christ. Third, because this divine action sets God radically over against the world both in his judgment and his grace and classifies all humanity within the sphere of sinful "flesh," even the (for Paul's contemporaries) ultimate distinction between Jew and Gentile is relativized. Hence justification becomes a key doctrine for facilitating the articulation of the truth that all come into the church having been accepted by God on the same basis, that of faith.

On the other hand, these aspects cannot simply be jumbled up under the general umbrella of justification; it is vital to distinguish between the various "meanings" of justification. In his recent work on the resurrection, Wright points helpfully toward an important distinction not always well observed by New Testament scholars: the distinction between reference and implication. Despite the shadow of twentieth-century philosophy of language, the distinction should be maintained. In Wright's illustration, to take the word "democracy," its *referent* is "government by the people." When one is talking about implication, however, democracy means "happiness (as spoken by a good democrat)" or "chaos (as spoken by a disgruntled dictator)."[22]

Applying this to the present discussion, it is important to distinguish between the *referent* of "justify" in Paul ("acquit" or "confer a righteous status on")[23] and its *implications*. I would prefer a more nuanced approach to that of James Dunn's *Theology of Paul the Apostle*, for example, where we see the following four statements in the conclusion to the section on justification by faith: (a) "Justification means acceptance by God, the God who justifies the ungodly who trust as Abraham trusted"; (b) "If justification means God accepting the sinner (5:8), it also means bestowing the blessing of peace on those who were formerly enemies (5:10)"; (c) "Justification by faith means Gentiles experiencing the blessing promised to Abraham, being granted a share in Israel's inheritance"; (d) "Justification means liberty."[24] Here referent and implication are all subsumed under the vaguer verb "mean."[25] It is important, by con-

22. N. T. Wright, *The Resurrection of the Son of God* (London: SPCK, 2003), 719.

23. Cranfield, *Romans*, 1:95.

24. Dunn, *Theology of Paul*, 385–86, 388.

25. What is perhaps worthy of further reflection, however, is whether it is possible to separate referent from implication in what is always by definition a polemical doctrine.

trast, to distinguish between the various relations between these levels of "meaning." As I have argued elsewhere, one of the problems with a number of New Perspective accounts of justification is that too much importance is frequently attributed to the function of justification as an ecclesiological doctrine, such that its fundamentally soteriological structure is relegated to secondary significance.[26]

In summary, then, returning to our main point: to regard justification as referring to the whole of salvation from a certain perspective, rather than to a part of salvation, solves at least some of the problems that attend assigning it to a certain stage in the salvation process.

Justification in Paul and New Testament Theology

By far the dominant aspect of justification for Paul, then, is God's confrontation with the sinner as ungodly, which paradoxically results in God's acceptance of the sinner. As a result, it is also the dominant sense of justification in New Testament theology, not because Paul is the dominant voice in New Testament theology but because he makes the most extensive contribution to the doctrine of justification. The other voices in the New Testament, however, force us to acknowledge that the biblical concept of justification is not a monolithic one.

Jesus

We can illustrate this diversity most clearly by examining two references to justification in the teaching of Jesus—two of the most explicit, since they employ the verb *dikaioō*, the only term usually translated as "justify." The first reference (in canonical sequence) to justification is Matthew 12:37: "For by your words will you be justified, and by your words will you be condemned." This comes in the context of Jesus' denunciation of the "brood of vipers" as those who cannot produce good fruit because they are not good (v. 34a); a good tree, by contrast, can produce good fruit: "The good man brings good things out of that good store-house, and the wicked man brings wickedness out of his wicked store" (v. 35). In 12:37 the reference to justification is clearly in the context of an eschatological acquittal; it stands in contrast with con-

---

Jüngel is interesting on the always-already polemical character of justification, in that it is always about (!) God's verdict on guilty humanity. See also Wright, "Letter to the Galatians," 234, for a different (though almost as strong) emphasis on justification as polemic.

26. Gathercole, *Where Is Boasting?*

demnation, and both future tenses certainly refer to the eschatological future of the day of judgment. Here *words* are the fruit that are referred to as the reason for justification. It is dangerous to attempt to be more orthodox than Jesus by insisting that "fruit" cannot be described as an instrumental cause of eschatological justification.

On the other hand, Jesus also uses the same language in Luke 18:14: "I say to you, this man went home justified rather than the other." "This man" is the tax collector who has called out for mercy from God although he is a sinner, in contrast to the Pharisee, who in the parable parades his obedience to that which he perceives to be what God requires from him. Justification here is clearly very close to the Pauline sense in Romans 4: it is a "justification of the ungodly," and it is not explicitly a justification that takes place at the eschaton; rather, it belongs to the *present* and marks initial acceptance before God.

James

Paul picks up very clearly the sense of justification in the parable above, and he is probably dependent upon an oral form of the parable later recorded by Luke. On the other hand, the description of justification that we saw in the Matthean saying is, mutatis mutandis, very close to what we see in the Epistle of James.

James, as is well known, makes the point very explicitly that justification is not by faith alone but by works (James 2:24). As the context makes clear, James understands justification to be linked to *future* salvation, much as in Matthew's Gospel.[27] Consequently, scholars who have attempted to solve the Paul/James tension by focusing on James's concern with eschatological justification have hit on an important point.[28] Others have tried to address (or perhaps circumvent) the problem by arguing that faith and works have very different senses in Paul and James: Paul contrasts trust in God (faith) with meritorious legalism (works of the law), whereas James contrasts nominal monotheism (faith alone) with works of charity.[29] And there is a good deal of merit in these observations as well.

The question needs to be addressed, however, from within the context of James's formulations; we have no references to justification in James beyond the statements in 2:21–25. The issue James is addressing here

---

27. The context leading up to the discussion of justification in James 2:14–26 is concerned with final salvation (see 2:12–13), and the meaning of the "save" word group in James probably refers consistently to eschatological salvation.

28. See, e.g., Moo, *James*, 141.

29. J. Jeremias, "Paul and James," *Expository Times* 66 (1954/1955): 368–71.

is that of what kind of faith God requires. In 2:20–26 James addresses his witless interlocutor (v. 20: *ō anthrōpe kene* ["you foolish fellow!"]) in the attempt to convince him that "faith without works is dead/useless," a statement repeated three times (vv. 17, 20, 26). In fact, justification is only mentioned in this final stage of the argument, after James has highlighted the futility of a faith that does not help the poor (vv. 14–17) and the fact that even the demons could subscribe to such a faith (vv. 18–19).

Within this framework, we can appreciate how James uses the language of justification, without blaming him for not simultaneously coming up with Paul's interpretation of "reckoning righteousness." Three points are particularly relevant to the discussion of James here. First, James understands justification predominantly as eschatological, although his usage cannot be confined to this sphere. Although his discussion is framed by the concern with what kind of faith avails eschatologically, he also brings in the examples of Abraham and Rahab, where the sense is not of eschatological justification. Second, James does not—as is perhaps commonly thought—confuse faith and works. He regards faith as working together with works (2:12) and "made perfect by works" (2:22). Third, James, crucially, regards future salvation as having pastoral implications for those who are resting on their doctrinal laurels. This pastoral situation must be seen as the setting for James's formulations.

Toward a Synthesis

The problem of the apparent differences between James and Paul has long been a *crux interpretum*, but it needs to be remembered that (as we have seen) the James/Paul tension is merely a manifestation a generation or so later of a Jesus/Jesus tension. Already in Jesus' teaching there is clear indication that God accepts sinners but that at the final judgment, vindication is for the righteous who have produced fruit. (It is not merely that those who have attained a superfluity of righteousness also accumulate rewards in heaven.)

Furthermore, it is also a Paul/Paul tension: Paul, too, can use the language of justification to describe the final vindication of God's people on the basis, from one angle, of their obedience. In Romans 2:13 Paul talks of justification as for the *doers*: "it is not the hearers of the Law who are righteous before God; rather, the doers will be justified." It will not do to write this off as a hypothetical reference to an empty set of "the righteous," for Paul goes on directly afterward to provide instances of these doers of the law who will be justified: the Gentiles who have the law written on their hearts.[30] There is not space to rehearse the argument in detail here, but it should be observed that the category of "doers of the Law" is picked up in 2:14 (cf. 2:26–27) as the Gentiles are defined precisely as those who do the law.[31] If this interpretation is correct, then it is not simply within the New Testament more broadly that we find this tension, but even within Paul. At the same time, it has to be recognized that this is an isolated example, perhaps because it occurs within the context of a debate with an imaginary Jewish interlocutor.[32]

Can this diversity, even within Paul himself, be accounted for? It can as long as we do not have a monolithic conception of justification whereby it only ever refers in the New Testament to the justification of the ungodly. A particularly important clue comes in the Jesus tradition from Matthew 12. The New Testament does not offer two ways of salvation, one by faith and one by works. Rather, the category of those who are justified by faith is coextensive with those who *will be justified* on the final day after a whole life of perseverance. The two groups are identical; there are none who begin in faith but, as a result of not obeying, are not vindicated. Similarly, for Paul, it does not make sense to speak of those who have somehow managed to obey outside faith. Obedience *is* "the obedience of faith" (Rom. 1:5, etc.).

For Paul, the categories of "those of faith" (Gal. 3:7) and "all who do good" in Romans 2:10 (cf. Rom 2:7, 13, 26–27) are one and the same, just as the "golden chain" of Romans 8:29–30 does not distinguish between different groups of people when it talks of those whom God foreknew, predestined, called, justified, and glorified. God's purpose, which begins with election and culminates in the final vindication of God's people, is not thwarted by any of his people being lost. As a result, Paul can speak of justification taking place "by the blood of Christ" (Rom. 5:9), perhaps also "by the Spirit" (1 Cor. 6:11), "through faith" (Rom. 3:22), and for "those who in persevering in good work seek glory, honor and immortality" (Rom. 2:7). Because God's work of salvation cannot be thwarted, it can be regarded as a singular work (or vice versa). Because it is a singular work, what is predicated of the people of God can (within certain parameters) be connected with the divine work in a variety of ways.

30. See Gathercole, "A Law unto Themselves."

31. See ibid., where I deal with, among others, the two main objections, that (a) they appear to do the law "by nature" (in fact, the word *phisei* belongs with the first half of the clause and refers not to a doing the law "by nature" but to the fact that the Gentiles are so "by birthright"), and (b) they do not do isolated bits of the law (in fact, the phrase *ta tou nomou* cannot be interpreted to refer to parts of the law; it is a general reference to the law in its entirety [cf. Rom. 2:26–27]).

32. See Gathercole, *Where Is Boasting?* ch. 6.

Righteousness and Works of the Law

This also seems a good opportunity to examine again Wright's approach to the concepts of "righteousness" and "works of the Law." It is particularly appropriate at the present time because of the publication of his Romans commentary; now one no longer has to gather together the numerous baskets full of fragments but can chew on the whole loaf. We will first treat righteousness and then "works of the Law."

Righteousness

It is very clear from the Romans commentary that Wright understands "righteousness" as synonymous with "covenant membership."[33] He sees this as originating in the relationship between Genesis 15:6 and the covenant ritual that God commanded Abraham to carry out: "The key statement of [Genesis] 15:6, cryptic and almost unparalleled as it is, appears to be proleptic, referring forward to the covenant ceremony about to take place. Its overall meaning must then be something like: 'God counted Abraham's faith as constituting covenant membership.'"[34] When this is then applied to the exegesis of Romans 4, the quotation of Genesis 15:6 has three contours: the two subsidiary craters are the bookkeeping metaphor, evoked by the "reckoning," and the forensic metaphor, which is suggested by the category of "righteousness." There is, however, the "third and deepest level of meaning" that dominates Romans 4, namely, "the covenant and membership within it."[35] So, Paul's use of Genesis 15:6 in Romans is expounded by Wright as follows:

> "Righteousness," when applied to humans, is, at bottom, the status of being a member of the covenant; "faith" is the badge, the sign, that reveals that status because it is its key symptom. Once that is grasped, the way is open not just for the rest of Paul's argument in the present passage to unfold smoothly, but also for the nuances carried by faith and the law later in the letter to be understood clearly.[36]

I am entirely in favor of understanding righteousness in covenantal terms; there is no chance to return to a previous generation's attempt to generalize the Jewish and Pauline understandings of righteousness as

---

33. Indeed, it was also clearly outlined in Wright's earlier work. On Paul, see in particular N. T. Wright, *The Climax of the Covenant: Christ and the Law in Pauline Theology* (Edinburgh: T&T Clark, 1991).

34. Wright, "Romans," 491.

35. Ibid.

36. Ibid.

generic good deeds, and the polemic of Wright and others against this line is important. There is still a problem, however, a problem that we shall see surfacing again when we look at his interpretation of "works of the Law" in a moment.

The principal difficulty concerns understanding "righteousness" in terms of *membership* within the covenant rather than as *doing what God requires* within the covenant. I would propose "doing what God requires" as the basic sense of righteousness in the Old Testament and early Judaism. The classic statement of this comes in Deuteronomy 6:24–25: "Then the Lord commanded us to observe all these statutes, to fear the Lord our God, for our good always, so as to keep us alive, as is the case today. If we are careful to observe all these commandments before the Lord our God, as he commanded us, that will be our righteousness." Here it is clear that righteousness is not constituted merely by covenant membership. The covenant has already been made at Horeb (Deut. 5:2). Now that the covenant has been established and the nation of Israel has by God's love been chosen as the covenant people, they must live lives of righteousness in response to God. Righteousness is, then, *what God requires*, or *doing* what God requires. The problem with this idea is that it carries connotations, for many, of a kind of self-righteous heaping up of merits or an attempt to make a claim upon God. But these ideas are far distant from Deuteronomy 6:25. Its sense of righteousness is also found frequently in the Old Testament.

It is also abundant in early Judaism in texts shortly prior to, and contemporaneous with, Paul. Righteousness is something that is "done": "everyone who does righteousness shall receive his reward" (Sir. 16:14 Hebrew). The righteous are "all those who walk in the way of righteousness, and do not sin like the sinners" (*1 Enoch* 82:4). *Jubilees* puts it similarly, in the mouth of Jacob: "And Jacob said: 'I will do everything just as you have commanded me because this thing is an honor and a greatness for me and a righteousness for me before the Lord, that I should honor them'" (*Jubilees* 35:2).[37]

The cash value of this for the interpretation of Paul is that when he speaks of the reckoning of righteousness, it is not just that Christians stand before God as members of the covenant but, rather, that *it is as if they have done everything that God requires.*

"Works of the Law"

We come now to the very closely related issue of Wright's treatment of works of Torah in Romans 3:20, 3:27–28, and 4:1–8. I am in agree-

37. The point that obedience leads to a righteous status is made throughout *Jubilees*; see 7:34–39; 20:2; 21:15; 30:17–23; 31:23; 32:9; 35; cf. *Testament of Abraham* 16:16.

ment with a substantial amount of Wright's exegesis of the relevant passages. The summary statement on 3:20, put in his characteristic style, expresses Paul's point admirably: "The appeal to Torah is like calling a defense witness who endorses what the prosecution has been saying all along."[38]

Examination of Wright's understanding of "works of the Law" shows that it is very clear what scholarly and popular view he is against: the idea that Paul's opponents were "proto-Pelagians, attempting to pull themselves up by their moral shoelaces" and who espoused "a theology of self-help legalism."[39] Second, one can see clearly Wright's approach to how Paul's contemporaries thought of works of the law as functioning: "The position he [Paul] is opposing can be stated thus: 'works of Torah' are the sign, in the present, of that membership in Israel, God's covenant people, which will be vindicated in the future when the long-awaited 'righteousness of God' is unveiled in action."[40]

For Paul, "works of the Law" is thus a way of talking about *possession* of the law rather than obedience to it. They function, for Paul's Jewish contemporaries, as evidence that God will undoubtedly save at the eschaton all who possess these badges. Third, in terms of the *content*, these badges, these works of the law, are seen primarily as "those things that marked out the Jews from their pagan neighbors, not least in the diaspora: the Sabbath, the food laws, and circumcision."[41] Hence we see such glosses as "the works of Torah," "the things that define Israel ethnically," and "the works of Torah that demarcate ethnic Israel."[42] The corollary to this understanding of "works of the Torah" is that the "Torah of works" in Romans 3:27 is "Torah seen as that which defines Israel over against the nations."[43]

We turn, then, to Romans 3:20a: "by works of Torah will no flesh be justified." Wright explains the statement as follows: "Paul's point here is that the verdict of the court, i.e., of God, cannot be that those who have 'works of Torah' on their record will receive the verdict righteous."[44] The big question here, however, is whether Paul would concede the point that his fellow Jews do "have" works of the law on their record. To put the question another way: are Paul's fellow Jews

---

38. Wright, "Romans," 459–60. I also share in Wright's criticism of Dunn's approach to works of the law (not very well known, as people tend to lump the two scholars together) that 4QMMT "cannot be used as a template for Paul's meaning of the phrase" because MMT is concerned with definition *among Jews*, which is not the issue for Paul.

39. Ibid., 461, 490.

40. Ibid., 460.

41. Ibid., 461.

42. Ibid., 481, 482.

43. Ibid., 480.

44. Ibid., 459.

guilty despite their works of the law or because of their lack of works of the law? Wright is arguing the former: they are guilty despite them. Let me offer some reasons I believe the latter to be the case—that those within the law here are guilty because of a lack of obedience to the law.

Wright has too minimal a view both of the nature of works of the law and of their function. In terms of what they are, first, he has argued that they are in particular the visible badges of the law. I have attempted elsewhere to demonstrate, however, that "works of the law," against the backdrop of the Old Testament and early Judaism, in fact means comprehensive obedience to the law.[45] Second, the function of works, then, is, for Paul's Jewish contemporaries, not primarily to mark them out as distinct from the Gentiles but to secure vindication at the eschatological judgment. This is what is most immediately in view in Romans 3:19–20: Paul is opposing the idea that his Jewish contemporaries will be vindicated by God at the final judgment on the basis of a wholehearted obedience to the law.

Paul's particular complaint is that this is impossible for the flesh, for the sinful person who has not received God's transforming grace in Christ. Paul is not opposed in principle to the idea of final vindication on the basis of obedience; in this respect he agrees with his Jewish interlocutor (Rom. 2:7–10). What he disputes is the ability of the flesh to obey sufficiently to attain this justification (Rom. 8:3, 7). Not only is it the case that sufficient obedience is impossible; according to 8:7, it is in fact impossible for the flesh even to begin to obey, for humanity, left alone, to come to terms with what God requires. It is, then, the *lack* of obedience to God's requirements that means that those within the law will not be justified through works of the law.

Romans 3:20, then, is Paul's argument that Israel has failed in the task of meeting God's requirement of obedience to Torah. On the other hand, I would enthusiastically affirm that 3:29–30 is about the inclusion of Gentiles. Although 3:20 is about obedience and justification being impossible for the flesh and the *referent* of justification is the acquittal of the unrighteous, it is a crucial *implication* for Paul that this means all having access to God on the same basis, that of faith. In this respect, I do not see that the Reformation emphases do an injustice to Paul's understanding of justification.

The portraits of Abraham and David follow the same pattern. Discussion of the nature of justification in Romans 4:1–8 then leads to the implication of worldwide faith in 4:9–12. To look very briefly at Abraham in 4:1–5, Paul contrasts the gift paradigm with the earning paradigm.

---

45. See Gathercole, *Where Is Boasting?* esp. chs. 2 and 7.

Here I see no problem with the idea that Paul is contrasting two soteriologies, his own and that of Judaism. Those who are unhappy with this do not sufficiently appreciate that verbs of repayment and recompense are frequently used in Judaism in connection with the eschatological reward for obedience. There are numerous other similar examples in the Jewish literature where eschatological salvation can be pictured as the prize for a race, or life that has been stored up through obedience to the law, and so on.[46]

In the light of this, then, Paul can be seen to be opposing the confidence of Jews in final vindication on the basis of obedience to the law. Again, this is not because he disagrees with the eschatological framework of his Jewish contemporaries or because he thinks obedience is unimportant but, rather, because he views obedience to Torah as impossible without the transforming power of Christ and the Spirit. "For what the Law was powerless to do in that it was weakened by the flesh, *God . . .*" (Rom. 8:3). "The mind of the flesh is enmity toward God, it does not submit to the Law of God, nor can it do so" (8:7). These provide a very helpful explanation of Paul's view of the relationship between Torah and flesh, which should not be neglected in the discussion of justification in Romans 3–4.

So let me summarize what Paul is denying and what he is affirming. Paul is saying "no" to the idea that God justifies on the basis of obedience to the law done in the flesh. Such obedience is impossible and cannot even be begun. Paul says "yes" to the alternative "instrumental cause" of *faith*, which he understands as *trusting God's promise*. By divine decision, this is reckoned as righteousness. That is to say, the believer is reckoned as having accomplished all that God requires. Justification, then, is not merely a reckoning as being in covenant membership. It is something bigger—God's creative act whereby, through divine determination, the believer has done everything that God requires. So, the doctrine of justification in Paul is quite individualistic, and this is not something of which Pauline interpreters should be ashamed. The doctrine does have a number of implications for the Christian community as a whole, but justification is inextricably tied to faith, which is the act whereby the individual trusts in God's promise. Consequently, in justification, the individual is accepted by God.

Conclusion

In conclusion, we can simply summarize the basic points in brief compass. As far as the basis of justification is concerned, Paul states in

46. See ibid., part 1.

Galatians and repeatedly again in Romans that the death of Christ is the ground of justification, although the present action of Christ is also a factor. Furthermore, contrary to the view of a number of scholars, Paul is interested in the concept of the forgiveness of sins; in fact, justification and forgiveness in Paul are almost indistinguishable. As far as the nature of justification is concerned, in Paul it is primarily concerned with God's determination of a new identity for the "ungodly," and this is particularly clear from the parallelism between the language of justification and that of the reckoning of righteousness. Justification does not constitute a part of salvation but is a way of speaking about salvation that highlights certain aspects, although one must distinguish between referent and implications when talking of justification in Paul. The central aspect is God's acceptance through his act of determining the believer really to be righteous. This frequently emerges in Paul's discourse as he opposes the view of his contemporaries that justification is attained through thoroughgoing obedience to the law. Righteousness, however, can only come as the gift of God to those who are not righteous but trust God's promise.

11

New Perspectives on Paul

N. T. WRIGHT

Introduction

I was grateful for the invitation to the Edinburgh Dogmatics Conference, which provided the contributions to this volume, and for the sensitive way in which the organizers responded to my comments on the initial outline of the program. I am aware that fresh interpretations of Paul, including my own, have caused controversy in evangelical circles, and particularly Reformed circles. My own name has been linked with proposals that have been variously dismissed, scorned, vilified, and anathematized.

Debate about these fresh interpretations of Paul draws together several different agendas. The question is sometimes treated as a variation on old modernist controversies, at other times as a clash between a Christian absolutism and a religious relativism, and at other times as a variation on a perceived Protestant/Catholic divide (or even a high-church/low-church divide), with the so-called New Perspective focusing on ecclesiology rather than soteriology and being condemned for so doing. And that is just the beginning. From time to time, correspondents draw my attention to various Web sites on which you can find scathing denunciations of me for abandoning traditional Protestant orthodoxy, and puzzled rejoinders from people who have studied my work and know that I am not saying what many of my critics suggest.[1] Faced with this kind of problem, it would take a whole book to unpick the strands, to disentangle them from other issues, to explain what the so-called New Perspective is and is not, and to argue exegetically step by step for a particular reading of Paul. This contribution instead will begin with two remarks about my aim and method, on the one hand, and the problem of the New Perspective, on the other. It will then explain what I think needs to be said about Paul and justification, sharpening up the issues here and there.

First, on aim and method. When I began research on Paul in autumn 1974, my aim was to understand Paul in general and Romans in particular better than I had done before, as part of my heartfelt and lifelong commitment to Scripture and to the *sola scriptura* principle, believing that the better the church understands and lives by Scripture, the better its worship, preaching, and common life will be. I was conscious of thereby standing methodologically in the tradition of the Reformers, for whom exegesis was the lifeblood of the church and who believed that Scripture should stand over against all human traditions. I have not changed this aim and method, nor do I intend to. Indeed, the present controversy often appears to me in terms of a battle for the Reformers' aims and methods—going back to Scripture over against all human tradition—against some of their theological positions (and, equally, those of their opponents, since I believe that often both sides were operating with mistaken understandings of Paul). I believe that Luther, Calvin, and many of the others would tell us to read Scripture afresh, with all the tools available to us—which is, after all, what they did—and to treat their own doctrinal conclusions as important but not as important as Scripture itself. This is what I have tried to do, and I believe I am honoring them thereby.

Allow me, if you will, a moment of autobiography, for reasons similar to those of Paul in Galatians 1 and 2. In my early days of research, before Sanders published *Paul and Palestinian Judaism* in 1977[2] and long before James Dunn coined the phrase "the New Perspective on Paul,"[3] I was

---

1. Cf. at amazon.com the comments that anonymous correspondents have appended to some of my books. See, e.g., N. T. Wright, "The Letter to the Romans: Introduction, Commentary, and Reflections," in *The New Interpreter's Bible*, 13 vols. (Nashville: Abingdon, 1994–2004), 10:393–770; *What Saint Paul Really Said* (Grand Rapids: Eerdmans, 1997); *The Climax of the Covenant: Christ and the Law in Pauline Theology* (Edinburgh: T&T Clark, 1991; Minneapolis: Fortress, 1992); *The Epistles of Paul to the Colossians and to Philemon* (Leicester, UK: Inter-Varsity; Grand Rapids: Eerdmans, 1987); *Paul: In Fresh Perspective* (Minneapolis: Fortress, 2005). For more details, see www.ntwrightpage.com.

2. See E. P. Sanders, *Paul and Palestinian Judaism* (Minneapolis: Fortress, 1977).

3. See J. D. G. Dunn, "Manson Memorial Lecture 4.11.1982: The New Perspective on Paul," *BJRL* 65, no. 2 (1983): 95–122.

puzzled by one exegetical issue in particular, which I here oversimplify for the sake of summary. If I read Paul in the then-standard Lutheran way, Galatians made plenty of sense, but I had to fudge (as I could see dozens of writers fudging) the positive statements about the law in Romans. If I read Paul in the Reformed way, of which, for me, Charles Cranfield remains the supreme exegetical exemplar,[4] Romans made a lot of sense, but I had to fudge (as I could see Cranfield fudging) the negative statements about the law in Galatians. For me then and now, if I had to choose between Luther and Calvin, I would always take Calvin, whether on the law or (for that matter) the Eucharist. But as I struggled this way and that with the Greek text of Romans and Galatians, it dawned on me, I think in 1976, that a different solution was possible.[5]

In Romans 10:3 Paul, writing about his fellow Jews, declares that they are ignorant of the righteousness of God and are seeking to establish "their own righteousness."[6] The wider context, not least 9:30–33, deals with the respective positions of Jews and Gentiles within God's purposes—and with a lot more besides, of course, but not least that. Supposing, I thought, Paul meant "seeking to establish their own righteousness" not in the sense of a *moral* status based on the *performance* of Torah and the consequent accumulation of a treasury of merit but in the sense of an *ethnic* status based on the *possession* of Torah as the sign of automatic covenant membership? I saw at once that this would make excellent sense of Romans 9 and 10 and would enable the positive statements about the law throughout Romans to be given full weight while making it clear that this kind of use of Torah, as an ethnic talisman, was an abuse. I sat up in bed that night reading through Galatians and saw that at point after point this way of looking at Paul would make much better sense of Galatians, too, than either the standard post-Luther readings or the attempted Reformed ones.

The reason for this explanation is to show that I came to the position I still hold (having found it over the years to be deeply rewarding exegetically right across Paul; I regard as absolutely basic the need to understand Paul in a way that does justice to all the letters as well as to the key passages in individual ones) not because I learned it from E. P. Sanders or Dunn but because of the struggle to think Paul's thoughts after him as a matter of obedience to Scripture. This brings me to the complexity of the so-called New Perspective and of my relationship to it.

4. See C. E. B. Cranfield, *A Critical and Exegetical Commentary on the Epistle to the Romans*, 6th ed. (Edinburgh: T&T Clark, 2001).
5. I first wrote on this in my 1978 Tyndale Lecture, N. T. Wright, "The Paul of History and the Apostle of Faith," *Tyndale Bulletin* 29 (1978): 61–88.
6. Unless otherwise indicated, Scripture quotations in this chapter are the author's translation.

When Sanders's book was published in 1977, I devoured it with both eagerness and puzzlement. Eagerness because his exposition of first-century Palestinian Judaism supported in all kinds of ways the picture to which I had been coming through my reading of Paul (I was not then well up in Judaism itself). Puzzlement because, when he came to Paul, Sanders seemed muddled and imprecise. This is partly, I now realize, because he was not dealing with theology (and so seemed confused about basic things, such as justification and salvation) but, rather, with religion, patterns of religion in particular. His agenda, there and elsewhere, included a desire to make Christianity and Judaism less antithetical—in other words, to take a large step away from the anti-Judaism of much Pauline scholarship. I need hardly say that I never embraced either Sanders's picture of Paul or the relativistic agendas that seemed to be driving it. Indeed, for the next decade, much of what I wrote on Paul was in debate and disagreement with Sanders, not least because his proposals lacked the exegetical clarity and rootedness that I regarded and still regard as indispensable. For me, the question has always been, "But does this make sense of the text?" not, "But will this fit into some abstract scheme somewhere?"

Many of those who joined the Sanders bandwagon, not least in America, did so because they shared his post-Holocaust reevaluation of Christian-Jewish relations and the implicit relativism that this engendered. I have spent considerable energy arguing against this position and explaining that Paul's critique of Israel is not based on, nor is it a product of, anti-Judaism as such, still less anti-Semitism, but involves a far more delicately balanced and nuanced theology that cannot be reduced to such slogans.

Likewise, when Dunn added his stones to the growing pile, I found myself in both agreement and disagreement with him. His proposal about the meaning of "works of the law" in Paul—that they are not the moral works through which one gains merit but the works through which the Jew is defined over against the pagan—I regard as exactly right. It has proved itself again and again in the detailed exegesis; attempts to deny it have, in my view, failed. But Dunn, like Sanders (and like some other New Perspective writers, such as John Ziesler),[7] has not, I think, arrived at the heart of Paul. Again, much of my writing on Paul, over the last twenty years at least, has been in implicit dialogue with Dunn, and I find his exposition of justification itself less than satisfying. For one thing, he never understands what I take to be Paul's fundamental covenant theology; for another, his typically Protestant antisacramentalism leads him to miss the point of Romans 6. I could go on.

7. See John Ziesler, *Paul's Letter to the Romans* (London: SCM, 1989).

I say all this to make it clear that there are probably almost as many New Perspective positions as there are writers espousing it—and that I disagree with most of them. Where I agree is as follows. It is blindingly obvious when you read Romans and Galatians—though you would never have known this from any of the theologians discussed in other essays in this volume—that virtually whenever Paul talks about justification, he does so in the context of a critique of Judaism and of the coming together of Jew and Gentile in Christ. As an exegete determined to listen to Scripture rather than abstract my favorite bits from it, I cannot ignore this. The only notice that most mainstream theology has taken of this context is to assume that the Jews were guilty of the kind of works righteousness that theologians from Augustine to Calvin and beyond have used to criticize their opponents; and although Sanders's account of Judaism needs much more nuancing, I regard the New Perspective's challenge to this point as more or less established. What I miss entirely in the "Old Perspective," but find so powerful in some modern Pauline scholarship, is Paul's sense of an underlying narrative, the story of God and Israel, God and Abraham, God and the covenant people, and the way in which this story came to its climax, as he says, "when the time had fully come" with the coming of Jesus the Messiah. How all this works out is still very controversial within the New Perspective, but at these points, for good exegetical and historical reasons, I find myself saying, "Here I stand."

What has happened, then? Like America looking for a new scapegoat after the collapse of the Cold War and seizing on the Islamic world as the obvious target, many conservative writers, having discovered themselves in possession of the Pauline field after the liberals tired of it, have looked around for new enemies. Here is something called the New Perspective; it seems to be denying some of the things we have normally taught; very well, let us demonize it, lump its proponents together, and nuke them from a great height. This has not made a pretty sight. Speaking as one of those who are regularly thus carpet bombed, what I find frustrating is the refusal of the traditionalists to do three things: first, to differentiate the quite separate types of New Perspective; second, to engage in the exegetical debates upon which the whole thing turns instead of simply repeating a Lutheran or similar line as though that settled matters; and third, to recognize that some of us at least are brothers in Christ who have come to the positions we hold not because of some liberal, modernist, or relativist agenda but as a result of prayerful and humble study of the text, which is and remains our sole authority. Of course, prayer and humility before the text do not guarantee exegetical success. We all remain deeply flawed at all levels. But this is precisely my point. If I am *simul justus et peccator*, the church, not least the church as the Scripture-reading community, must be *ecclesia catholica semper reformanda*. Like Calvin, we must claim the right to stand critically within a tradition. To deny either of these would be to take a large step toward precisely the kind of triumphalism against which the Reformers themselves would severely warn us. But if we are siblings in Christ, there are appropriate ways of addressing one another and of speaking about one another, and I regret that these have not always characterized the debate. There is much more that I could say under both these initial headings, but this must suffice for now. I turn to what I regard as the central issues around which the debate ought to turn.

Understanding Righteousness in Paul: The Central Issues

Let me, as a good Calvinist, offer you five points about Paul that are crucial in the present debates, justification itself being the fifth. Many other things are, of course, vital to Paul, not least Christology, about which I have written much; all of these need careful integration into the picture, for which now is not the time. Ideally, one would walk slowly round the piece of the Pauline jigsaw labeled "justification," commenting on each other piece of the jigsaw and noting how justification fits into it. Obvious examples, each of which is dear to my heart and most of which I have written about elsewhere, are the cross, the resurrection, the Spirit, the Jewish law, union with Christ, the sacraments, election, and love.[8] Please do not think that because I am unable to expound any of these because of space, I am forgetting or marginalizing them. I simply state each point in the barest outline, relying on my other works, not least my recent Romans commentary, to back me up with details.[9]

The Gospel

I begin where Romans begins—with the gospel. My proposal is this. When Paul refers to "the gospel," he is not referring to a system of salvation, although certainly the gospel implies and contains this, nor even to the good news that there now is a way of salvation open to all but, rather, to the proclamation that the crucified Jesus of Nazareth has been raised from the dead and thereby demonstrated to be both Israel's Messiah and

8. See, e.g., Wright, *Climax of the Covenant*.
9. Wright, "Romans." See also "Redemption from the New Perspective," in *Redemption*, ed. S. T. Davis, D. Kendall, and G. O'Collins (Oxford: Oxford University Press, 2004), 69–100.

the world's true Lord. "The gospel" is not, "You can be saved, and here's how"; the gospel, for Paul, is, "Jesus Christ is Lord."

This announcement draws together two things, in derivation and confrontation. First, Paul is clearly echoing the language of Isaiah: the message announced by the herald in Isaiah 40 and 52 has at last arrived. Saying, "Jesus is Messiah and Lord," is thus a way of saying, among other things, "Israel's history has come to its climax," or, "Isaiah's prophecy has come true at last." This is powerfully reinforced by Paul's insistence, exactly as in Isaiah, that this heraldic message reveals God's righteousness, that is, God's covenant faithfulness, about which more anon. Second, since the word "gospel" was in public use to designate the message that Caesar was the Lord of the whole world, Paul's message could not escape being confrontational; Jesus, not Caesar, is Lord, and at his name, not that of the emperor, every knee shall bow. This aspect lies at the heart of what I have called "the fresh perspective on Paul," the discovery of a subversive political dimension not as an add-on to Paul's theology but as part of the inner meaning of "gospel," "righteousness," and so on.[10]

For Paul, the announcement or proclamation of Jesus as Lord was itself the "word of God" that carried power. Putting together the various things he says about the preaching of the gospel, the word, and the work of the Spirit, we arrive at the following position: when Paul enters a town and declares that Jesus is Lord, no doubt explaining who Jesus was, the fact and significance of his death and resurrection, and so on, then the Spirit is at work mysteriously in the hearts and minds of the listeners. As a result, when some of them believe in Jesus, Paul knows that this is not because of his eloquence or clever argument but because the announcement of Jesus as Lord functions as (in later technical language) the means of grace, the vehicle of the Spirit. And since the gospel is the heraldic proclamation of Jesus as Lord, it is not first and foremost a suggestion that one might like to enjoy a new religious experience. Nor is it even the take-it-or-leave-it offer of a way to salvation. It is a royal summons to submission, to obedience, to allegiance; and the form that this submission and obedient allegiance takes is faith. This is what Paul means by "the obedience of faith." Faith itself, defined conveniently by Paul as belief that Jesus is Lord and that God raised him from the dead, is the work of the Spirit, accomplished through the proclamation. "No one can say 'Jesus is Lord' except by the Holy Spirit" (1 Cor. 12:3 NRSV). But this already jumps ahead to my fourth point, and before we arrive there, we must take in the second and third.

---

10. See N. T. Wright, "A Fresh Perspective on Paul?" *BJRL* 83, no. 1 (2001): 21–39; *Paul: In Fresh Perspective*, ch. 4.

The Righteousness of God

The second point concerns the phrase "the righteousness of God," *dikaiosynē theou*. I became convinced many years ago, and time and exegesis have confirmed this again and again, that Paul always uses this phrase to denote not the status that God's people have from God or in God's presence but the righteousness of God himself. This is not to say that there is no such thing as a righteous status held by believers. There is. But it is to deny that the latter is the referent of Paul's phrase *dikaiosynē theou*. Here a Pauline exegesis rooted in Paul's own understanding of Jewish scripture and tradition must challenge the fuzzy thinking that, as evidenced in other essays contained in this volume, I discover characterized most of the great, but basically Latin-speaking, theologians.

The main argument for taking *dikaiosynē theou* to denote an aspect of the character of God himself is the way in which Paul is summoning up a massive biblical and intertestamental theme, found not least in Isaiah 40–55, which is vital for him.[11] God's *dikaiosynē*, God's *tsedaqah*, is the aspect of God's character because of which, despite Israel's infidelity and consequent banishment, God will remain true to the covenant with Abraham and rescue Israel nonetheless. This righteousness is a form of justice; God has bound himself to the covenant, or perhaps we should say that God's covenant is binding upon God, and through this covenant God has promised not only to save Israel but also thereby to renew creation itself. The final flourish of Isaiah 55 is not to be forgotten, especially when we come to Romans 8. Righteousness, please note, is not the same thing as salvation; God's righteousness is the *reason* he saves Israel.

But this covenant fidelity, this covenant justice, is not purely a matter of salvific activity. As Daniel 9 makes clear, it is a matter of God's severe justice upon covenant-breaking Israel, and only then a matter of God's merciful rescue of penitent Israel. This is why the gospel—the announcement that Jesus Christ is Lord—contains within itself, as Paul insists in Romans 2:16, the message of future judgment as well as the news of salvation. What God's righteousness never becomes in the Jewish background that Paul is so richly summing up is an attribute that is passed on to, reckoned to, or imputed to God's people. Nor does Paul treat it in this way. What we find, rather, is that Paul is constantly (especially in Romans, where all but one of the occurrences of the phrase are found)[12] dealing with the themes that, from Isaiah to 4 Ezra, cluster together with

11. See Wright, "Romans."
12. See ibid., notes on Rom. 2:16.

the question of God's righteousness: How is God to be faithful to Israel, to Abraham, to the world? How will the covenant be fulfilled, and who will be discovered to be God's covenant people when this happens?

This is precisely what Romans 9–11 is about, not as an appendix to the letter but as its proper climax. This is anticipated in several earlier parts of the letter that are conveniently screened out by the great tradition in its quest for a non-Jewish soteriology—not least the second half of Romans 2 and the first nine verses of Romans 3. It can also be anticipated in Romans 4, where Paul is demonstrably arguing about God's faithfulness to the Abrahamic covenant, not simply using Abraham as an example of someone justified by faith.

Part of the tragedy of Reformation exegesis, not least Lutheran exegesis, is that this entire line of thought was screened out. Thus even Ernst Käsemann, who sees clearly that *dikaiosynē theou* must refer to God's own righteousness, cannot allow that it has anything to do with the covenant, but insists, against the evidence, that it has become a technical term denoting "God's salvation-creating power" with a cosmic reach.[13] He fails to notice a point that is central and crucial: that the covenant with Israel was always designed to be God's means of saving and blessing the entire cosmos. You get the cosmic reach, as in Genesis 12, as in Isaiah 40–55, as in the Psalms, as in Romans 8, as in 1 Corinthians 15, not by bypassing the covenant but by fulfilling it.

What, then, can we say about the status of "righteous" that, in many Pauline passages, is enjoyed by the people of God in Christ? For Paul, there is a clear distinction. God's own righteousness is *dikaiosynē theou*. The status of "righteous" that people enjoy as a result of God's action in Christ and by the Spirit is, in Philippians 3:9, *hē ek theou dikaiosynē*, the righteous status which is "from God." Ignoring this distinction and translating *dikaiosynē theou* as "a righteousness from God," or something like that, makes nonsense of several passages, most noticeably Romans 3:21–26 (as, e.g., in the appalling and self-contradictory New International Version), where the great theme is the way in which God has been faithful to the covenant, the astonishing way whereby all alike, Jewish sinners and Gentile sinners, are welcomed, redeemed, justified.

You can see this most clearly if you remember the context of the Jewish law court, which forms the background for Paul's forensic use of the *dikaiosynē* theme. Despite some odd recent attempts to deny this, if you want to understand forensic justification, you must go to the law court and find how the metaphor works. In the Jewish law court that Paul would have known, there is no director of public prosecutions;

---

13. See Ernst Käsemann, "'The Righteousness of God' in Paul," in *New Testament Questions of Today* (London: SCM, 1969), 168–82.

there is a judge, with a plaintiff and a defendant appearing before him. When the case has been heard, the judge finds in favor of one party and against the other. Once this has happened, the vindicated party possesses the status of "righteous"—not itself a moral statement, we note, but a statement of how things stand in terms of the now completed lawsuit. It all depends on what you mean by "righteous." But this status of righteousness has nothing to do with the righteousness of the judge. For the judge to be righteous, it is necessary that he or she try the case fairly, refuse bribes or other favoritism, uphold the law, and take special note for the helpless, the widows, and so on. When either the plaintiff or the defendant is declared righteous at the end of the case, there is no sense that in either case the judge's own righteousness has been passed on to the individual by imputation, impartation, or any other process. What the individual has is a status of "righteous" that comes *from* the judge. Let me stress, in particular, that when the judge finds in favor of one party or the other, he or she quite literally makes that party righteous because "righteous" at this point is *not* a word denoting moral character but only and precisely the status that you have when the court has found in your favor. If this had been kept in mind in earlier centuries, a great deal of heartache and puzzlement might have been avoided.

What, then, about the "imputed righteousness"? This is fine as it stands; God does indeed "reckon righteousness" to those who believe. But this is not, for Paul, the righteousness either of God or of Christ except in a very specialized sense, to which I shall return. Only two passages can be invoked in favor of the imputed righteousness being that of God or Christ. The first proves too much, and the second not enough. The first is 1 Corinthians 1:30–31, where Paul says that Christ has become for us wisdom from God, and righteousness, sanctification, and redemption. Wisdom is the main point he is making, and the other three nouns come in as a way of saying, "And everything else as well." "Yea, all I need, in thee to find, O Lamb of God, I come"; this line sums it up well. I doubt if this will sustain the normal imputation theology, because it would seem to demand equal airtime for the imputation of wisdom, sanctification, and redemption as well. The second passage is 2 Corinthians 5:21, which is not, as a matter of good exegesis, a statement of soteriology but of apostolic vocation.[14] The entire passage is about the way in which Paul's new covenant ministry, through the death and resurrection of Jesus, is in fact God's appointed means for establishing and maintaining the church. "So that we might become God's

14. See N. T. Wright, "On Becoming the Righteousness of God: 2 Corinthians 5:21," in *Pauline Theology*, ed. D. M. Hay, 4 vols. (Minneapolis: Augsburg Fortress, 1991–1997), 2:200–208.

righteousness in him" means that in Christ those who are called to be apostolic preachers indeed embody God's own covenant faithfulness. I do not expect to convince by this microcosmic summary of the point, but it deserves careful exegetical consideration, not a dismissal with a wave of the hand and a reference to Brother Martin.

Is there, then, no "reckoning of righteousness" in, for instance, Romans 5:14–21? Yes, there is; but this is not God's own righteousness or Christ's own righteousness that is reckoned to God's redeemed people but, rather, the fresh status of "covenant member," and/or "justified sinner," which is accredited to those who are in Christ, who have heard the gospel and responded with "the obedience of faith." But this too is pushing toward my fifth point, and I must proceed with the third.

Final Judgment according to Works

The third point is remarkably controversial, seeing how well founded it is at several points in Paul. Indeed, from the contributions in this volume and other papers presented at the Edinburgh Dogmatics Conference, it seems that there has been a massive conspiracy of silence about something that was quite clear for Paul (as indeed for Jesus). Paul, in company with mainstream Second Temple Judaism, affirms that God's final judgment will be in accordance with the entirety of a life led—in accordance, in other words, with works. He says this clearly and unambiguously in Romans 14:10–12 and 2 Corinthians 5:10. He affirms it in that terrifying passage about church builders in 1 Corinthians 3. But the main passage in question is Romans 2:1–16.

This passage has often been read differently. As one of the other authors in this volume has shown, Augustine had problems with it (perhaps the only thing in common between Augustine and E. P. Sanders). This is hardly surprising; here is the first statement about justification in Romans, and lo and behold it affirms justification according to works! The doers of the law, Paul says, will be justified (Rom. 2:13). Shock, horror; Paul cannot (so many have thought) have really meant it. So the passage has been treated as a hypothetical position that Paul then undermines by showing that nobody can actually achieve it or, in Sanders, for instance, as a piece of unassimilated Jewish preaching that Paul allows to stand even though it conflicts with other things he says. But all such theories are undermined by exegesis itself, not least by observing the many small but significant threads that stitch Romans 2 into the fabric of the letter as a whole. Paul means what he says. Granted, he redefines what "doing the law" really means; he does this in chapter 8 and again in chapter 10, with a codicil in chapter 13. But he makes the point most compactly in Philippians 1:6: "he who began a good work in you will bring it to completion at the day of Christ Jesus." The "works" in accordance with which the Christian will be vindicated on the last day are not the unaided works of the self-help moralist. Nor are they the performance of the ethnically distinctive Jewish boundary markers (Sabbath, food laws, and circumcision). They are, rather, the things that show that one is in Christ; the things that are produced in one's life as a result of the Spirit's indwelling and operation. In this way, Romans 8:1–17 provides the real answer to Romans 2:1–16. Why is there now "no condemnation"? Because, on the one hand, God has condemned sin in the flesh of Christ (let no one say, as some have done, that this theme is absent in my work; it was and remains central in my thinking and my spirituality)[15] and, on the other hand, because the Spirit is at work to do within believers what the law could not do—ultimately, to give life, but a life that begins in the present with the putting to death of the deeds of the body and the obedient submission to the leading of the Spirit.

I am fascinated by the way in which some of those most conscious of their Reformation heritage shy away from Paul's clear statements about future judgment according to works. It is not often enough remarked upon, for instance, that in the Thessalonian letters and in Philippians, he looks ahead to the coming day of judgment and sees God's favorable verdict not on the basis of the merits and death of Christ, or because he simply casts himself on the mercy of the judge, but on the basis of his apostolic work. "What is our hope and joy and crown of boasting before our Lord Jesus Christ at his royal appearing? Is it not you? For you are our glory and our joy" (1 Thess. 2:19–20; cf. Phil. 2:16–17). I suspect that if you or I were to say such a thing, we could expect a swift rebuke of "Nothing in my hand I bring, simply to thy cross I cling." The fact that Paul does not feel obliged at every point to say this shows that he is not as concerned as we are about the danger of speaking of the things he himself has done—though sometimes, to be sure, he adds a rider, which proves my point, that it is not his own energy but what God gives and inspires within him (1 Cor. 15:10; Col. 1:29). He is clear that the things he does in the present by moral and physical effort will count to his credit on the last day, precisely because they are the effective signs that the Spirit of the living Christ has been at work in him. We are embarrassed about saying this kind of thing; Paul clearly is not. What on earth can have happened to a *sola scriptura* theology that it should find itself forced to screen out such emphatic, indeed celebratory, statements?

---

15. See, e.g., at two quite different levels, N. T. Wright, *The Crown and the Fire* (London: SPCK; Grand Rapids: Eerdmans, 1992); and *Jesus and the Victory of God* (London: SPCK; Minneapolis: Fortress, 1996), ch. 12.

God's verdict, when it is positive, can be denoted by the verb "justify." This carries its full forensic sense, rooted in the ancient Jewish belief that the God of Israel, being the Creator of the world and also the God of justice, would finally put the world to rights—in other words, that he would conduct a final assize. On that day there will be "glory, honor, immortality and the life of the age to come" for all who do right (Rom. 2:7); in other words (2:13), they will be justified, declared to be in the right. This ought to have highlighted long ago something that I believe has played too little part in discussions of Paul: justification by faith, to which I shall come in a moment, is the *anticipation in the present* of the justification that will occur in the future, and gains its meaning from this anticipation. What Augustine lacked, what Luther and Calvin lacked, what Regensburg lacked as a way of putting together the two things it tried to hold on to was Paul's eschatological perspective, filled out by the biblical fusion of covenantal and forensic categories. But before we take up the subject of justification, I want to address a question that Paul seldom touches explicitly but about which we can reconstruct his thought quite accurately: the *ordo salutis*. This is just as well because it has played an important role in Protestant discussions of soteriology and it lies at the heart of today's controversies about justification.

Ordo salutis

I understand the *ordo salutis* to refer to the lining up, in chronological sequence, of the events that occur from the time when a human being is outside the community of God's people, stuck in idolatry and consequent sin, through to the time when this same erstwhile sinner is fully and finally saved. This question has been closely bound up with that of justification, but this and the next section will suggest that when Paul uses the word and its cognates, he has in mind one step only within this sequence, and—critically, as you will see—not the one that the word has been used to denote in much Christian dogmatics. At this point I am implicitly in dialogue with a general trend, at least since the sixteenth century, to make "conversion" and "justification" more or less coterminous—a trend that has been sped on its way when "conversion" is understood as "the establishment of a personal relationship with God" and justification has been understood in a "relational" sense, with the meaning not of membership in the covenant, as in the Old Testament, but of this personal relationship between the believer and God. I have already described how Paul understands the moment when the gospel of Jesus as Lord is announced and people come to believe it and obey its summons. Paul has a regular technical term for this moment, and it is neither "justification" nor "conversion" (though he can employ the latter from time to time); the word in question is "call." "Consider your call," he says to the Corinthians (1 Cor. 1:26); "God called me by his grace," he says of himself (Gal. 1:15). (This is why Krister Stendahl's suggestion that we should think of Paul's "call" as opposed to his "conversion" misses the point.[16] For Paul, the word "call" denoted not merely a vocation to a particular task but also, more fundamentally, the effective call of the gospel, applied by the Spirit to the individual heart and life, resulting in a turning away from idolatry and sin and a lifelong turning to God in Christ in believing allegiance.)

But if the call is the central event, the point at which the sinner turns to God, what comes before and after? Paul himself has given the answer in Romans 8:29–30. Although he does not often discuss such things, he here posits two steps prior to God's call through the gospel: God's foreknowledge and God's marking out ahead of time, the mark in question being the mark of the image of the Son. (I translate with a paraphrase because of the problems associated with the word "destiny" within the word "predestination.") These serve to emphasize, admittedly, the sovereignty of God in the call itself, whereas Paul never engages with the questions we want to ask about how precisely these things work out. (The closest he comes is Romans 9, which simply restates the problem for us; the parallel statement in Ephesians 1:3–14 is a celebration rather than an explanation.)

But what matters for our purposes even more is the question of what comes *after* the call. "Those he called, he also justified" (Rom. 8:30). In other words, Paul uses "justify" to denote something other than, and logically subsequent to, what we have often thought of as the moment of conversion, when someone who has not before believed the gospel is gripped by the word and the Spirit and comes to believe it, to submit to Jesus as the risen Lord. Here is the central point in the controversy between what I say about Paul and what the tradition, not least the Protestant tradition, has said. The tradition has used "justify" and its cognates to denote conversion, or at least the initial moment of the Christian life, and has then debated broader and narrower definitions of what counts. My reading of Paul indicates that he does not use the word like this, and my method, shared with the Reformers, insists that I prefer Scripture itself to even the finest traditions of interpretation. The fact that the Christian tradition has, since at least Augustine, used the word "justify" to mean "become a Christian," whether broadly or narrowly conceived, is neither here nor there. For Paul, justification is

16. See Krister Stendahl, *Paul among Jews and Gentiles* (Philadelphia: Fortress, 1976), ch. 1.

something that *follows on from* the call through which a sinner is summoned to turn from idols and serve the living God, to turn from sin and follow Christ, to turn from death and believe in the God who raised Jesus from the dead. This directs us to my fifth and final point.

But before we take up that point, we note that the final verb in Paul's sequence is not "sanctified." He would say that this has already happened to all baptized believers (see 1 Cor. 6:10–11). Instead it is "glorified." Paul regards it as a fixed point that those who belong to the Messiah by faith and baptism already share his glorious life, his rule over the world, and that this rule, this glory, will one day be manifest. This cannot be developed here, but I note, as a point that much dogmatics has yet to come to terms with, the fact that both Paul and John the Seer place great emphasis not just on being saved, not just on being raised from the dead, but on sharing the glorious rule of Jesus Christ as Lord over God's new world. What this sharing will consist of, who or what will be in subjection under this rule, and so on, are questions that have fallen off most people's radar screens. It is time we put them back on.

I hope I have offered enough in this short section to convince you of two things. First, my understanding of how Paul supposed someone became a Christian is, I think, basically orthodox and indeed Reformed. God takes the initiative, on the basis of his foreknowledge; the preached word, through which the Spirit is at work, is the effective agent; belief in the gospel, that is, believing submission to Jesus as the risen Lord, is the direct result. My central point is that *this is not what Paul is referring to when he speaks of "justification."* But the substance of what Reformed theology, unlike Paul, has referred to by means of this word remains. Faith is not something someone does as a result of which God decides to grant him or her a new status or privilege. Becoming a Christian, in its initial moment, is not based on anything that a person has acquired by birth or achieved by merit. Faith is itself the first fruit of the Spirit's call. And those thus called, to return to Philippians 1:6, can be sure that the One who began a good work in them will complete it at the day of Christ.

Second, it is simply not true, as people have said again and again, that I deny or downplay the place of the individual in favor of a corporate ecclesiology. True, I have reacted against the rampant individualism of Western culture and have tried to insist on the antidote of a biblically rooted corporate solidarity in the body of Christ. But this in no way reduces the importance of every person being confronted with the powerful gospel, and the need for each one to be turned around by it from idols to God, from sin to holiness, and from death to life.

Justification

What, then, is justification if it is not conversion itself, not the establishment of a relationship between a person and God, but something that is, at least logically, consequent upon it? This is where confusion inevitably creeps in. I have argued many times that Paul uses *dikaioō* and its cognates to denote something other than conversion itself. But several critics have not listened to this and instead have imagined that what I say about Paul's use of the *dikaioō* word group is my proposed description of his theology of conversion, and they have then charged me with all kinds of interesting heresies. To make things clear, let me use instead a near synonym and speak here not of "justification" but of "vindication," recognizing that this is itself controversial.

My proposal has been, and still is, that Paul uses vindication language, that is, the *dikaioō* word group, when he is describing not the moment when, or the process by which, someone comes from idolatry, sin, and death to God, Christ, and life but, rather, the verdict that God pronounces consequent upon this event. The word *dikaioō* is, after all, a declarative word, declaring that something is the case, rather than a word for making something happen or changing the way something is.[17] (Nor do we need to get around this, as many have done, by saying that when God declares something to be the case, God brings it into being; that is not the point here.) And if we work backward from the future vindication I spoke of earlier, we can see what this declaration amounts to and why Paul insisted on it, especially in Romans and Galatians.

The language of vindication, the *dikaioō* language, is, as we have seen, law court language. Law court imagery is appropriate because God is the God of justice, who is bound to put the world to rights, has promised to do so, and intends to keep his promises. But the means by which God will do so, from Genesis 12 onward, is through the covenant God has made with Abraham; and so, God's covenant faithfulness, on the one hand, and God's justice, on the other, are not two quite different things but closely interlinked. Both are indicated, as we have seen, in the phrase *dikaiosynē theou*. When we talk of God's vindication of someone, we are talking about God's declaration, which appears as a double thing to us but, I suspect, a single thing to Paul: the declaration (a) that someone is in the right (his or her sins having been forgiven through the death of Jesus) and (b) that this person is a member of the true covenant family, the family that God originally promised to Abraham and has now created through Christ and the Spirit—the single family that consists equally of believing Jews and believing Gentiles.

17. See Wright, "Romans."

I submit that this way of lining things up draws together the various categories that are otherwise left untidily around the place: forensic in Luther versus adoption in Calvin, law court versus incorporative in Schweitzer and Sanders. Once you grasp Paul's underlying covenantal theology, these dichotomies are overcome. My first main point in this subsection is therefore that these two things—declaring sinners to be in the right, with their sins forgiven, and declaring someone to be a member of the single multiethnic covenant family—go very closely together in Paul's mind and that to point out the importance of the latter (belonging to the family) in passages such as Romans 3 or Galatians 3 in no way undermines the importance of the former (being one of those now declared "in the right" in God's law court). The underlying point here is crucial: the reason God established the covenant with Abraham, according to Scripture in general and Paul in particular, was to undo the sin of Adam and its effects and thereby to complete the project of the good creation itself. Thus God's declaration of forgiveness and declaration of covenant membership are not ultimately two different things. I freely grant that some of those who have highlighted the importance of the Jew-plus-Gentile point in Paul have used it as a way of saying that Paul is therefore not, after all, interested in God's dealing with sins and putting sinners in a right relation to himself. But the fact that people draw false inferences one way is no reason we should draw them the other way. Let me take two obvious examples.

First, in Romans 3:21–31, a vital and central passage by anyone's showing, Paul makes what most commentators in the Reformation tradition regard as a strange shift in verse 29, when he asks, "Or is God the God of the Jews only?" (Notice how the New International Version, for instance, omits the word "or.") If he had been speaking all along simply about individual sinners being put right with God, we should indeed regard this as a sudden intrusion of ethnic questions. But he has not. As Romans 4 will reveal, when we allow it to play its full role, he has been talking about God's faithfulness to the covenant with Abraham and about God's creation of a single family from both halves of sinful humanity. God's declaring that sinners are now in a right relation to himself and God's declaring that believing Jews and believing Gentiles belong in the same family are inextricably bound up with one another.

The same point emerges in Galatians 2:11–21. Here, beyond cavil, the point of vindication is not "how someone becomes a Christian" but the question of table fellowship: with whom may I, indeed must I, share table fellowship? Peter's action in separating himself from Christian Gentiles did not imply that they needed to perform moral good works; it was implying that they needed to become physically Jewish. Paul's argument against him concerned not the mechanism of how people come from being sinful idolaters to forgiven members of Christ's people but the equality, within the people of God, of all who believe the gospel, Jew and Gentile alike. This controversy, indeed, dominates the entire letter in a way that, alas, I think Martin Luther never saw (though specialists may correct me).

What, then, is this vindication, this *dikaiōsis*? It is God's declaration that a person is in the right—that is, (a) that the person's sins have been forgiven and (b) that he or she is part of the single covenant family promised to Abraham. Notice the opening phrase: God's *declaration that*. Not "God's bringing it about that" but God's authoritative declaration of what is in fact the case. This is the point where some reviewers have accused me of semi-Pelagianism. That might be so if I intended to denote, with the word "justification," what the tradition has denoted. But I do not. Paul, I believe, uses "vindication/justification" to denote God's declaration about someone, about (more specifically) the person who has been "called" in the sense described above. Vindication is not the same as call.

We now discover that this declaration, this vindication, occurs twice. It occurs in the future, as we have seen, on the basis of the entire life a person has led in the power of the Spirit—that is, it occurs on the basis of "works" in Paul's redefined sense. And near the heart of Paul's theology, it occurs in the present *as an anticipation of that future verdict*, when someone, responding in believing obedience to the call of the gospel, believes that Jesus is Lord and that God raised him from the dead. This is the point about justification by faith, to revert to the familiar terminology: it is the anticipation, in the present, of the verdict that will be reaffirmed in the future. Justification is not "how someone becomes a Christian." It is God's declaration about the person who has just become a Christian. And just as the final declaration will consist not in words so much as in an event, namely, the resurrection of the person concerned into a glorious body like that of the risen Jesus, so the present declaration consists not so much in words, though words there may be, but in an event, the event in which one dies with the Messiah and rises to new life with him, anticipating that final resurrection. In other words, baptism. I was delighted to discover, as you discover in reading this volume, that not only Chrysostom and Augustine but also Luther would here have agreed with me.

Traditional Protestants may not like this much, but it is, I submit, what Paul is saying. Before I draw some broader conclusions from all this, notice three things that follow. First, Paul's doctrine of what is true of those who are in the Messiah does the job, within his scheme of thought, that the traditional Protestant emphasis on the imputation of Christ's righteousness did within that scheme. In other words, that which imputed righteousness was trying to insist upon is, I think, fully taken care of in (for instance) Romans 6, where Paul declares that what is true of the Messiah is true of all his people. Jesus was vindicated by God as Messiah after his penal death; I am in the Messiah; therefore I, too, have died and been raised. According to Romans 6, when God looks at the baptized Christian, God sees him or her in Christ. But Paul does not say that God sees us clothed with the earned merits of Christ. This would be the wrong meaning of "righteous" or "righteousness." He sees us within the *vindication* of Christ, that is, as having died with Christ and risen again with him. I suspect that it was the medieval over-concentration on righteousness, on *justitia*, that caused the Protestant Reformers to push for imputed righteousness to do the job they rightly saw was needed. But in my view, they have thereby distorted what Paul himself was saying.

Second, it emerges that justification, for Paul, is not (in Sanders's terminology) how one "gets in" to God's people but about God's declaration that someone *is* in. In other words, it is all about assurance—as we should have known from reading Romans. I have said it before: If we are thinking Paul's thoughts after him, we are not justified by faith by believing in justification by faith. We are justified by faith by believing in the gospel itself—in other words, that Jesus is Lord and that God raised him from the dead. If, in addition, we believe in justification by faith itself, we believe that—amazingly, considering what God knows about us—we are now and forever part of the family to whose every member God says what he said to Jesus at his baptism: you are my beloved child, with you I am well pleased.

Third, it follows at once that justification is the original *ecumenical* doctrine. The first time we meet justification, that is, in Galatians 2, it is about people from different cultures and traditions sharing table fellowship on the basis of nothing other than their shared faith in Jesus as Messiah and Lord. Once we relocate justification, moving it from the discussion of how people become Christians to the discussion of how we know that someone is a Christian, we have a powerful incentive to work together across denominational barriers. One of the sad ironies of the last four hundred years is that, at least since 1541, we have allowed disputes about how people become Christians—what we thought was denoted by the language of justification—to divide us when the doctrine of justification itself, urging us to unite across our cultural divides, went unheard. Not that there are not large and important problems in ecumenical relations. I am horrified at some of the recent Anglican-Roman statements, for instance, and on topics such as the papacy, purgatory, and the cult of saints (especially Mary), I am as Protestant as the next person for (I take it) good Pauline reasons. But justification by faith tells me that if my Roman neighbor believes that Jesus is Lord and that God raised him from the dead, then he or she is a brother or sister, however much I believe my neighbor muddled, even dangerously so, on other matters.

Conclusion

Let me conclude with four brief propositions about the importance of taking at least this version of the New Perspective seriously, and with one flagrantly homiletic plea.

First, to restate the point of method. I remain committed to understanding Paul in his own right and his own terms against all traditions about him, including my own. I remain convinced that Luther and Calvin would say Amen to this point of principle. And I believe, and have argued in my various exegetical works, that this reading of Paul makes far more sense of his letters, in whole and in their various parts, and in their mutual relations, than all other readings known to me. Part of the exegetical task is to relate Paul to the Jewish world of his day, and this reading, I believe, does it far better than the traditional one, though debates naturally remain about many aspects of the Jewish context.

Second, this reading of Paul allows fully not only for the challenge to each person to hear and believe the gospel and live by it but also for three other contexts, each of which is vitally important to Paul, to have their place. These three other contexts are the cosmic, as in Romans 8; the ecclesiological, as in Paul's constant emphasis on the unity of Jew and Gentile in Christ; and the political, as mentioned earlier. Many have tried to play these off against each other, but I believe they are instead mutually reinforcing. The united multiethnic church is a sign of God's healing and remaking of the cosmos and also thereby a sign to Caesar and his followers that his attempted unification of the world is a blasphemous parody. This is part of what Ephesians and Colossians are all about, although that is another story. It is also, I believe, a point in urgent need of emphasis today.

Third, this New Perspective reading of Paul enables us to understand—crucially for some current debates in my church at least—why Paul is very tolerant of differences on some points (particularly food, drink, and holy days) and completely intolerant on others (particularly sexual ethics). The boundary lines he insists on blurring (in, e.g., Romans 14 and 1 Corinthians 8) are precisely those between different ethnic communities, particularly Jew and Gentile. The boundary lines he draws more firmly are those between the holy lifestyle required of those who have died and been raised with the Messiah and the unholy lifestyle of those who behave as if they had not and were still living "in the flesh." This, too, is urgent today.

Fourth, I discover an irony in the anti–New Perspective reaction in specifically Reformed circles. The New Perspective launched by Sanders and taken up eagerly in many American contexts was always a reaction not to Reformed readings of Paul but to Lutheran ones and the broader Protestantism and evangelicalism that went along for the Lutheran ride, particularly in its negative assessment of Judaism and its law. Had the Reformed reading of Paul, with its positive role for Israel and the law, been in the ascendancy rather than the Lutheran one, the New Perspective might not have been necessary, or not in that form. For myself, it may surprise you to learn that I still think of myself as a Reformed theologian, retaining what seems to me the substance of Reformed theology while moving some of the labels around in obedience to Scripture—itself, as I have suggested, a good Reformed sort of thing to do.

I close with a plea. I have lived most of my life in and around evangelical circles in which I have come to recognize a strange phenomenon. It is commonly assumed that Luther and Calvin got Paul right. But often, when people think of Luther and Calvin, they see them, and hence Paul, through three subsequent lenses provided by Western culture. The Enlightenment highlighted the abstract truths of reason over against the messy facts of history; many Protestants have put Lessing and Luther together and still thought they were reading Paul. The Romantic movement highlighted inner feeling over against outer, physical reality; many have thence supposed that this was what Paul, and Luther and Calvin, were really saying (hence the knee-jerk Protestant antisacramentalism). More recently, existentialism has insisted that what matters is being true to my inner self rather than being conditioned by history, mine or anyone else's; many people, not only Rudolf Bultmann, have read Paul and Luther in this light.

At a popular level, this mess and muddle shows up in a general sense that anything inward, anything to do with strong religious emotion, anything that downplays outward observance, must be striking a blow for the Pauline gospel of justification by faith. This is as worrying as it is absurd. All these movements are forms of dualism, whereas Paul believed in the goodness and God-givenness of creation and in its eventual promised renewal. Together they reinforce the Gnosticism that is a poison at the heart of much contemporary culture, including soi-disant Christian culture.

It is time to turn away from all this, to rub our eyes and look clearly at the path by which we and our culture have come. It is time to turn back again, following the old *sola scriptura* principle, to the source and origin of one of the great doctrines of the New Testament: that when, through

God's effective call (*sola gratia*) in the preaching of the gospel of Jesus Christ (*solus Christus*), someone comes to believe that Jesus is the risen Messiah and Lord, God thereupon (*sola fide*) declares in advance what God will declare on the last day when he raises that person from the dead: this person is in the right, his or her sins have been forgiven, this person is part of the single, true, worldwide covenant family promised to Abraham, the sign of the coming new creation and the countersign to the boast of Caesar. Justification is ultimately about justice, about God putting the world to rights, with God's chosen and called people as the advance guard of this new creation, charged with being and bringing signs of hope, of restorative justice, to the world. Let us put the justice back in justification and, as we do so, remind ourselves whose justice it is and why. *Soli Deo gloria!* Having thus stolen Luther's slogans, I thought I might end with "Here I stand"; but let me, rather, say it in Paul's language: *hōde hestēka; allo ou dynamai.*

Contributors

Henri A. Blocher (D.D., Gordon-Conwell Theological Seminary) is Knoedler Professor of Theology at Wheaton College. He has taught at the Faculté Libre de Théologie Evangélique in Vaux-sur-Seine, outside of Paris, for over forty years. He is the author of several books, including *Original Sin* and *Evil and the Cross*.

Mark Bonnington (Ph.D., University of Nottingham) is tutor in New Testament at St. John's College in Durham. He is also the author of a forthcoming commentary on 1 Corinthians.

Simon Gathercole (Ph.D., University of Durham) is senior lecturer in New Testament at the University of Aberdeen. He is the author of *Where Is Boasting?* and *The Preexistent Son: Recovering the Christologies of Matthew, Mark, and Luke*.

Anthony N. S. Lane (D.D., University of Oxford) is professor of historical theology and director of research at London School of Theology. He is author of a number of books, including *A Concise History of Christian Thought*, *John Calvin: Student of the Church Fathers*, and *Justification by Faith in Catholic-Protestant Dialogue*.

Bruce L. McCormack (Ph.D., Princeton Theological Seminary; Dr. theol. h.c., Friedrich Schiller University) is the Frederick and Margaret L. Weyerhaeuser Professor of Systematic Theology at Princeton Theological Seminary. A world-renowned Barth scholar, he is a frequent writer and lecturer on topics of Reformed theology.

A. T. B. McGowan (Ph.D., University of Aberdeen) is principal of Highland Theological College, Dingwall, Scotland and honorary professor of Reformed doctrine at the University of Aberdeen. He is the author of *The Federal Theology of Thomas Boston* and editor of *Always Reforming: Explorations in Systematic Theology*.

Nick Needham (Ph.D., University of Edinburgh) is lecturer in church history at Highland Theological College. He is the author of an introduction to Augustine's theology entitled *The Triumph of Grace* and three volumes of a projected five-volume history of the Christian church entitled *2,000 Years of Christ's Power*.

Carl Trueman (Ph.D., University of Aberdeen) is professor of historical theology and church history at Westminster Theological Seminary. He is the author of several books, including *Luther's Legacy*, *The Claims of Truth*, and *Reformation: Yesterday, Today, Tomorrow*.

David F. Wright (D.D., University of Edinburgh) is emeritus professor in patristic and Reformed Christianity at the University of Edinburgh, where he taught for almost forty years. He has produced notable works on Bucer, Calvin, Knox, and Peter Martyr Vermigli. He has also edited collections of essays, dictionaries, and encyclopedias, particularly regarding the history and theology of the early church and the Reformed tradition.

N. T. Wright (D.D., University of Oxford) is the bishop of Durham. A prolific author with over fifty books to his credit, Wright has taught New Testament studies at the University of Cambridge, McGill University, and the University of Oxford.

Karla Wübbenhorst is pastor of Westminster-St. Paul's Presbyterian Church in Guelph, Ontario. She has taught at the University of Aberdeen, Presbyterian College (Montreal), and McGill University.

Scripture Index

Genesis

6:5 207
8:21 207
12 251, 258
15:6 195, 236

Leviticus

16 224

Deuteronomy

5:2 237
6:24–25 237
6:25 237
27:26 40

1 Kings

21:29 31n23

Psalms

3:8 57
19:11–14 217
22 34n28
32 69
33:9 227
98:2 223
103:14 213
111 58
130:4 113
139:23–24 217
145:13 143

Ecclesiastes

10:1 212

Isaiah

40 249
40–55 223, 250, 251
43:26 31n23
52 249
53 216

55 250
57:17–18 31n23
64:6 212

Ezekiel

16:14 53n77
16:60–61 53n77
18 212n52

Daniel

9 250
12:3 211n51

Habakkuk

1:13 212

Wisdom of Ben Sira

16:14 237

Ecclesiasticus

3:30 44

Matthew

3:2 143
5:19–20 214
5:22 214
5:28 214
5:48 212
6:9 61
12 235
12:34 232
12:35 232
12:37 232

Luke

10:29 61, 62
17:5 145
18 65
18:13–14 59
18:14 233
24:47 143, 145

John

1:16 70
3:5 210n43
6:29 67

Acts

10 42n49
10:48 42n49
13:39 158

Romans

1:5 235
1:17 57, 69, 106n21
1:21–23 229
2 251, 253
2:1–16 253, 254
2:7 235, 255
2:7–10 239
2:10 235
2:13 61, 65, 234, 235, 253, 255
2:14 235
2:16 250
2:26–27 235, 235n31
3 185, 220, 251, 259
3–4 240
3:4 28
3:19–20 239
3:19–26 185
3:20 237, 238, 239
3:21 107, 108, 223
3:21–22 175, 223
3:21–26 15, 223, 224, 251
3:21–31 259
3:22 109, 174, 235
3:23–26 216
3:24 59, 61, 109
3:24–25 220
3:24–26 225
3:25 114n48, 224
3:25–26 223
3:26 214
3:27 238
3:27–28 237
3:28 61, 63, 65, 65n38

Subject Index

absolutization, and "Joint Declaration," 214

acquittal. *See* forgiveness of sins

actes du concile de Trente, avec le remède contre la poison, Les (Calvin), 206, 209

almsgiving, 44–46

Ambrose
  and baptism, 42
  on faith, 45, 48
  and good works, 44n53
  and justify/condemn antithesis, 29
  on mercy of God, 50
  and merit, 53
  on sin, 47n58

Amor Dei (Burnaby), 67, 68n46

Antidote to Trent. See *actes du concile de Trente, avec le remède contre la poison, Les* (Calvin)

apocalyptic theme, 168, 174, 175

Aristotle, 87n32, 136n79

Arminianism, 151

Arminius, Jacobus, 151

Article 5 of Regensburg Colloquy
  Calvin's reaction to, 123
  Cruciger's reaction to, 124
  on faith, 127, 128
  on good works, 127, 128
  history and development of, 121–23
  and Holy Spirit, 126, 127, 128n35
  Luther's reaction to, 124
  and merit of Christ, 126
  Protestant reactions to, 123–25

and righteousness, 126, 129, 130
  on sanctification, 127
  teachings of, 125–28
  translation of, 143–45
  and twofold righteousness, 125–26, 128–30

assurance
  Barth and, 159
  Calvin and, 102, 104, 172
  christological doctrine and, 212–13, 214–15
  Cyprian and, 49
  "Joint Declaration" and, 212–13, 214–15
  justification and, 221, 261
  U.S. dialogue on "Joint Declaration" and, 213n56

atonement
  Barth and, 176n29
  christological doctrine and, 21, 37, 220–21, 225
  Harink and, 176n29
  imputation and, 33, 161
  Judaism and, 20
  Justin Martyr and, 33
  Romans 3:21–26, 20–21

Augsburg declaration. *See* "Joint Declaration on the Doctrine of Justification"

Augustine
  Burnaby on, 67
  and divine act of justification, 56, 57–58, 60–61, 64–65, 66, 69–70, 72
  and doctrine of justification, 55–56